THE COMRADES AND THE MULLAHS

THE COMRADES AND THE MULLAHS

CHINA, AFGHANISTAN AND THE NEW ASIAN GEOPOLITICS

ANANTH KRISHNAN
STANLY JOHNY

HarperCollins *Publishers* India

First published in India by HarperCollins *Publishers* 2022

HarperCollins Publishers India, Cyber City, Building 10-A, Gurugram, Haryana-122002, India
www.harpercollins.co.in

2 4 6 8 10 9 7 5 3 1

P-ISBN: 978-93-5489-521-0
E-ISBN: 978-93-5489-544-9

Cover design: Saurav Das
Cover photograph: Reuters

Map on pages vi–vii by L. Balamurugan

Typeset in 11.5/15.2 Bembo Std at
Manipal Technologies Limited, Manipal

Printed and bound at MicroPrints India, New Delhi

MIX
Paper
FSC FSC® C218906

This product is made of FSC®-certified and other controlled material.

HarperCollins Publishers, Macken House, 39/40 Mayor Street Upper, Dublin 1, D01 C9W8, Ireland

Contents

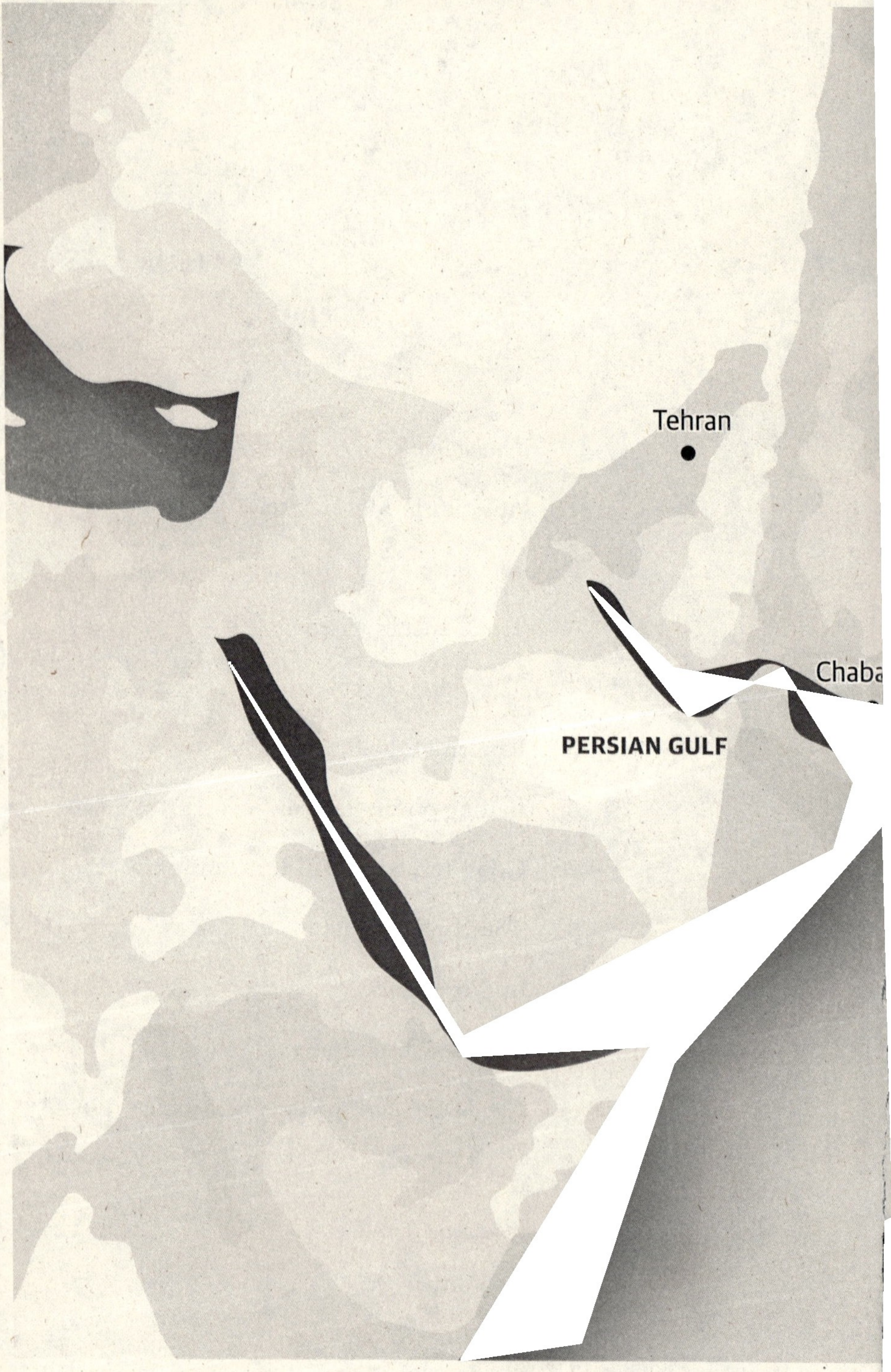

Tehran
Chaba
PERSIAN GULF

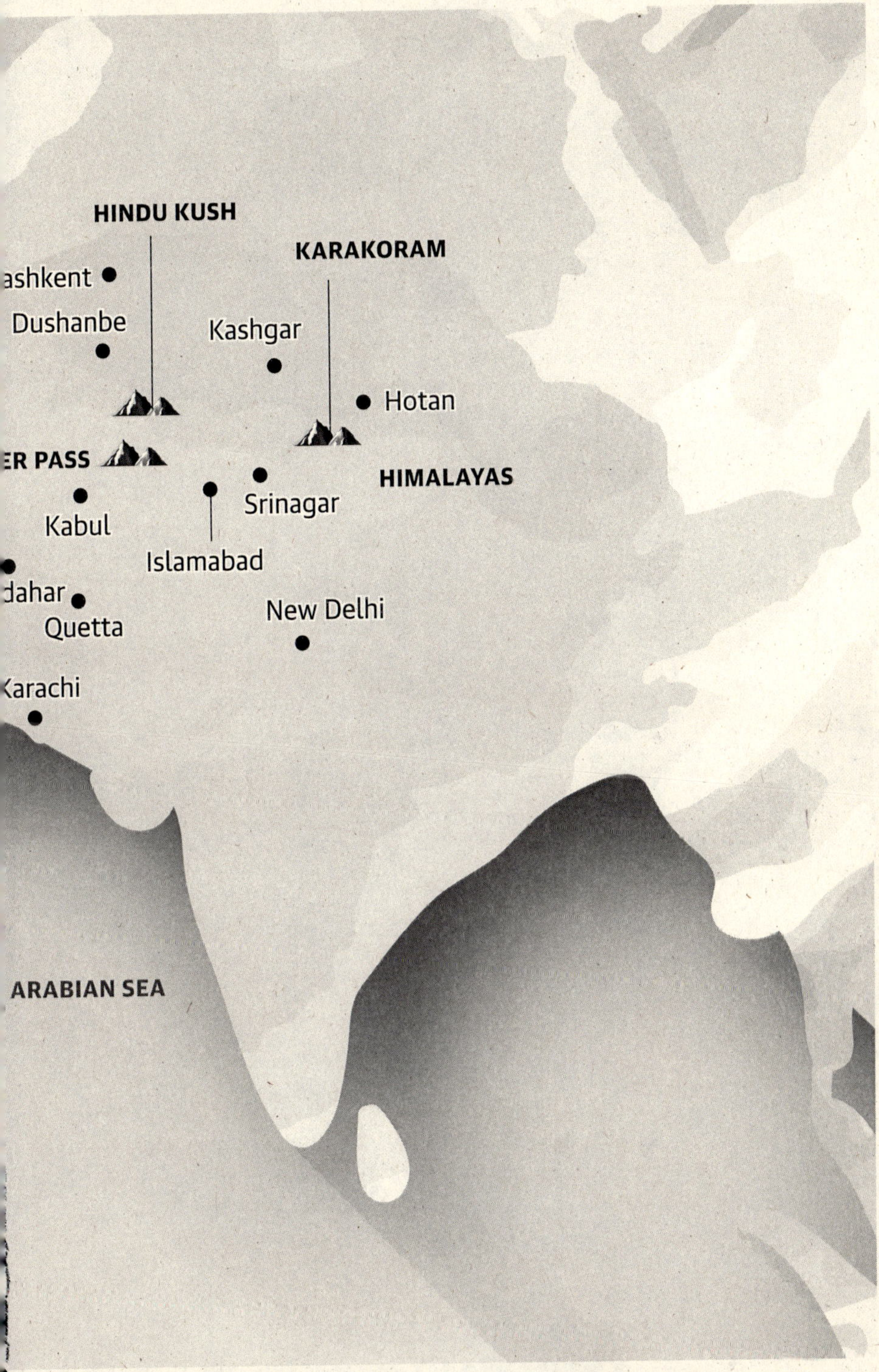
HINDU KUSH
KARAKORAM
ashkent
Dushanbe
Kashgar
Hotan
ER PASS
HIMALAYAS
Srinagar
Kabul
Islamabad
dahar
Quetta
New Delhi
Karachi
ARABIAN SEA

Introduction

THE REMNANTS OF AN ARMY, A FAMOUS OIL ON CANVAS by the nineteenth-century artist Elizabeth Butler, is a lasting image of the first Anglo-Afghan War (1839–42). It depicts William Brydon, a medical officer in the British Indian Army, arriving in Jalalabad from Kabul on horseback in 1842. Both Brydon, who was wounded, and his horse, look exhausted.

Brydon was the only survivor of the 16,000 soldiers and camp followers who were retreating from Kabul after the British invasion went awry. The British would invade Afghanistan two more times. On both occasions, they would fail to bring the whole country under their control. Finally, in 1919, after the third Anglo-Afghan War, Britain recognized Afghanistan's independence and promised that it would not extend military expeditions beyond the Khyber Pass in the mountains of the Hindu Kush.

The British Army was neither the first nor the last force that crossed the Khyber Pass. As the British general, George Molesworth, put it, 'every stone' in those mountains 'has been soaked in blood'.[1] Afghanistan has a long history of foreign invasions and resistance. From Alexander the Great to the British, and from the Soviets to the Americans, invading forces saw Afghanistan as a stepping stone for expanding their influence in Asia.

Take a look at any map, and Afghanistan's importance is self-explanatory. It sits at the meeting point of South, Central, West and East Asia. On its east and south, Afghanistan shares a border with Pakistan, which is the country's gateway to South Asia. On its west sits Iran, a major power in the Middle East. On the north, it shares a vast border with the Central Asian republics of Tajikistan, Turkmenistan and Uzbekistan, which were part of the Soviet Union during the last century and under imperial Russia in the nineteenth century. To the northeast, Afghanistan shares a small border with China and India (with Pakistan-occupied Kashmir [PoK]).

This book tells the story of the latest great power that sought – and failed – to remake Afghanistan, and what its failure will mean for the world, and particularly for the growing ambitions of its great rival – a superpower-in-waiting that happens to sit right next door. If it is still unclear how the messy and chaotic US withdrawal, and the stunning fall of Kabul to the forces of the Taliban on 15 August 2021, which invoked comparisons to the fall of Saigon, may affect the exercise of American power in the long term, there is little doubt that the exit has opened both opportunities and challenges for China, America's most potent competitor in the twenty-first century.

In the nineteenth century, Afghanistan found itself in the middle of the Great Game between the British and Russian empires. In the twentieth century, it was caught in the Cold War between the US and the Soviet Union. What will the twenty-first-century rivalry between the US and China – the most important geopolitical contest of our times – mean for Afghanistan? Attempting to unravel this question was what prompted us to write this book.

The book is divided into ten chapters that offer a descriptive and historical view of Afghanistan's civil war, foreign interventions and the evolution of its polity. The first half of this book focuses on America in Afghanistan – its entry and exit – while the second half deals with the rising influence of China on its neighbour to the west.

The first chapter maps America's decades-long interference, direct and indirect, in Afghanistan, which culminated in its withdrawal in August 2021. The US made a direct military intervention in the country in 2001, after the 11 September terrorist attacks by al-Qaeda. But the US also played a military role in the country long before that through its proxies, since the late 1970s. When communists took power in Kabul and the Soviets sent troops to Afghanistan, the US saw both a challenge – to its influence in South Asia and the Middle East – and an opportunity – to trap the Soviets in Afghanistan. Washington joined hands with Saudi Arabia and Pakistan and provided money, weapons and training to various Mujahideen Islamist factions in Afghanistan that fought both the People's Democratic Party of Afghanistan (PDPA) regime in Kabul and the Soviet Red Army.

The US-backed Mujahideen ultimately succeeded in ending communist rule in Afghanistan and establishing an Islamic government. The US effort did, however, lead to unforeseen ramifications that would alter the course of Afghanistan's history. The second chapter looks at the Taliban's origins, ideology and their rise to power. During the anti-Soviet civil war, the various Mujahideen factions, divided over ethnicities and ideologies, stood united against the common enemy. But once the communist regime fell, they started fighting against each other, plunging

Afghanistan into a deadly civil war. The country was divided into several fiefs, each controlled by different warlords. The Taliban rose from this anarchy as an anti-Mujahideen Islamist movement that promised security to the public. With their ideological and theological roots in the vast Deobandi madrassa networks in southern Afghanistan and north-western Pakistan, the Taliban, backed by Pakistan's military establishment, emerged as the most powerful insurgency against the Mujahideen and would eventually take Kabul in 1996.

The Taliban's hold on power would, however, last only five years. The third chapter follows the arc of their fall from power and their second coming, in part thanks to Pakistan hosting them and helping enable their return. The US invasion of 2001 toppled the Taliban regime and drove them underground. The Taliban were defeated, but not destroyed. When the US declared an early victory and started working to establish a new Islamic republic, keeping the remnants of the Taliban out, the insurgents retreated to Pakistan's and Afghanistan's mountainous territories, which had always provided refuge to guerrillas. Pakistan, which formally joined the US-led war on terror, was, however, not ready to shun its ties completely with the Taliban. With Pakistan's help, the Taliban regrouped and started attacking government positions and coalition troops in Afghanistan. By the time the US realized Pakistan's double game, it was too late. The Taliban had already become a nationwide insurgent group that would prove difficult to defeat.

Chapter four reconstructs the events that led to the Taliban's return to Kabul, starting with the withdrawal agreement that the US signed with the Taliban in February 2020. When Soviet troops withdrew from Afghanistan in 1989, many thought that the communist government of Mohammad Najibullah would collapse immediately. But to their surprise, Najibullah, backed by India and the Soviet Union, clung on to power. His regime fell in 1992, a few months after the disintegration of the Soviet Union. With the US exit, however, the government of President Ashraf Ghani collapsed stunningly on 15 August 2021, just two weeks before the US troops completed their withdrawal.

Exit America, enter China. If the collapse of Kabul was rapid, the chain of events that led to the dramatic fall was years in the making. America's gradually waning appetite to sustain its ultimately failed effort to rebuild Afghanistan coincided with an expanding Chinese footprint in the region, particularly after the launch of the Belt and Road Initiative (BRI) in 2013. Chapter five delves into the past and present of China's presence in Afghanistan, going back to connections forged along the old Silk Road and through the travels of scholar–monks. We chart the rise and fall of Chinese influence in Afghanistan, and how ties are today poised on the cusp of a new era.

What do opinion makers in Beijing think of Afghanistan's future, and how is Beijing responding to the US exit? If the fall of Kabul brought immediate celebration in Beijing, seen as yet another example of the decline of Western power, there was an equal amount of concern on what a vacuum in Kabul could mean for the region and the potential for instability to spill over across the Afghanistan-China border. In chapter six, we look at where on the spectrum of celebration to caution we are likely to find China's approach to Afghanistan in this new era. The debates in Beijing suggest that its approach is likely to be calibrated somewhere in the middle. China does not want to repeat the mistakes of the West and pour in billions, let alone set boots on the ground. It is, on the other hand, increasingly willing to insert itself as a power player and use its deep pockets to influence the Taliban's behaviour.

Chapter seven explores China's engagement with the Taliban and a contradiction that lies at the heart of this relationship – a hardening of China's policy towards its own Muslims, especially in its western Xinjiang region, even while China's official media is rebranding the Taliban, once viewed widely in China as a hard-line jihadist organization, as 'grassroots' liberators and sons of the soil. Indeed, China's stepped-up diplomacy in the Middle East and Afghanistan, and its forwarding a narrative of being the new 'good power' (read different from the West), coincided with a harsh crackdown on Islam at home. We examine how Beijing is managing this contradiction, and how the rising tide of Islamophobia in China will likely impact its engagement with Muslim countries.

Security, not conquest, is China's abiding priority. For all the schadenfreude at the expense of the US, Chinese strategic thinkers remain essentially cautious about how deep Beijing's involvement in Afghanistan should become. In chapters eight and nine, we explain why China's domestic drivers are key to understanding its geopolitical ambitions. Understanding the Communist Party's motivations at home offers the clearest picture of its impulses abroad. With regard to both Afghanistan and Pakistan, we explain how domestic considerations loom large above all others: the Xinjiang factor and preserving the stability of China's western frontier regions. Chapter eight delves into Xinjiang's history and troubled assimilation into the People's Republic, and how the party's Xinjiang policy impacts China's foreign policy. China's relationship with Pakistan is the focus of chapter nine, and how increasingly for Beijing, the road to Kabul runs through Islamabad. Instability in Afghanistan, we argue, is further reaffirming an already close relationship as China leans even more on the country it now calls its 'iron brother' to safeguard its security interests in the region.

There is little doubt that the growing closeness between China and Pakistan is perhaps India's single biggest foreign policy challenge. In the book's last chapter, we look at the changes in Afghanistan through an Indian lens, as New Delhi confronts the prospect of rising Chinese and Pakistani influence in a country that it has historically enjoyed warm ties with. Indeed, the only period when Kabul had a government that was inimical to India's interests was when the Taliban were in power from 1996 to 2001. In 2021, India faces the same dilemma it did in 1996. Should it deal with the Taliban or shun any kind of political contact, as it did in the 1990s? Now, the Taliban appear to be stronger than they were twenty-five years ago. With China's stated willingness to work with the Taliban, they also have more space to diversify their foreign policy. For now, their grip on the country appears to be tight. This leaves India with few options. We explore, in the book's last chapter, what those options are.

Through history, it is Afghanistan's strategic and geographical position that brought one great power after another inside its borders. In the summer of 327 BCE, Alexander the Great and his Greek-Macedonian army crossed the Hindu Kush range through the Khyber Pass. After taking what is today's Afghanistan and the eastern satrapies of Persia, Alexander moved towards India. In the seventh century, Arabs took the region and introduced Islam. Then came Mongols, Timur and the British.

One of the defining factors of nineteenth-century geopolitics was the Great Game, or the power contest between imperial Russia and the British empire. The British saw Afghanistan as a buffer state between Russia and then undivided India. In December 1838, the British governor general, Lord Auckland, ordered the invasion of Afghanistan. British Indian troops crossed the Khyber Pass, toppled Dost Mohammad's regime, and installed their protégé Shah Shujah Durrani in Kabul's royal palace. But

Auckland's strategy proved wrong. Dost Mohammad's son, Akbar Khan, mobilized a tribal army and launched guerrilla attacks against the British. When the invasion became unsustainable, the British decided to withdraw. As they left, most of their troops – barring William Brydon, who was immortalized in *The Remnants of an Army* – were massacred. Dost Mohammad went on to recapture Kabul.

More than a century later, the Soviet Union repeated the same mistakes of the British. In 1989, the Soviet Red Army withdrew from the country. It took only another twelve years before a different superpower, this time the US, became the next invader. And just like the British and the Soviets did, the Americans got rid of the existing regime and installed a new one. After twenty years of war and occupation, the US finally struck a deal with the very group it ousted and packed its bags, just like the great powers before it.

Superpowers suffering military setbacks at the hands of weaker forces create a perception of great power fatigue, if not weakness, that prompts both their allies and rivals to rethink their strategic assessments. The British never recovered from their misadventure in the Suez Canal in 1956, when they supported the invading Israeli army against Gamal Abdel Nasser's Egypt. This marked the end of their time in the Middle East. After the American withdrawal from Vietnam in 1975, a triumphant Soviet Union sent troops to Afghanistan in 1979 (the Soviets, of course, miscalculated America's resolve, while the US ended up creating a Vietnam for the Soviets in Afghanistan). The Soviet withdrawal from Afghanistan in 1989 marked the beginning of the unravelling of the Soviet empire. Within a few months of their pullback, Soviet-backed communist regimes in Eastern Europe fell one after another, eventually leading to the collapse of the Union of Soviet Socialist Republics.

The inability of the world's most powerful military power and the largest economy to defeat a group that began as a ragtag militia of hard-line madrassa students may well be remembered as one of the geopolitical shocks of the twenty-first century. With the withdrawal of its last troops, the US no longer has a military presence in South Asia. As far as practical purposes go, its alliance with Pakistan is all but over. The withdrawal will allow the US to refocus its resources, away from the mountains of Afghanistan to the waters of the Indo-Pacific where it is confronting a rising China and trying to build new partnerships and alliances to deal with the China challenge.

This book tells the story of Afghanistan's encounter with the latest great powers that have sought to shape its future. In writing this story of great powers and great ambitions, we are acutely aware that it is the people of Afghanistan who should rightfully be at the centre of any story about their country. Indeed, it is the great tragedy of Afghanistan that through the long arc of its history, outside powers have viewed the country as merely a chessboard on which to play their great games, as a land with resources and treasures to exploit. The people who live on that land have always been secondary in their calculations, although the people have borne the brunt of great games that cost them a great deal.

As this book goes to press, the people of Afghanistan are in the midst of an unprecedented economic and humanitarian crisis. Reports of food shortages are widespread, with both the new Taliban regime and civil society organizations asking for foreign assistance, without which an already stressed economy, teetering on the brink, may well collapse. We write this book with the belief that those who do not learn from history are condemned to repeat its mistakes. This is a story of power after power failing to learn from the past. We also write with the hope that repeating the mistakes of the past need not be an inevitability. Nothing would be more tragic for the people of Afghanistan.

Ananth Krishnan
Hong Kong
December 2021

Stanly Johny
Chennai
December 2021

1

America in Afghanistan

On 9 May 1978, eleven days after the communists captured power in Afghanistan through a coup, Pakistan's military dictator Muhammad Zia-ul-Haq wrote a letter to US President Jimmy Carter, warning him of the dangers the regime in Kabul posed to regional security. Gen. Zia, who had himself come to power in Pakistan through a military coup less than a year ago, was certain that the growing Soviet influence in Afghanistan would present a multi-pronged threat to Pakistan. 'We know that the Afghan barrier has been breached and our country lies directly in the path of the flood which rolled out of Czarist Russia in the last century and is now flowing in full force towards the Indian Ocean and the Persian Gulf,' he wrote, conveying an unmistakable sense of alarm.[1]

For Zia, the change of regime in neighbouring Afghanistan posed twin challenges. One, a hostile regime meant security complications given that both countries had an unsettled border.

The pro-Soviet People's Democratic Party of Afghanistan (PDPA) not just endorsed the previous regimes' position that the Durand Line, the international border between Pakistan and Afghanistan, was a colonial imposition, but also advocated a Pashtun-controlled 'Greater Afghanistan'.[2] Two, Zia, who was heavily influenced by Islamist politics, saw communism as a mortal ideological enemy. He wanted the US to help combat this enemy in Pakistan's backyard.

Gen. Zia's military regime had initiated talks with the deposed Afghan President Mohammed Daoud Khan. Khan, a senior member of Afghanistan's ruling dynasty, captured power in 1973 through a palace coup and declared the country a republic. The communists were initially allies of Daoud Khan. But when the new President established a one-party dictatorship and turned against his political rivals, the PDPA started scheming against him. On 28 April 1978, pro-PDPA soldiers stormed the presidential palace and assassinated President Khan and most of his family members. The PDPA renamed the country the Democratic Republic of Afghanistan.

'In our estimation,' Zia wrote in the letter to Carter, 'the advent of the leftist regime in Kabul is an event of historic proportions. The change is of a fundamental nature which will have a profound impact on the balance of power in our region and beyond. Its consequences for Pakistan are incalculable.'[3] In a blunt warning to the US, he said, 'Nothing will stop the Soviet Union from pursuing its expansionist policies if events encourage it to believe that smaller countries are expendable in the overall context of America's global strategy.' He wanted a meeting with President Carter to discuss the Afghan situation and explore the possibilities of US–Pakistan cooperation in countering their common enemy: communism.

Carter, a Democrat who came to power after the humiliating American withdrawal from Vietnam, agreed with Zia's assessment.

He wrote back to the Pakistani dictator on 9 June 1978, saying: 'We agree fully that Soviet domination of Afghanistan would be a development of great seriousness for South Asia and the entire free world. Those of us who share this view must cooperate closely over the coming weeks and months.'[4] But Carter wasn't ready for an immediate summit meeting with Zia, partly because the administration had its own apprehensions on the direction Pakistan was taking under the military dictatorship and partly because the Central Intelligence Agency (CIA) was yet to make an assessment on the American options in Afghanistan. Carter asked Zia to wait for the summit and in the meantime continue the communication and cooperation through the ambassadors. But Zia, faced with the red scare, wasn't willing to wait.

The Revolt Begins

The 1970s had been particularly bad for the US in the Cold War. It had been stuck in an unpopular and unwinnable war in Vietnam. In August 1971, India and the Soviet Union signed the Treaty of Friendship and Cooperation, which allowed the Soviets to deepen their influence in South Asia, a matter of high concern for Washington. In 1975, the US withdrew from Vietnam in ignominy and watched from afar the communists unifying the country. In 1978, Afghanistan came under communist rule. So the US, having suffered several setbacks, was looking for an opportunity to turn around its fortunes and score some points in its ongoing Cold War games.

Enter Afghanistan, whose new rulers, who had pushed a number of changes including expanding education, gender equality and land reforms, were dealing with discontent and a backlash from elements in the country's conservative society. Afghanistan's tribal elders, for instance, who had enjoyed autonomy under both the Islamic Emirate and Daoud Khan's republic, were aghast at the new centralized one-party dictatorship of the godless communists.

Gen. Zia, who was highly influenced by the political Islamist preachings of Abul A'la Maududi and the movement he founded, Jamaat-e-Islami, decided to back the Islamist opposition inside Afghanistan against the PDPA regime. Protests broke out in several parts of Afghanistan, largely led by tribal elders.[5] The Afghan government responded to the protests with force, which led to more resentment and counter-violence. Hafizullah Amin, the foreign minister in the PDPA regime and number two in the ruling party, directly accused Pakistan of providing support 'for the subversion in Afghanistan'.[6]

The Islamist upsurge in neighbouring Iran in 1978, which culminated in the overthrow of the secular monarchy of Shah Mohammad Reza Pahlavi in early 1979, had an electrifying impact on Islamist movements across the region. The year 1979 also saw the siege of the Masjid al-Haram (the Grand Mosque) in Mecca and the raid of the American embassy in Islamabad by radical Islamists. In Afghanistan, ethnic warlords and tribal elders, emboldened by the developments elsewhere and the support coming from across the border, launched an armed rebellion against the communist regime.

The Afghan government was facing multiple challenges. Noor Muhammad Taraki, the President, consolidated power in his hands but could not establish order across the country. Despite the regime using force against the rebels, more and more enclaves of insurgency sprang up. The ruling party was divided between two factions: Khalq (led by Taraki) and Parcham (led by his internal rivals, including Babrak Karmal). Within Khalq, President Taraki fell out with his one-time protégé, Foreign Minister Amin, who would eventually overthrow Taraki and have him killed.

As a divided communist government struggled to suppress the Islamist insurgency, the CIA found an opportunity in the crisis. In January 1979, the CIA deputy director Frank Carlucci wrote a memorandum to the White House in which he listed out options for covert action in Afghanistan and the risks. The communist government's policies had offended 'many deeply religious, conservative Afghans' in the countryside where Kabul did not have much control, Carlucci wrote in the memo. 'A tribal rebellion has been underway for several months in Afghanistan's eastern provinces, and the government is finding it increasingly difficult to maintain public order in other outlying areas of the country.' He said armed groups were operating from Pakistani territories and supported by Saudi donors.

The CIA concluded that it was in American interests that the PDPA government fall and be replaced by a non-communist regime. Carlucci suggested the US launch a propaganda war against the Afghan government highlighting its attempts 'to force an atheistic philosophy on a sincerely religious population'. This, the CIA believed, would help its efforts at attracting more donors for the rebels from Saudi Arabia and other Islamic countries. It also suggested measures to mobilize support among Afghan exiles for the insurgents and provide assistance to the rebels.[7] President Carter, who had taken a guarded approach to Pakistani dictator Zia's letter a few months ago, eventually changed his position.

Even as the US was half-heartedly exploring options in Afghanistan, the pro-American monarchy in Iran fell and was replaced with a Shia theocracy that termed America 'the Great Satan'. With the collapse of the Shah regime, the US lost one of its lasting allies in the Middle East. These developments seemed to have influenced Carter's thinking on Afghanistan. On 3 July 1979, he signed the first order for secret aid for the anti-Soviet jihad in Afghanistan. The very same day, Zbigniew Brzezinski, his National Security Advisor (NSA), wrote a note to the President saying the aid was going to induce a Soviet military intervention in Afghanistan.[8]

Brzezinski, a Polish-American scholar and diplomat and a dedicated Cold Warrior, was right. The Soviet Union sent troops to Afghanistan on the Christmas eve of 1979 to prop up the fledgling PDPA regime. But it was a risky bet. In the Soviet intervention, the US found both a challenge and an opportunity. The challenge was that if the Soviet Union stabilized Afghanistan, communism could spread to other countries in South Asia and the Middle East. On the other side, the presence of the Red Army in a deeply religious conservative country, where rebellions against the communist government had already begun, was an opportunity for the Americans to create a Vietnam for the Soviet Union.

On 26 December, two days after the Soviet intervention, Brzezinski sent a memo to President Carter in which he called on the US to accelerate its support for the insurgency. In his view, the US was facing 'a regional crisis' as both Iran and Afghanistan were in 'turmoil'. The fall of the Iranian regime, he believed, had led to the collapse of the balance of power in Southwest Asia. Earlier, the US had banked on the Shah's regime as a bulwark against communism in the Middle East. The loss of Iran could lead the Soviets to expand their presence right down to the edge of the Arabian Peninsula and Oman Gulf. Brzezinski's solution was the US doubling down on the Islamists. He asked President Carter to send more money and weapons to Afghanistan, besides providing technical assistance. But there was a problem. The US would need to rely on Gen. Zia's Pakistan to execute this strategy. And when Zia had sought America's help, Carter had remained non-committal.

Brzezinski advocated a change in America's policy towards Pakistan and asked the President to overlook Washington's own nuclear non-proliferation policy while dealing with Islamabad. He also said the US should act in 'concert with Islamic countries both in a propaganda campaign and in a covert action campaign to help the rebels'.[9] Carter agreed. The US launched a propaganda blitzkrieg to mobilize support of Muslim countries against the Soviet Union. It started sending more money to the rebels and made efforts to coordinate with Pakistan and China to provide weapons and training. Saudi Arabia, equally worried about communist presence in a Muslim country, was already on board. This was the beginning of a new era of America's involvement in Afghanistan, which would take drastic turns in the years that followed. For Gen. Zia, it was a pivotal moment. He was finally getting what he asked for: America's direct assistance in the fight against communism in his backyard.

The Mujahideen

In the beginning, Carter's administration officials were not confident the US could create a Vietnam for the Soviets. Brzezinski himself believed that the guerrillas were badly organized and poorly led. 'They have no sanctuary, no organized army, and no central government – all of which North Vietnam had,' he said to President Carter. 'The Soviets are likely to act decisively, unlike the United States, which pursued in Vietnam a policy of "inoculating" the enemy.' But despite the odds, the Carter administration concluded that it was 'essential' for the US that 'Afghani resistance continues'.[10] They wanted to get the Soviet Union bogged down in the Afghan morass.

In February 1980, Brzezinski travelled to Pakistan to put the new policy into action. At Khyber Pass, a 32-km path through the intimidating Hindu Kush range which Rudyard Kipling called a 'narrow sword cut in the hills',[11] he toured an Afghan refugee camp. He told the refugees, who had fled the civil war in Afghanistan, that the 'world is outraged' at their plight.[12] Pointing his left hand towards the Afghan border, which is just 20 km away, Carter's NSA said, 'That land over there is yours. You will go back to it one day, because your fight will prevail and you'll have your homes and your mosques back again, because your cause is right and God is on your side.'[13] He was cheered with applause. Deputy Secretary of State Warren Christopher, who was accompanying the NSA, added: 'The American people admire your fight for freedom and believe in the long run you will persevere.' The crowd responded in chorus: 'Inshallah.'[14]

Pakistan had direct access to the Mujahideen who were already fighting the PDPA government. With US support, Pakistan emerged as the lynchpin of the new jihad. Under Turki Al Faisal, the Saudi intelligence chief, the Kingdom sent wooden boxes full of cash dollars to bankroll the rebellion. Several Mujahideen groups sprang up across Afghanistan's countryside, mostly along ethnic lines. In Panjshir Valley, a narrow valley in north-central Afghanistan that is surrounded by mountains, Ahmad Shah Massoud, the legendary Tajik commander, and his mentor Burhanuddin Rabbani, would fight off the Soviets. In Herat and Mazar-e-Sharif, Ismail Khan, the Shia Hazara warlord, would set up his own bases. The Hezb-e-Islami, led by Pashtun warlord Gulbuddin Hekmatyar, who would later earn the nickname the 'Butcher of Kabul', would become the fiercest Islamist opponent of the Soviets. There were countless other small militias that were brought together in the civil war by their common antipathy towards the Soviets.

President Ronald Reagan, Carter's successor, steadily expanded the programme to help the Mujahideen, code-named 'Operation Cyclone'. If, in 1980, the Carter administration allocated $30 million for the Mujahideen, the Congressional allocation would rise to $250 million in 1985 and $650 million in 1987.[15] Between

1979 and 1992, the US distributed at least $3 billion to various Mujahideen factions in Afghanistan.

The focus of their campaign was to turn the Afghan civil war into a global jihad against the Soviet Union. With help from Pakistan's Inter-Services Intelligence (ISI) and the Saudi intelligence, thousands of Muslim radicals were recruited from across the world and moved to the training camps in Pakistan or the battlefields in Afghanistan. Journalist Ahmad Rashid writes that some 35,000 Muslim radicals from forty Islamic countries joined Afghanistan's civil war between 1982 and 1992. 'Tens of thousands more came to study in Pakistani madrassas. Eventually, more than 100,000 foreign Muslim radicals were directly influenced by the Afghan jihad.'[16]

The main objective of Operation Cyclone in the early 1980s was to 'harass' the Soviet troops in Afghanistan because even the CIA was not sure the Mujahideen could defeat the Red Army. The Soviets had total monopoly over Afghanistan's skies. And they carried out retribution strikes for every Mujahideen guerrilla attack, targeting both the rebels and their supporters. The Soviet air strikes led to large-scale casualties and triggered waves of refugees. The incessant bombardment and high casualties further drove chunks of the population away from the communist regime. While the balance of power in the conflict remained in favour of the Soviet troops, the Mujahideen, like any successful guerrilla force, did one thing: they survived, denying the superior Red Army a conclusive victory. They captured pockets of territories in Afghanistan from where they continued to target the Russian and Afghan soldiers.

This stalemate eventually led the Reagan administration to decisively shift its policy goal in Afghanistan from harassing the Soviet troops to seeking the ouster of Soviet troops from the country. In March 1985, President Reagan signed the National Security Decision Directive (NSDD) 166, setting new policy goals and ordering measures to achieve them. 'The ultimate goal of our policy is the removal of Soviet forces from Afghanistan and the restoration of its independent status,' Reagan wrote in the order. He instructed that the US should boost the intelligence support to its covert action programme in Afghanistan and 'improve the military effectiveness of the Afghan resistance in order to keep the trends in the war unfavourable to the Soviet Union'. He also ordered the intelligence agencies to ensure 'that resistance groups in Afghanistan are receiving increased supplies and are using them in combat'.[17]

Within a year, Reagan had authorized the supply of hundreds of Stinger anti-aircraft missiles to the Mujahideen.[18] Until then, the US had stayed away from supplying US-made high-tech weapons, maintaining a plausible deniability policy. The Stinger, a man-portable air defence system, practically ended the Soviet superiority in the air.[19] When the Mujahideen started bringing down Soviet jets one by one from the Afghan skies, there was even more pressure on the Kremlin where the new general secretary, Mikhail Gorbachev, was already looking for a way out from Afghanistan.

The US, on its part, escalated the conflict in three ways. First, the distribution of the Stinger missiles raised the morale and operational capability of the Mujahideen; second, the CIA directly supported the ISI's efforts to recruit Islamist radicals from across the world to join the Afghan Mujahideen; and third, American, British and Pakistani intelligence started sending armed insurgents to the Soviet Union's Central Asian republics that share a long border with Afghanistan.[20]

The Soviets had ventured into Afghanistan to expand communist influence to the Muslim world. Instead, they saw Islamist insurgency spreading to the soft Islamic underbelly of the USSR in Central Asia. Unable to turn around the war and faced with growing complications at home at a time when Soviet finances were already in a shambles, Gorbachev decided to pull back the troops by 1989, ending a decade-long intervention. Afghanistan upheld its reputation of being 'a graveyard of empires'.[21]

When the Soviets withdrew from Afghanistan, many thought the communist government then headed by President Mohammad Najibullah would collapse quickly. Having met their 'ultimate goal', as President Reagan called it, the US stopped supplying weapons to the Mujahideen and reduced financial aid substantially. The Cold War was nearing its end, particularly after the fall of the communist governments in East Europe. Najibullah, with an archipelago of cities and towns under his government's control spread across the country, clung on to power even as the Mujahideen took over much of Afghanistan's countryside.

But the collapse of the Soviet Union in 1991 was a body blow to Najibullah's government. When military and financial aid from Moscow dried up, his government steadily lost control. In 1992, the PDPA government fell apart and the Tajik faction of the Mujahideen, led by Rabbani and Massoud, captured Kabul. Both the Soviet Union and the communist regime in Afghanistan became history. The US, the victor of the Cold War and the centre of the new unipolar world, would quickly lose all interest in Afghanistan. But Afghanistan would not lose interest in America.

The Road to 9/11

Osama bin Laden was a twenty-two-year-old student at King Abdulaziz University in Jeddah, Saudi Arabia, when Leonid Brezhnev, the drunken, impulsive General Secretary of the Communist Party of the Soviet Union, sent the Red Army to Afghanistan in 1979. Son of a wealthy Saudi builder, Bin Laden 'felt outraged that an injustice had been committed against the people of Afghanistan'.[22] Within days of the Soviet intervention, Bin Laden travelled to Afghanistan, according to his own account. When the Mujahideen groups were scrambling for resources and recruits, Bin Laden emerged as a liaison officer between the Saudi intelligence, the ISI and the jihadists. He channelled millions of dollars to the Mujahideen, partly from the profits of his family's construction business and partly through donations he raised from wealthy Arab businessmen for the cause of jihad.

In 1984, Bin Laden co-founded Maktab al-Khidamat, with the goal of channelling money and fighters from across the world to Afghanistan.[23] He also recruited thousands of radicals from across the Arab and Muslim world – Egyptians, Algerians, Lebanese, Kuwaitis, Turks and Tunisians – and sent them to Afghanistan. He built tunnels into mountains for Mujahideen hospitals and arms depots, and cut roads in Mujahideen-controlled territories. Towards the end of the 1980s, he joined combat against the Soviets. 'Yes, I fought there, but my fellow Muslims did much more than I. Many of them died and I am still alive,' Bin Laden later told journalist Robert Fisk in an interview.[24]

When the Soviet troops pulled back from Afghanistan, Bin Laden, like other Mujahideen leaders, felt triumphant. 'We beat the Soviet Union. The Russians fled,' he said.[25] Back in Saudi Arabia, he was welcomed as a hero of jihad. He was close to Prince Turki, the Saudi intelligence chief, and had direct access to the top echelons of the Saudi monarchy – what Steve Coll called 'a substantial relationship with the Saudi intelligence'.[26]

But the relationship did not last long. Having 'defeated' the Soviet Union, Bin Laden, who had thousands of battle-hardened Arab Mujahideen under his command, wanted to continue the jihad. He had already split with Maktab al-Khidamat and secretly founded his own militarist network, al-Qaeda, aimed at taking up jihadist causes elsewhere in the world. Saudi Arabia's decision to welcome American troops to the Kingdom after the Iraqi invasion of Kuwait in 1990 angered Bin Laden. The Saudi royals would soon find Bin Laden's radicalism a threat to stability in the Kingdom and expel him from the country. He would return to Afghanistan and then move to Sudan, where the regime of Omar Bashir would initially welcome him. In Sudan, Bin Laden set up bases for his Arab Mujahideen, the foot soldiers of al-Qaeda, besides taking up infrastructure projects, including the 800-km Khartoum–Port Sudan road.

Soon, Bin Laden's jihadist training camps became an issue of international concern. Under regional and international pressure, the Bashir regime decided to send him away. But the Saudis, who had already revoked Bin Laden's citizenship, would not take him back.[27] Finally, Sudan agreed to let Bin Laden go to a country of his choice.

Afghanistan was his obvious choice. The country was going through another bad phase of the intra-Mujahideen civil war. After the Soviets left, the Afghan Mujahideen factions, who had lost their common enemy, started fighting with each other. The capture of Kabul by Tajiks angered the Pashtun Islamists, who were backed by the ISI. Shia, Sunni, Tajik, Uzbek and Pashtun militias started attacking each other, plunging Afghanistan into chaos and bloodshed. The Taliban rose from this anarchy.

By the time Bin Laden arrived back in Afghanistan in May 1996, the Taliban, the most radical Islamist faction among the Mujahideen, had already captured much of the country and were preparing to march on to Kabul. Bin Laden sought a close relationship with Mullah Mohammad Omar, the Taliban's reclusive emir. Omar welcomed him with open arms, beginning a friendship that would shake the world in 2001.

The Taliban captured Kabul in September 1996 and declared the establishment of the Islamic Emirate of Afghanistan. The Mujahideen government of Rabbani and Massoud fled to Panjshir Valley. Almost 90 per cent of Afghanistan came under the Taliban's firm control. Mullah Omar oversaw the Taliban administration from Kandahar, while a council of clerics ran the day-to-day affairs from Kabul.

To Bin Laden, the Taliban regime offered him the best chance to start a global jihad against the West and its allies in the Muslim world. With safe sanctuary and the protection of the national government, he set up an al-Qaeda base in Afghanistan. Within a few months of his arrival, Bin Laden had issued a fatwa, 'Declaration of War against the Americans Occupying the Land of the Two Holy Places', referring to the US presence in Saudi Arabia, which hosts Islam's two holiest mosques. First published in *Al Quds Al Arabi*, a London-based newspaper, in August 1996, the fatwa called upon the world's Muslims to rise against 'the Jewish-Crusader alliance' and 'expel, humiliate and defeat the enemy out of the sanctities of Islam'.[28]

In February 1998, less than two years into Taliban rule, Bin Laden and his co-jihadists, including Ayman al-Zawahiri, the current leader of al-Qaeda, issued another statement in the name of the 'World Islamic Front'. In the fatwa titled 'Jihad and Jews and Crusaders', they claimed that the US, through its 'occupation' of Muslim lands, had 'declared war on Allah and his Messenger and Muslims'. In the statement, they said:

> The ruling to kill the Americans and their allies – civilians and military – is an individual duty for every Muslim who can do it in any country in which it is possible to do it, in order to liberate the al-Aqsa Mosque [in Jerusalem] and the holy mosque [Mecca] from their grip, and in order for their

> armies to move out of all the lands of Islam, defeated and unable to threaten any Muslim … We – with Allah's help – call on every Muslim who believes in Allah and wishes to be rewarded to comply with Allah's order to kill the Americans and plunder their money wherever and whenever they find it. We also call on Muslim ulema, leaders, youths, and soldiers to launch the raid on Satan's US troops and the devil's supporters allying with them, and to displace those who are behind them so that they may learn a lesson.[29]

Six months after the fatwa was announced, al-Qaeda bombed American embassies in Kenya and Tanzania, killing 224 people. It was a wake-up call for the US. In October 2000, al-Qaeda struck again, carrying out a suicide attack on USS *Cole*, a guided missile destroyer of the US Navy that had anchored off Aden, Yemen; seventeen American Navy sailors were killed. The rise of al-Qaeda brought American attention back to Afghanistan. The CIA started coordinating with Ahmad Shah Massoud, who was commanding the Northern Alliance, the anti-Taliban grouping based in the northern districts of Afghanistan, and Amrullah Saleh, one of Massoud's close aides who would become a key figure in the post-Taliban administration, to hunt for Bin Laden. They neither captured Bin Laden nor found out what he was up to.

For Bin Laden, the attacks in Kenya and Tanzania and on USS *Cole* were only the beginning. He was already planning a huge attack on the American mainland, a threat the US did not take seriously. On 11 September 2001, al-Qaeda attacked the US, ramming hijacked planes into the World Trade Center (WTC) twin towers in New York and the Pentagon in Virginia. Another hijacked plane crashed in a field in Shanksville, Pennsylvania. Close to 3000 people, including nineteen al-Qaeda terrorists, were killed in the attacks.

For the US, it was a moment of tremendous shock and grief. The last time the US mainland had been attacked by foreign forces was on 7 December 1941, when Japan staged a surprise attack on Pearl Harbor, Hawaii, decimating America's Pacific fleet. The attack led to the US joining the Second World War. On the day the planes rammed into the twin towers, President George W. Bush was in Sarasota, Florida, to interact with students at the Emma E. Booker Elementary School. After the second plane hit the WTC, White House Chief of Staff Andrew Card, who was with the President, walked up to Bush and whispered in his ear, 'America is under attack.'[30] Immediately after the 9/11 attacks, the US asked the Taliban regime to hand over Osama bin Laden.

The Taliban had consistently resisted international pressure to expel Bin Laden. After 9/11, the Taliban faced a dilemma. They did not want to disown Bin Laden after providing him refuge. But if they didn't do so, an American attack was certain. Factions within the Taliban considered cutting ties with al-Qaeda and Bin Laden. But Mullah Omar was adamant. He told his inner circle in September 2001:

> You just care about your posts and your money, your ministries, but I don't care about mine. My position is bigger than yours, but I don't care about it ... I am ready to lose my leadership, but not to hand over Osama to the Americans or send him to another country.[31]

He kept his word. Osama bin Laden was not handed over to the US. On 7 October 2001, the US began an invasion of Afghanistan, twelve years after the Soviet Union, unable to defeat the America-backed Mujahideen Islamist, withdrew from the country.

Another Vietnam

The US invaded Afghanistan to defeat al-Qaeda, which had carried out the 9/11 attacks, and get rid of the Taliban, which harboured the attackers. The Taliban regime fell within weeks of the American attack and most of its leaders retreated to Afghanistan's mountainous countryside or to Pakistan. The al-Qaeda bases and camps in Afghanistan were destroyed and its networks disrupted. A new US-backed government was installed in Kabul, replacing the Taliban's Islamic Emirate.

It seemed like the US had made convincing gains in the first outpost in the global war on terror declared by President George W. Bush. But in the long run, the war did not proceed as the Americans had expected. The invasion of Afghanistan would go down in America's history as its longest war. After twenty years of fighting, the US had to enter into an agreement with the Taliban and withdraw its troops from the country in August 2021, just days before the twentieth anniversary of the attacks on 11 September. If the US had started its covert operations in Afghanistan in 1979 to create a Vietnam for the Soviet Union, Afghanistan would turn out to be another Vietnam for the Americans themselves.

It is hard to miss the similarities between the way the US exited Vietnam in 1975 and the way it withdrew from Afghanistan in 2021. Well before its actual withdrawal, the US had realized it could not win the Afghan war, much like it realized in the 1960s that the Vietnam war was lost. US involvement in Vietnam went back to the last years of French colonial rule. In Vietnam, the US first backed France against the Viet Minh guerrillas. After France exited Vietnam in 1954, the US backed South Vietnam against the communist-led North. Initially, American involvement was limited to advisory roles. But after the US destroyer USS *Maddox* was attacked by North Vietnamese torpedo boats in the Gulf of

Tonkin off the Vietnamese coast in August 1964, the Lyndon Johnson administration steadily escalated the American role.

At its peak, in 1968, American troop deployment in Vietnam reached 549,500 personnel.[32] By the late 1960s, it became evident to American leaders that they could not win the war. Richard Nixon, who was elected President in 1968, assigned Henry Kissinger, the National Security Advisor, to hold talks with communist North Vietnam, seeking 'peace with honor'.[33] The Americans were actually prolonging a war they had already lost. The goal was not to defeat North Vietnam but to stop it from taking over the South, the American ally. Daniel Ellsberg, who leaked the Pentagon Papers, the documents on US involvement in Vietnam from 1945 to 1967 that Washington had kept away from the public, called this approach the 'stalemate machine'.[34]

By the late 1960s, American public opinion had largely turned against the war. Despite massive troop deployment, both the US and its South Vietnamese allies had failed to make substantial gains. America's search and destroy operations in communist-dominated villages in the South and its air campaign in the North only fuelled Vietnamese hostility. The US had dropped more than three times as many bombs on Vietnam as the Allied forces had during the Second World War.[35] Besides, the South Vietnamese regime was unpopular, oppressive and weak at the same time. In a visit to Saigon, the South's capital, a few months after he assumed the presidency, Nixon promised peace and asked the communists to reciprocate. He badly wanted a deal, and Kissinger was his bet.

Nixon first started 'Vietnamizing' the war: reducing US troop presence in Vietnam and shifting the focus from direct participation in land war to training and advisory roles, while continuing with air strikes. At the same time, Kissinger started talks with Le Duc Tho, a North Vietnamese revolutionary and diplomat. When talks were deadlocked, the US offered to pull out of the South as a compromise. In 1973, the US, North Vietnam and representatives of South Vietnam and Viet Cong, the communist guerrillas from the South, signed the Paris Peace Accords. The North and the South agreed to a ceasefire and to continue holding peace talks, while the US agreed to pull troops out of Vietnam.

In Afghanistan, veteran diplomat Zalmay Khalilzad, who started direct negotiations with the Taliban, became the new Kissinger. Just as Nixon wanted to get out of Vietnam, Presidents Donald Trump and Joe Biden wanted to get out of Afghanistan. The US negotiated with the Taliban from a position of weakness, like it did with the Vietnamese communist guerrillas. The Afghan war had similarly become a 'stalemate machine': the US-backed Kabul government couldn't defeat the Taliban and the Taliban couldn't take over the whole country as long as the Americans stayed. America's allies in Afghanistan stood divided. The government of the Islamic Republic of Afghanistan was known for infighting, chronic corruption and incompetence.

Like Nixon's 'Vietnamization', President Barack Obama had started 'Afghanizing' the war: pulling out most troops and moving the remainder to training and advisory roles. If the US had 90,000 troops in Afghanistan at its peak (and 41,000 from coalition partners) in 2011, the numbers fell to 7000 in 2016, Obama's last year in office.[36] The Afghan war also turned unpopular in America. One of the key campaign promises of Donald Trump was to wind down America's foreign interventions. Trump won the presidency in 2016, but the US could not have unilaterally pulled out, especially when the Taliban were on the offensive. That would have left a lasting stain on America's already battered reputation as the world's pre-eminent military power. Hence, it needed a deal, and finding one was Ambassador Khalilzad's mission. When the US was forced to pull out of Vietnam, the South and

North governments had not reached any settlement other than a ceasefire. The plan was for talks to continue, towards a final agreement. The ceasefire did not last long. Two years after the US pulled out, the communists captured Saigon and the government crumbled like a house of cards.

In the case of Afghanistan, the situation was worse. There wasn't even a ceasefire. The US–Taliban agreement was signed in February 2020 when Trump was the President.[37] When Joe Biden became the US President, he practically endorsed the Trump–Taliban agreement, and announced that the US troops would pull back by 11 September, which he later advanced to 31 August.[38] But fifteen days before the US could complete its withdrawal, the Taliban had captured Kabul.

New Great Game

While defending his decision to pull back forces, President Biden said on 31 August that he was left with only two options after the withdrawal agreement was signed by the Trump administration with the Taliban: either honour the deal, or renege on it and send in thousands of more troops to escalate the war. 'I was not going to extend this forever war, and I was not extending a forever exit,' he said.[39] He brought the forever war to an end. What did the US gain from it?

Biden clearly sought to reinterpret America's foreign policy from a realistic, national security point of view. 'To those asking for a third decade of war in Afghanistan, I ask: What is the vital national interest? In my view, we only have one: to make sure Afghanistan can never be used again to launch an attack on our homeland,' he said. He said the US had invaded Afghanistan not because it was ruled by the Taliban but because the 11 September attacks originated from Afghanistan.

> I respectfully suggest you ask yourself this question: If we had been attacked on September 11, 2001, from Yemen instead of Afghanistan, would we have ever gone to war in Afghanistan – even though the Taliban controlled Afghanistan in 2001? I believe the honest answer is 'no.' That's because we had no vital national interest in Afghanistan other than to prevent an attack on America's homeland and our friends. And that's true today.[40]

Biden had set this realist tone for his Afghan policy after the decision to pull back troops. On 8 July, he had said, 'America didn't go to Afghanistan to nation-build.' He added, 'We went for two reasons: one, to bring Osama bin Laden to the gates of hell, as I said at the time. The second reason was to eliminate al Qaeda's capacity to carry out more attacks on the United States from that territory. We accomplished both of those objectives – period.'[41] He was clearly de-emphasizing the Taliban's return to power in Afghanistan. The new argument was that the Taliban were not America's main enemy and defeating them was not the primary objective.

While it is true that America went to Afghanistan because the 9/11 attacks originated from that country, Biden's assessment of the Taliban was not shared by his predecessors, as their actions suggest. The Taliban had offered to surrender on modest terms – Mullah Omar, their leader, was to be allowed to return home – in December 2001, but President George W. Bush rejected the offer and his Department of Defense vowed to defeat them.[42] America did not pull back from Afghanistan after the Taliban regime fell and the insurgents retreated to the Afghan mountains and Pakistan. America did not withdraw after Bin Laden was killed in 2011 either. The US stayed on in Afghanistan, propping up the Islamic

Republic because American leaders were of the view that a return of the Taliban to power would derail the global war on terror.

While there is little evidence to suggest that the Taliban have changed over the past twenty years, American foreign policy thinking has clearly changed during this period. If the US saw the Taliban, which hosted al-Qaeda, as part of the problem in 2001 and removing them from power as a key goal of the war on terror, in 2021, it has virtually delinked a victorious Taliban from the war on terror. The Taliban are now a problem of the Afghans, not of Americans, according to the Biden doctrine. In their last days in Afghanistan, the American military coordinated with the Taliban to ensure Kabul airport security. The Department of State even said that the Taliban and the Haqqani Network, a designated terrorist group, 'are two separate entities'.[43]

When the US invaded Afghanistan, it was touted as the first step in what George W. Bush called a global war on terrorism. 'The Taliban regime … is not only repressing its own people, it is threatening people everywhere by sponsoring and sheltering and supplying terrorists. By aiding and abetting murder, the Taliban regime is committing murder,' Bush told a joint session of the US Congress on 20 September 2001. He asked the Taliban to hand over terrorists, or 'share in their fate'. 'Our war on terror begins with al Qaeda, but it does not end there. It will not end until every terrorist group of global reach has been found, stopped and defeated,' Bush told cheering lawmakers.[44]

In 2001, al-Qaeda was largely concentrated in Afghanistan. The US invasion and the fall of the Taliban led to al-Qaeda's disintegration. The terrorist outfit was driven underground, but was not defeated or decimated. Over the years, new branches of al-Qaeda sprang up in different parts of the world. Of them, the deadliest was al-Qaeda in Iraq (AQI), which was led by Abu Musab al-Zarqawi after the US invasion of Iraq in 2003. The Jordan-born terrorist was killed in a US strike in 2006, but AQI transformed into the Islamic State of Iraq, which later became the dreaded Islamic State (IS) that declared a caliphate and established a proto-state across Iraq and Syria in 2014.

The IS's physical infrastructure was destroyed in coordinated and separate war efforts by a group of powers, including the US, Iran, Iraq, Kurdish and Shia militias, Syria and Russia. But the rump of the outfit continued to operate in parts of Syria and Iraq until the end of 2021. The IS has also established provinces in other parts of the world, including the IS West Africa Province (ISWAP) and the IS Khorasan Province (ISKP) that claimed responsibility for the 26 August 2021 Kabul blasts in which over 200 people were killed, including thirteen Americans. Al-Qaeda has also established a strong presence in Africa, particularly in the Sahel region, where they have carried out dozens of attacks in recent years, killing hundreds of people.

If al-Qaeda was an organized terrorist machinery concentrated in Afghanistan in 2001, it's now a decentralized amalgam that has metastasized across the world, as Biden himself claimed.[45] The US can take credit for disrupting al-Qaeda's networks in Afghanistan, which it thinks neutralized the terrorists' capability to strike the American mainland, and for killing Osama bin Laden. But the question American policymakers and the public faced at the time of US withdrawal from Taliban controlled Afghanistan was whether, to meet these modest objectives, it had been required to stay twenty years in the country, spend over $2 trillion and lose over 2300 soldiers in a war that also killed hundreds of thousands of Afghans.

The Soviet Union's forced withdrawal from Afghanistan in 1989 had caused irreparable damage to its global power. Moscow looked on helplessly as communist regimes in East Europe fell in 1989. All the Muslim-majority Soviet republics in Afghanistan's neighbourhood and other parts of East Europe declared independence, which eventually led to the disintegration of the USSR itself. In contrast, today's US is a stronger and a more flexible power than the Soviet Union of 1989. It has suffered geopolitical setbacks in the past and bounced back. No doubt the forced withdrawal from Afghanistan and the return of the Taliban to power will dent its power and embolden its rivals. But the withdrawal from Afghanistan and larger continental Asia also allows the US to mobilize its resources and shift strategic focus towards a bigger challenge it's facing in East Asia: China.

The US saw a series of setbacks, including the defeat in Vietnam, in the decade before it decided to indirectly interfere in Afghanistan in 1979. Still, by late 1979, the US was back in action, thanks to the Soviet intervention in Afghanistan. Biden's America, having suffered a crushing defeat in Afghanistan, would be reluctant to launch another direct military intervention in the near future. But the US, which is seeking to return to realism from neoconservatism, would wait for its rivals, especially China, to commit blunders, like the Soviets, emboldened by America's defeat in Vietnam, did in 1979, or other strategic opportunities. Afghanistan is not the end of American power. It is possibly the beginning of a new Cold War, this time played out between the US and China.

2

The Rise of the Mullahs

IN THE SPRING OF 1996, THE TALIBAN, WHICH HAD TAKEN southern Afghanistan under its control, organized a conference of its fighters, commanders and mullahs in downtown Kandahar, the movement's political and spiritual base. The city hosts one of the holiest shrines in the country: the Shrine of the Cloak of the Prophet Muhammad (Kirka Sharif), which keeps a robe that Afghans believe was worn by the Prophet. According to legend, the cloak, a camel-fur garment woven by the Prophet Enoch, was presented by God to the Prophet Muhammad after his Night Journey to heaven (*Mi'raj*) on al-Buraq, a winged horse.[1]

Next to the shrine is the tomb of King Ahmad Shah Durrani, the patriarch of the Durrani dynasty and the founder of the modern state of Afghanistan. The legend is that King Durrani, who ruled the country from 1747 to 1772, brought the cloak to Kandahar from Bukhara in 1768. According to one account, Durrani saw the sacred cloak in Bukhara, in modern Uzbekistan, which was a centre of Islamic learning, and asked the locals if he could borrow it. The keepers, fearing that the mighty Shah might steal it, refused his request. Durrani then pointed to a stone in the ground and promised he would never take the robe away from the stone. He kept his word. When he took the cloak to Kandahar, the Durrani capital, he took it along with the stone, which now stands at his grave.[2]

Very rarely has the cloak been shown to the public. Inside the mosque, it is kept in a small silver box, which, in turn, lies inside two larger boxes. The head keeper holds the keys to the silver box. According to tradition, Afghanistan's king would seek permission to take the cloak out if the country faced great danger. The robe was taken out when there was a catastrophic cholera outbreak in Afghanistan in the early twentieth century. Qari Shawali, the former keeper of the cloak, said in December 2001 that during his lifetime, only three men tried to look at the robe. The first was King Mohammed Zahir Shah. 'When the chest was opened, he became afraid and began trembling,' Shawali said. 'Maybe he was a sinner.'[3] The second, he said, was Pir Ahmed Gailani, the leader of the Qadiriyyah Sufi order and a relative of King Zahir. The third was Mullah Mohammad Omar, the Taliban leader, in 1996.

Those who assembled before Kirka Sharif in central Kandahar in 1996 for the Taliban Shura (consultative council) were clueless as to what they were going to see. Then Mullah Omar appeared on the roof, with the sacred cloak in his hands. He held it aloft before a cheering crowd, who named him 'Amir ul-Momineen', the 'commander of the faithful'. Omar's appearance with the relic was at a critical juncture in the Taliban's history. The militants had not reached Kabul yet. The rank and file were divided on whether the Taliban should press ahead with the offensive on Kabul which had been in a blockade for months. But what happened in Kandahar, as Steve Coll wrote, was Mullah Omar's 'coronation' as the leader of the most powerful Islamist insurgency in Afghanistan. The mullahs and militants assembled before Kirka Sharif would pledge themselves to the new commander. Omar wanted the war to go on. Within a few months the Taliban would capture Kabul and establish the Islamic Emirate of Afghanistan.[4]

The Commander

The roots of the Taliban go back to the Mujahideen movement against the Soviet troops in Afghanistan in the 1980s. Many of the Taliban's early leadership, including Omar and his deputy Mullah Mohammad Rabbani, fought the Soviets with various Mujahideen factions, which were supported by the United States' Central Intelligence Agency (CIA), Pakistan's Inter-Services Intelligence (ISI) and Saudi Arabia's General Intelligence Directorate. Omar had served as a deputy commander of the militant group Harakat Inquilab i-Islami (Islamic Revolution Movement) that was led by Muhammad Nabi Muhammadi, an influential Pashtun Mujahideen leader from Kandahar, who studied in Pakistan's madrassas.[5] Omar fought the Soviets in Kandahar, Zabul, Herat and Farah.

Born in a village outside Kandahar some time between 1959 and 1962, Omar lost his father at a very young age. He grew up in Urozgan, a central province, with his mother and stepfather, who was a madrassa teacher. He attended religious schools and then, as a teenager, moved to Kandahar, Afghanistan's second largest city, in the 1970s. In a country that was taking initial steps of economic and social modernization, first under the leadership of President Mohammed Daoud Khan and then the communists, Kandahar was an emerging centre of urban life. University-educated youth from rich families dominated the city's social and economic networks while the poor with only religious schooling, known as Talibs (a Talib is a seeker of knowledge in Pashto), confined themselves to the madrassas. Omar belonged to the second category.[6] When the civil war broke out, both the elite and the Taliban (plural form of Talib) joined the fighting. But the latter never made it to the leadership of the Mujahideen. They were, including Omar, the muscles of the jihad.

While commanding a small unit of the Mujahideen in Sangesar outside Kandahar, Omar came under heavy Russian assault. The Red Army 'pushed forward and soon we could see them from our trenches', Mullah Abdul Salam Zaeef, who later served as the Taliban's ambassador to Pakistan, wrote in his memoir. 'The area was littered with bodies ... The battle turned into a hand-to-hand fight, with grenades flying over our heads.'[7] A piece of shrapnel struck Omar in the face and took his right eye. After many rounds of attacks, the Russians retreated. That night, Omar and his comrades got together to celebrate their survival. Omar, with a bloody bandage on his face, sang a ghazal to his fellow militants:

> My illness is untreatable, oh, my flower-like friend
> My life is difficult without you, my flower-like friend.[8]

After the Soviets pulled back from Afghanistan in 1989, the Mujahideen turned their focus towards the communist government of Mohammad Najibullah. His regime did not survive long after the collapse of the Soviet Union in 1991. Najibullah took refuge at the UN office in Kabul after his government fell in 1992. The Mujahideen would quickly form the government under the leadership of Burhanuddin Rabbani and Ahmad Shah Massoud, both Tajik leaders. Abdul Rashid Dostum, the Uzbek commander, would offer his support to the new government. Nabi Muhammadi, Mullah Omar's commander in Harakat Inquilab i-Islami, would go on to become Vice President in the Mujahideen government. Omar would leave the battlefield and retreat to a madrassa in

Sangesar. A Talib with limited political clout and practically no support from the country's tribal leaders or powerful warlords, Omar, who was in his early thirties, did not stand a chance of building a political career in the Mujahideen-led Afghanistan. Nor did he show any ambition for one. In Sangesar, he started teaching the Quran to madrassa students, earning himself the title Mullah (provider of knowledge). His country, however, would soon start falling into chaos.

Civil War

Post-communist Afghanistan was deeply divided along ethnic lines. After Najibullah's government fell, the warlords lost their common enemy and ethnic fault lines started re-emerging. Under the Mujahideen government, the Tajiks, the second biggest ethnic group in Afghanistan after the Pashtuns, took control of Kabul for the first time since the modern Afghan state was formed. Tajiks make up some 27 per cent of Afghanistan's population. Their unprecedented political ascent triggered resentment among the majority Pashtuns, who constitute about 42 per cent of the population and have traditionally dominated the country's politics.[9]

In 1992, when the Mujahideen took power, the situation in Afghanistan was slipping from bad to worse. Fifteen years of war had exhausted the country. It had one of the world's lowest life expectancies (fifty-one years)[10] and the largest refugee problem (about 3.5 million Afghan citizens were living in Pakistan and around 3 million in Iran).[11] The new government was expected to unify the country, offer stable governance, end violence and address critical issues such as providing security, fixing the economy, offering public services and improving ties with neighbouring countries. But Rabbani and Massoud failed to meet any of these expectations.

With the two failing to unify the country under their leadership, warlords, representing different ethnicities, started to fight each other. The Tajiks controlled Kabul and the north-eastern provinces that are home to the Tajik population. Gulbuddin Hekmatyar, the Pashtun Islamist leader who commanded Hezb-e-Islami, controlled a small region south and east of Kabul. In Herat and surrounding provinces, Ismail Khan, the Shia Hazara warlord, had carved up his fiefdom. Dostum, who controlled northern provinces, initially backed the Mujahideen government, but would break with it and join Hekmatyar to attack Kabul.

Pakistan had played a critical role during the Mujahideen resistance against the communists. But the rise of the Tajiks to power in Kabul upset Pakistan's calculations as well. Massoud was not one of the favourites of Pakistan's military establishment, which had supplied money and weapons to the Mujahideen factions. Pakistan also saw the Rabbani government, which was recognized by India, as hostile to its vital interests in Afghanistan. Islamabad wanted its proxy to be on the throne in Kabul. The ISI started backing Hekmatyar, who turned Kabul into a graveyard with heavy shelling from the mountains surrounding the city. In the south, the Pashtun provinces were ruled by a Jalalabad-based Mujahideen Shura but nobody was effectively in control. Kandahar, the capital of the Durranis and the traditional centre of Pashtun life, was divided up by a group of Mujahideen commanders among themselves. There was no central authority. Life was chaotic. Crimes, including robbery, rape and murder, were rampant. Afghanistan, which poet Muhammad Iqbal once called 'the heart of Asia', was falling apart.[12]

It was against this background that a group of Talibs in Kandahar came together to launch a new movement to restore order. Most of them were Mujahideen fighters and had studied in Deobandi madrassas in Pakistan and Afghanistan, had known each other for years and shared common aspirations for Afghanistan. 'We all knew each other – Mullahs Omar, Ghaus, Mohammed Rabbani and myself – because we were all originally from Urozgan and had fought together,' Mullah Mohammed Hassan, who was the governor of Kandahar, told journalist Ahmad Rashid in an interview. The mullahs wanted to end anarchy, restore peace, disarm the militias and unite people under Islam. They saw only one way to achieve all of these goals: by enforcing the Sharia, the Islamic code, across Afghanistan. As Olivier Roy and Mariam Abou Zahab write in their book *Islamist Networks*, their political strategy consisted only of 'the Sharia, the whole Sharia, and nothing but the Sharia'.[13]

The mullahs saw themselves as God's pure soldiers destined to fight corrupt warlords and Mujahideen commanders. They believed that the answer to the chaos, lawlessness and continuing conflicts in Afghanistan was to re-establish the Islamic order created by the Prophet Muhammad in the seventh century. And they didn't have to think twice about who their leader should be. Mullah Omar, the man who had lost an eye in the jihad against the Soviet Red Army, was the obvious choice. 'We selected Mullah Omar to lead this movement. He was the first among equals. And we gave him the power to lead us and he has given us the power and authority to deal with the people's problems,' Mullah Hassan, who would go on to become the acting head of the Taliban's Shura in 1997, said after the Taliban took Kabul.[14]

There are many stories about how Omar mobilized the Taliban under his command. 'The most credible story,' writes Rashid in his book, 'is that in the spring of 1994, Sangesar neighbours came to tell him that a commander had abducted two teenage girls.' They were taken to a military camp and repeatedly raped. Omar, along with thirty Talibs who had sixteen rifles among them, attacked the base. They freed the girls and hanged the warlord from the barrel of a tank. From his base, they captured arms and ammunition, beginning a long journey of bloody militancy. This story was told and retold in Kandahar's lawless neighbourhoods where Omar's stature as a simple, devout mullah who could be ruthless to his enemies started growing. In another incident, the Taliban attacked two local commanders who had fought each other with tanks in a Kandahar bazaar over the possession of a young boy. Omar's forces killed the commanders and hanged them in public.[15] Gradually, the people in Kandahar started approaching the Taliban for protection from warlords and to settle local disputes. Omar and his Taliban, having tasted victory, were ready to pick up more fights. 'We were fighting against Muslims who had gone wrong. How could we remain quiet when we could see crimes being committed against women, and the poor?' Omar later said.[16]

The initial small successes and their growing popularity in Kandahar prompted the Taliban to expand their operations. On 12 October 1994, Omar assembled some 200 madrassa students and led them to Spin Boldak, a key border crossing between Afghanistan and Pakistan. They took the crossing after heavy fighting and seized a huge arms depot on the border that was guarded by Gulbuddin Hekmatyar's men. This was the Taliban's first major territorial victory, which earned them the attention of Pakistan's generals; their patience with Hekmatyar, who was unable to take Kabul despite his brutal military campaign, had been wearing thin. The capture of one of the busiest border crossings of Afghanistan also allowed the Taliban to collect taxes from the Afghan–Pakistan transport mafia. Their coffers started swelling.

What started as a local madrassa students' movement was now growing as a militia with more and more weapons and money. Their rise immediately acquired geopolitical implications with help coming in from Pakistan. Omar set his goals higher. The Taliban were no longer looking to resolve the troubles of the local residents of Kandahar. Omar wanted to wage a jihad against all Mujahideen warlords. 'We took up arms to achieve the aims of the Afghan jihad and save our people from further suffering at the hands of the so-called Mujahideen,' Omar told Pakistani journalist Rahimullah Yusufzai in 1995, in the midst of his military campaign. 'We had complete faith in God Almighty. We never forgot that. He can bless us with victory or plunge us into defeat.'[17]

The Ascent

After the Taliban's victory at Spin Boldak, Pakistan sent a convoy of trucks carrying rice, clothes and medicines to Turkmenistan via Afghanistan – which Pakistan Interior Minister Naseerullah Babar called the 'peace convoy' – without securing the permission of Kandahar's warlords.[18] At Kandahar the trucks were hijacked by a Mujahideen commander, who asked Pakistan to pay ransom to release them. On 3 November 1994, the Taliban intervened again, staging a surprise attack. They released the trucks, shot and killed the commander, and hanged his body from the barrel of a tank for everyone to see.[19] It was a message from Mullah Omar. They were the new leaders of Kandahar. On the same day, the Taliban launched an attack on the city.[20] Some warlords did not even resist while some others cut deals with the Taliban in return for their safety, and the soldiers they commanded joined the Taliban's ranks. Within two weeks, this little-known militia commanded by a little-known mullah had taken over Afghanistan's second largest city.

They also captured a vast quantity of arms and ammunition. Pakistan found the Taliban the most reassuring proxy in an otherwise fractured Afghanistan. The victory in Kandahar turned around the Taliban's prospects. Thousands of madrassa students from the seminaries controlled by the Jamiat Ulema-e-Islam (JUI) across Pakistan and Afghanistan flocked to Kandahar to join the Taliban. For them, Mullah Omar was the 'prince of all believers'.[21]

With thousands of fighters under his command, Omar would order more attacks, capturing province after province. Forces of surrendered commanders, battle-hardened men, including pilots, tank commanders and front-line infantry officers – some of whom had fought the Soviets and some others who had served the communist army – would join the Taliban's ranks. In three months, twelve out of thirty-two provinces would come under the Taliban's total control.[22]

By mid-1995, with southern and eastern Afghanistan under their control, the Taliban moved west and then north, determined to capture Kabul and other provinces held by ethnic warlords. In September, after initial setbacks, they took Herat, Afghanistan's third largest city.[23] And then they marched on towards Kabul. The Taliban blockaded the capital, which was already under attack from the forces of Hekmatyar. They attacked both Hekmatyar's forces and the government of President Rabbani. On 7 March 1996, Hekmatyar signed a power-sharing accord with President Rabbani in which both sides agreed to cooperate against the Taliban.[24] The fighting dragged on for months, without any breakthrough. The prolonged military campaign and the coming together of their rivals had created fissures and confusion within the Taliban. One belief was that the war had entered a stalemate: the Taliban could not take Kabul and the Kabul government could not take Kandahar. Sections within the Taliban pushed for talks with Rabbani and Massoud to reach a political settlement. But Mullah Omar, now an ambitious warlord himself, did not favour any settlement with the government. He wanted to take his jihad to its logical conclusion: the military takeover of Kabul and establishment of the Taliban's monopolistic rule over the country.

On 30 March, amid growing uncertainty within the movement, the Taliban called a Shura in Kandahar. Hundreds of mullahs from across the country assembled in the city to discuss the future course of action. In the meeting, the hardliners led by Omar and his close associates emerged stronger. Omar was given the title Amir ul-Momineen here.[25] It was after this council that Omar appeared on the roof of Kirka Sharif, the holy mosque in Kandahar, holding up the Prophet's cloak. He re-emphasized the jihad against the Mujahideen. With the new title and the loyalty of the whole of the Taliban and the ulema, Mullah Omar ordered the war to continue.

The Taliban thereafter adopted a two-pronged strategy: it continued to shell Kabul, retaining military pressure on President Rabbani and Massoud, while at the same time attacking other provinces and cutting through their weak defence lines. The plan was to surround Kabul and force it to surrender. In early September, the Taliban seized Jalalabad, capital of the eastern Nangarhar province and a key city linking Kabul to Peshawar in Pakistan. The victory gave the Taliban control over the major land route between Afghanistan's capital and Pakistan. Now, with almost two-thirds of the country under their control, the Taliban attacked Kabul with full force from the southeast and southwest despite a United Nations Security Council (UNSC) call for a ceasefire.

On 26 August, when it became evident that they couldn't stop the Taliban from entering the city, President Rabbani, Defence Minister Massoud and their associates retreated to the Panjshir Valley in the north, the base of Massoud's guerrilla movement. The next day, the Taliban entered the city. Mullah Omar, who was in Kandahar, declared amnesty to 'all former government supporters'.[26] But not to the leader of the former communist regime. One of the first things the Taliban did after taking Kabul was to raid the UN compound, seize Mohammad Najibullah, who was under UN protection, torture him to death, drag his body through the streets of Kabul and hang it from a lamp post outside the Arg, the presidential palace in the capital that had been Najibullah's seat of power for five years.[27] The Taliban immediately declared the

Islamic Emirate of Afghanistan, marking a new beginning. Within two days, the new Taliban government was recognized by Pakistan.

Ideology

As soon as they were in power, the Taliban started enforcing their version of a strict Islamist code on Afghan society. Mullah Omar appointed his deputy, Mullah Muhammad Rabbani (not related to Burhanuddin Rabbani), head of a six-man council that would run the day-to-day affairs of the government. They issued a host of decrees, radically altering the social and religious lives of Afghans. Women were banned from working in public offices, girls were kept out of school and men were required to grow their beards. The Taliban proscribed public music, the sale of CDs and even kite flying. They established a new Ministry of Prevention of Vices and Promotion of Virtues that would enforce the new moral code on Afghans.[28] Women and men were segregated. If women did not wear a burqa covering the entire body, they would be beaten up by the Taliban's moral police, who patrolled the streets.[29] Capital punishment was widely used. Kabul's sports stadium was turned into a public execution ground. Gambling was forbidden. Those captured for theft were subjected to surgical amputation, and adultery was punishable by stoning to death in public.[30]

The Taliban claimed that these measures, driven by their interpretation of the Sharia, were prerequisites to establish order in the civil war-torn Afghanistan, as well as to cleanse society of its communist and Mujahideen vices and create an ideal Islamic country. In an interview, Mullah Omar listed the Taliban's goals: 'To end the mischief in the country, to establish peace and security, to protect life, wealth and honour and to enforce the Sharia, do jihad against the leaders who were devoted to power, and endeavour to make the land of Afghanistan an exemplary state.'[31] To achieve these goals, the Taliban moved to establish a tightly held religious totalitarian system in which loyalty and submission to the Amir ul-Momineen was unquestionable. Obeying the supreme leader was God's wish (*fardh*) and hence could not be violated. If he called for jihad, the faithful were to take weapons and join him. Those who disobeyed would be punished.[32]

There were not many modern examples for the system the Taliban put in place in Afghanistan. Especially in Afghanistan, a multi-ethnic and multi-religious society where Islam, the majority religion, had coexisted with other faiths for centuries, the Taliban's extremist interpretation of Islam and its violent enforcement was alien. A vast majority of Afghanistan's Muslims are Sunni, who follow the Hanafi school of thought, one of the four major schools of Sunni Islamic jurisprudence. More than 10 per cent of the population are Shia.[33] The country also had sizeable Hindu and Sikh communities until the outbreak of the civil war,[34] as well as a vibrant Jewish community whose roots can be traced back to the medieval period. According to one legend, the Pashtuns were the descendants of one of Israel's lost tribes, who were expelled from the Kingdom of Israel after its conquest by the Assyrians in 722 BCE.[35] While Islam remained the major religion of the state, different communities lived in harmony and minorities were free to follow their faiths. But most of the minority communities started leaving the country after the civil war broke out in the late 1970s.

This culture of harmony and coexistence started changing at this time, a period which also saw the political Islamization of Afghanistan. When the communists captured the state and centralized power in their hands, eating into the autonomy the tribal and religious leaders had traditionally enjoyed, there was resentment and resistance. Later when the Soviets came, Afghans, who had a history of fighting the mighty British empire in multiple wars until they got freedom, saw the Soviets as an invading army and started armed resistance. The geopolitics of the Cold War turned this Afghan resistance into a regional conflict between radical Islamism, backed by the US and Pakistan, and the communist government in Kabul, backed by the Soviet Union. This was the period when radical Islamist movements took root in Afghanistan.

The Taliban were a late entrant into this Afghan cauldron. Gen. Zia-ul-Haq, the Pakistani dictator who was influenced by the teachings of radical Islamist cleric Abul A'la Maududi and the party he founded, Jamaat-e-Islami, leaned on the Jamaat model Islamist groups in Afghanistan such as Hekmatyar's Hezb-e-Islami and Rabbani's Jamiat-e Islami to drive his regional agenda. The Pakistan–US–Saudi arms and money pipeline specifically supported these Islamist groups against the communists. But Gen. Zia's Islamization drive at home helped all kinds of Islamic parties, including those who were critical of the Jamaat-e-Islami and its concepts of Islamic state and revolution. One of them was the Jamiat Ulema-e-Islam, the political party of the Deobandi madrassa networks, an Islamic revivalist movement, in Pakistan. The roots of the Taliban can be traced to these Deobandi madrassa networks, which flourished across Pakistan and Afghanistan, with help from the Pakistani state and Saudi money, during the Afghan civil war in the 1980s. Deobandism, which originated in colonial India, is the Islamic basis of the Taliban's ideology.

The Revivalists

In 1867, a group of religious scholars came together and founded Darul Uloom (House of Learning) in Deoband in today's Indian state of Uttar Pradesh, with the main goal of reforming prevalent Islamic practices.[36] A decade prior to this, Indians' resistance to colonial rule had been crushed by the British and Mughal rule had come to an end. There was generally a sense among Muslims that the period of Islamic glory was fading. The solution the Deobandi clerics found was to launch a movement to restore the key tenets of Islam in Muslim life and fight the British with greater strength. So in the political sphere, the Deobandis remained staunchly anti-colonialist, and within Islam, they emerged as revivalists who wanted to purify the practice of Islam.

They were inspired by Shaikh Ahmed Sirhindi, the seventeenth-century Sufi who called for the reform of Sufi practices. Shah Wali Ullah, one of the most prominent Islamic scholars of South Asia in the eighteenth century, further developed Sirhindi's ideas and argued for the reintroduction of the Quran and Hadith into the Sufi *tariqa* (path).[37] Shah Wali Ullah was greatly inspired by Ibn Taymiyyah, the fourteenth-century Islamist revivalist scholar, who sanctioned *takfir* (making a declaration of apostasy against a fellow Muslim who does not follow the 'true' beliefs of Islam).[38] Muhammad Abd al-Wahhab, the eighteenth-century Arabian scholar whose puritanical interpretation of Islam would come to be called Wahhabism (Salafism), had also been inspired by Ibn Taymiyyah.[39] There are similarities between the interpretation of Islam by Abdul Wahhab, and by the Deobandis. While both the Wahhabis and Deobandis claim that they follow the purest path of Islam based on the Quran and Hadith, there are theological differences between them. The Deobandis, who emerged as a reform movement from Sufi Islam, did not completely cut off their ties with the Sufi tradition. Both the Deobandis and the Barelvi Sufis follow the Hanafi school of jurisprudence (a majority of Afghans follow the Hanafi school), and Abu Hanifa is their imam.[40] On the other side, there is no consensus among the Wahhabis (also called Salafis) whether they should follow any particular school (*fiqh*). Some Salafis have denounced *taqlid* (adherence to any of the four schools of Sunni Islamic law) and believe in the direct and literal interpretation of the Quran and Hadith.[41]

Shah Wali Ullah's teachings had been taken to the Pashtun region north of Punjab in 1820 by his grandson, Shah Ismail. Ahmed Sirhindi was also revered by many Afghans who followed the Naqshbandi Sufi order. Later, when the Darul Uloom Deoband was founded, the preaching of Ahmed Sirhindi and Shah Wali Ullah was incorporated into the curriculum. The Deobandi seminaries spread across the subcontinent and many students from Afghanistan travelled to them for studies. In 1879, there were twelve Deobandi madrassas across India. 'By 1967 when Deoband celebrated its first centenary, there were 9,000 Deobandi madrassas across South Asia,' writes Rashid.[42]

The Deobandis, with strong anti-colonial roots, could never separate themselves from politics. In 1919, twenty-five leading Deobandi clerics came together to form the Jamiat Ulema-e-Hind (JUH) as a political platform of their madrassas with the twin goals of defending the core tenets of Islam and fighting the British. The JUH joined with the Indian National Congress during the Khilafat protests and later opposed Partition.[43] The Deobandi clerics from the Pashtun belt, however, disagreed with their counterparts in northern India, particularly on Partition and the Muslim League. In 1945, they split with the JUH and created the Jamiat Ulema-e-Islam, the party that would benefit from Gen. Zia's Islamization drive during the Afghan Mujahideen civil war.[44]

After Partition, Deobandi madrassas spread faster in Pakistan, especially in the North West Frontier Province (NWFP; now Khyber Pakhtunkhwa) and Balochistan. Under Mufti Mehmood, who would go on to become the chief minister of NWFP in 1972, the JUI would develop a strong presence in the Pashtun belt.[45] But the JUI faced an internal crisis when Gen. Zia started directly supporting the Afghan Mujahideen. The JUI saw the Jamaat-e-Islami, Zia's Islamist ally and the lynchpin of his Afghan strategy, as a political and ideological rival. The JUI wanted to reform Islamic practices and fight 'innovations' within Islam, but there was no consensus among its rank and file on the political role of Islam. However, for the Islamist Jamaat, Islam is both the order of life and an ideology of state power.

One section within the JUI opposed Zia's support for the Afghan Mujahideen, while another took a favourable position on the issue. This eventually led to a split in the JUI in 1980, after the death of Mufti Mehmood, into the JUI-F, led by Maulana Fazalur Rahman, Mufti Mehmood's son, and the JUI-S, headed by Samiul Haq, another prominent Deobandi cleric. The JUI-S supported Zia's campaign in Afghanistan.

Zia operated in Afghanistan largely through the Jamaat-e-Islami network. The JUI lacked the political clout to influence the Pakistani establishment's Afghan policy but the civil war opened up all kinds of opportunities for Islamic parties. When Zia's regime promoted opening of madrassas across Pakistan, especially in the border areas with Afghanistan where tens of thousands of Afghan refugees had settled, the JUI factions treated it as an opportunity to expand their networks. Funds were easily available, coming in both from the government and Saudi Wahhabi donors. If there were only 900 madrassas in Pakistan in 1971, by the end of the Zia era in 1988, there were 8000 registered madrassas, and 25,000 unregistered ones, educating over half a million students.[46]

Besides, Samiul Haq, whose JUI-S openly supported Zia's intervention in Afghanistan, established contacts with the Mujahideen leaders who had links with his madrassas. One of them was Nabi Muhammadi, leader of the Harakat Inquilab i-Islami. Muhammadi had studied in Samiul Haq's Darul Uloom Haqqania in Akora Khattak, Khyber Pakhtunkhwa, one of the largest Deobandi seminaries in Pakistan. It's not a coincidence that Mullah Omar was a commander of the Harakat Inquilab i-Islami during the anti-communist civil war. The Haqqania seminary would later become one of the largest training and recruiting grounds for the Taliban.[47]

A host of key historical events in the late 1980s in the region would change the political prospects of the JUI and the Deobandis in Pakistan and Afghanistan. Gen. Zia would die in a plane crash in 1988. A year later, the Soviet troops would withdraw from Afghanistan. A year after the disintegration of the Soviet Union in 1991, the communist government would fall in Afghanistan, and the country would plunge into an intra-Mujahideen civil war. In Pakistan, after the fall of the Zia regime, the Jamaat-e-Islami would lose its political clout. In the 1993 elections in Pakistan, the JUI-F of Fazalur Rahman supported Benazir Bhutto's Pakistan People's Party, which emerged victorious.

When Bhutto became Prime Minister, the corridors of power opened for the JUI-F. Maulana Rahman, who after his initial reticence would establish contacts with the Deobandi militias in Afghanistan, was appointed chairman of the Standing Committee of Foreign Affairs.[48] In this capacity, the maulana was able to influence Pakistan's foreign policy. This was also a time when the Pakistani generals were growing impatient with Hekmatyar's failed siege of Kabul. Pakistan wanted an alternative proxy, and they found one when the Taliban successfully attacked and seized Spin Boldak in 1994. For the Taliban, the Deobandi networks turned out to be an endless source of manpower in their fight.[49] With foot soldiers coming from the madrassa networks, political support from the JUI-F, which was close to power in Islamabad, and military support from the ISI, the Taliban rose quickly in an anarchic Afghanistan where the Mujahideen warlords were fighting each other.

The Deobandis had taken a restrictive view of the role of women in society and a puritanical approach to Islamic practices. But the Taliban took Deobandism to new extremes. The Taliban's quest to create a society based on the realities of the seventh century, resolute opposition to modernity, embrace of brutal violence, total disregard for the role of women in society, and sectarian hatred towards Shias and other minorities were beyond what the Deobandis originally taught in their seminaries. Also, the Taliban's quest for power and the readiness to fight a war for the establishment of an Islamic state and society were far from the Islamic revivalism of the Darul Uloom Deoband.

That is perhaps because the socio-political milieu of Afghanistan in the 1980s and 1990s from which the Taliban rose was influenced by different Islamic ideologies. The anti-communist civil war gained traction immediately after the Shia Islamic revolution in neighbouring Iran. During the civil war, millions of dollars as well as Arab fighters came in from Saudi Arabia and other Gulf states. With them also came Wahhabi ideas. The Jamaat-e-Islami, which believes in an Islamic state and revolution, had retained an overarching ideological presence throughout the civil war, though the factions it supported couldn't sustain their gains in the conflict. The traces of all these ideologies can be found in the Taliban's worldview.

In Iran, the Shia mullahs had established a theocracy after the 1979 Islamic revolution. The Taliban established a Sunni theocracy in Afghanistan in 1996, although the Taliban banned elections (which are permissible in Iran), calling them un-Islamic. The Taliban's restrictions on women, sectarian antipathy towards Shias and extreme views on what they call 'idolatry' are comparable with the Wahhabi extremist approach in these matters. In the Kingdom of Saudi Arabia, founded in 1932 and where Wahhabism is the state religion, men and women were segregated in public places and women were barred from driving until recently. But again, the Wahhabi ulema are not in power in Saudi Arabia, while under the Taliban regime, the clergy is directly in power. When it comes to ideas relating to Islamic society and state, the Taliban's views are closer to those of the Jamaat-e-Islami. In effect, the Taliban built a Sunni Islamist theocracy with a puritanical Wahhabi social view based on the traditional madrassa networks of Deobandism. Despite their embrace of ideas from other streams of Islam, the Taliban never cut off their ties with their Deobandi past. They were rather proud of it. Rahmatullah Hashemi, a Taliban spokesman, once famously said, 'Every Afghan is a Deobandi.'[50]

The Fall

The brutal religious state the Taliban established in Afghanistan allowed Mullah Omar to tighten his grip on power. The former Mujahideen commanders, including Ahmad Shah Massoud and Burhanuddin Rabbani, formed an alliance called the United Front (or Northern Alliance) and continued to resist the Taliban's rule from Panjshir Valley and the surrounding Northern Provinces. But at no point during the Taliban's six-year rule did the Northern Alliance manage to pose a serious challenge to the Taliban's grip on Kabul. On the other side, the Taliban kept expanding its territories, taking control of almost 90 per cent of the country by 1998. There was practically no resistance from civil society because the Taliban did not tolerate it.

The regime was internationally isolated. Besides Pakistan, only two countries – the United Arab Emirates and Saudi Arabia – offered diplomatic recognition to the Islamic Emirate. The public executions, suppression of women's basic rights and the systemic persecution of minorities, especially Shias, led to widespread international condemnation of the Taliban's regime. In March

2001, Mullah Omar ordered the destruction of the 2500-foot tall Buddha statues in Bamiyan, built in the sixth and seventh centuries, because they were 'idolatrous' and 'the infidel's gods'.[51] The Taliban's ties with al-Qaeda and Osama bin Laden further complicated their relations with the outside world. Bin Laden had become the world's most-sought-after terrorist by 2008, and he was a guest of the Taliban regime.

But Mullah Omar did not bother too much about international criticism or his regime's isolation. At home, he remained the supreme leader. He continued to live in Kandahar, ruling over the whole country, and travelled to Kabul, which was the administrative capital of the Islamic Emirate, just once during his six-year rule.[52] Omar consolidated power into his hands and commanded loyalty of both the top leadership and the rank and file of the Taliban. A December 1998 diplomatic cable from the US embassy in Islamabad noted that Omar 'maintains an idiosyncratic, almost obscurantist, leadership style', making policy decisions, 'but generally leav[ing] the day-to-day matters to his key lieutenants'.[53] If someone questioned his authority, they were purged, as happened with Mullah Muhammad Rabbani, who disagreed with Omar on the Taliban hosting Bin Laden.[54]

In Bin Laden, Omar saw a Mujahideen comrade and an ideological brother. In the December 1998 cable, American diplomats in Pakistan shared concerns that Omar, 'perhaps under the influence of bin Laden and other extremists – may have become more sympathetic to pan-Islamist thinking. For example, he was quoted at least twice in 1998 as criticizing the US presence in the Gulf, which is not usually a great concern of Afghans.'[55] Despite mounting international pressure, he refused to disown Bin Laden or expel him from Afghanistan. But this friendship would also lead to Omar's own undoing. After the terrorist attacks of 11 September, which Bin Laden planned and executed from Taliban-controlled Afghanistan, the US would invade the country, bringing an end to Mullah Omar's regime. Omar would flee his residence in Kandahar, while the Taliban would retreat to Afghanistan's mountains or Pakistan across the border. After twelve years of a life in hiding, the Amir ul-Momineen would die of bad health, which the world would come to know only two years later. But the movement he founded would not only survive but return to capture Kabul another day.

3

The Generals' Proxies

ON 13 SEPTEMBER 2001, TWO DAYS AFTER THE TERRORIST attacks on the World Trade Center (WTC) and the Pentagon in the United States, Richard Armitage, the Deputy Secretary of State, met with Mahmud Ahmed, the chief of Pakistan's ISI. Mahmud was in the US for high-level talks with the CIA and the Pentagon. On 11 September, he was with Republican Congressman Porter Goss and Democratic Senator Bob Graham for a breakfast meeting in Washington, DC, discussing the threats posed by Osama bin Laden and al-Qaeda, when an American Airlines Boeing 767 crashed into the north tower of the WTC in New York City.[1] Mahmud, a three-star rank army general, had been appointed the head of Pakistan's spy agency on 20 October 1999, a few days after Gen. Pervez Musharraf captured power through a military coup. Mahmud was seen as Musharraf's man and he ran the spy agency, which had close ties with the Taliban at a time when Bin Laden was steadily expanding al-Qaeda's operations from a Taliban-controlled Afghanistan.

In their meeting, Armitage, a former naval officer-turned-diplomat, submitted seven 'non-negotiable' requests to the ISI chief. The US had already concluded that al-Qaeda was behind the 9/11 attacks. Al-Qaeda was harboured by Mullah Mohammad Omar's Taliban and Pakistan's ties with the Taliban were hardly a secret. The Bush administration wanted to know if Pakistan was 'with us or against us' in the coming war. The specific requests, handed to Mahmud in a 'non-paper', or an unofficial memo, were:

- Stop al-Qaeda operatives at your border, intercept arms shipment through Pakistan and end all logistical support for Bin Laden;
- Provide the US with blanket overflight and landing rights to conduct all necessary military and intelligence operations;
- Provide territorial access to US and allied military intelligence and other personnel to conduct all necessary operations against the perpetrators of terrorism or those that harbour them, including use of Pakistan's naval ports, air bases and strategic locations on borders;
- Provide the United States immediately with intelligence;
- Continue to publicly condemn the terrorist acts against the US or its friends and allies;
- Cut off all shipments of fuel to the Taliban and any secret other items en route to Afghanistan that can be used in a military offensive capacity or to abet the terrorist threat; and
- Cut off ties with the Taliban regime if they continue to support Osama bin Laden.[2]

Armitage asked Mahmud to hand over the 'non-paper' to Gen. Musharraf immediately. Mahmud had called his boss before the meeting to discuss the talking points, and the general asked him to report back as soon as the meeting was over.[3] He did as he was asked. On the same day, in Islamabad, Wendy Chamberlin, America's newly appointed ambassador to Pakistan, met Musharraf to present her credentials. After the ceremony, in which four other ambassadors were also present, Musharraf invited Chamberlin for a private meeting. Foreign Secretary Imam ul-Haque and the President's Military Secretary, Brigadier Nadeem Taj, attended this meeting. Musharraf had a call with Colin Powell, the US Secretary of State, who repeated the American requests to the general that his deputy had handed to Mahmud.

In the meeting, Chamberlin told Musharraf that the US was determined to act and had already been assured of support by the North Atlantic Treaty Organization (NATO) and the United Nations. 'There was an operational need to go after the terrorist who launched these heinous attacks … We believe strongly that the Taliban are harbouring the terrorists who are responsible for the attacks,' the ambassador told the Pakistani dictator. That must have sounded like a warning to Musharraf, whose government had deep ties with the Taliban regime. Musharraf sensed that the sands of geopolitics in the Afghan–Pakistan region were shifting. Chamberlin also told him there was no scope for negotiations with the Taliban. 'There was absolutely no inclination in Washington to enter into a dialogue with the Taliban. The time for dialogue was finished as of September 11,' she said.[4]

On 14 September, Musharraf discussed the seven-point memo from Washington with his senior military and government colleagues. Musharraf was in a precarious position. Any decision to join an America-led war against the Taliban would trigger protests from Pakistan's Islamic parties. But on the other side, Musharraf, after taking power two years earlier by toppling a democratically elected government, was facing international isolation. The Cold War-era cooperation between Pakistan and the US was in the past. The US Congress had suspended aid to Pakistan and frozen sales of F-16 fighter jets over its nuclear programme. In 1998, Pakistan went nuclear, after India did, which invited further sanctions from the US. In the same year, as the army chief, Musharraf took Pakistan to the brink of a nuclear war with India by sending militants to Kargil in Kashmir.

Now, the US was offering an opportunity for Pakistan to end its isolation and re-enter the good graces of the US. Musharraf also feared that if Pakistan did not accept the American request, it would weaken the country's regional standing further and help India. He persuaded his generals to join hands with the US. On the same day, he met Ambassador Chamberlin again for ninety minutes and told her that Pakistan would accept all of America's requests 'without conditions and that his military leadership concurred'. He also said the US should not alienate the Afghan people during the war. 'You are there to kill terrorists, not make enemies,' he said, adding that, 'Pakistan wants a friendly government in Kabul.'

Chamberlin was happy with the outcome of the meeting. She told the State Department that 'Musharraf is personally on board and so is his military leadership'. Despite his acceptance of American requests, Musharraf still wanted to explore the possibility of diplomacy before going to war. He sent Mahmud, the ISI chief, to Kabul to persuade Mullah Omar to hand over Bin Laden and other al-Qaeda operatives to the Americans. Mahmud would travel twice to Kabul in February, but return empty-handed. Despite Omar's intransigence, Mahmud believed that the Taliban regime was weak and confused and that they could be pushed to act against al-Qaeda. He told Chamberlin that the US should give more time to diplomacy before launching the attack. 'I implore you not to act in anger. Real victory will come in negotiations,' Mahmud told the ambassador. 'We should get the Afghans to do the job for us. If the strategic objective is al-Qaeda and Osama, it's better for the Afghans to do it.' An outright Pakistani deep state man, Mahmud had other concerns as well. 'If the Taliban are eliminated,' he warned, 'Afghanistan will revert to warlordism.'

Mahmud's arguments would have made sense from the point of view of realpolitik. But Chamberlin knew the mood in DC. The US, hit at home for the first time since the Pearl Harbor attack, wanted to strike back. President George W. Bush's war council had already begun preparations and there was bipartisan support for the counter-attack. She told the spymaster what she had told his President. 'The time for negotiation was past. People around the world needed to be protected from Bin Laden and the people around him … We need to move forward with our military plans,' she said.

The message was clear. Mahmud agreed. 'No matter what happens, Pakistan stands behind you,' he assured the ambassador. A week later, President Bush called Musharraf from Camp David where his National Security Council was making the final preparations for the war. Bush wanted direct assurances from the general of Pakistan's support. He believed that 'no country wielded more influence in Afghanistan than its eastern neighbour' and its support was pivotal. He asked Musharraf if he was with America. 'The stakes are high,' the general told him. 'We are with you.'[5] But neither Bush nor Chamberlin realized back then that Pakistan had other plans.

Second Home

As promised, Musharraf offered all support for the American invasion of Afghanistan. Pakistan cut off diplomatic ties with the Taliban regime. The general sent thousands of troops to guard the porous Afghan–Pakistan border. American fighter jets flew over Pakistani airspace on their way to bomb Taliban destinations. The US military would also get access to Pakistani bases. Musharraf was rewarded for his cooperation. The Bush administration lifted sanctions on Pakistan, designated the country a major non-NATO ally and offered help for counterterrorism operations. The US also opened its markets for Pakistani goods, and the US Congress, which had earlier cut off aid, would agree to provide billions in economic assistance. Musharraf's military regime, which had been an international outcast till a few months ago, was now rising as America's most important ally in the war on terror.

For Musharraf, this opportunity to gain international legitimacy presented a challenge inside Pakistan. By joining the US in a war on the Taliban, he was breaking with a decades-old consensus within Pakistan's military establishment. Support for Islamist militant groups, especially in India and Afghanistan, had been a central part of Pakistan's security policy. In Afghanistan, this strategy served Pakistani interests very well. They fought the mighty Soviet Red Army through the proxies in the 1980s, helped the Taliban capture Kabul in the 1990s and made sure that a pro-Pakistan government was formed in the Afghan capital so that there wouldn't be a strategic encirclement by India. The war on terror threatened to unravel this policy.

Musharraf, therefore, saw Pakistan joining the war as a tactical necessity rather than a strategic shift. He committed Pakistan's support for America's war, but he never went after the Taliban once their regime was toppled. Most of the Taliban fighters and mullahs retreated either to the mountains in Afghanistan's southern Pashtun heartland or across the border to Pakistan. Despite Pakistani reinforcements on the border, large swathes of the Durand Line, the 2670-km long contested frontier between Pakistan and Afghanistan, remained porous. The border, drawn in 1893 by Mortimer Durand, a British diplomat of the Indian Civil Service, and accepted under British colonial influence by the Afghan emir, Abdur Rahman Khan, divided the region's Pashtun population into two countries.[6] The border remained difficult to be manned throughout its history with people, mainly Pashtuns, travelling freely on both sides. For the Taliban, with strong roots in the Pashtun regions of Pakistan, especially Quetta in Balochistan, it was not difficult to retreat to Pakistan, which their spokesperson Zabihullah Mujahid called a 'second home' after the American invasion.[7]

Most of the Taliban top brass, including Mullah Omar, would slip away from public attention. Once the Taliban regime was toppled, the American focus shifted to fighting al-Qaeda and building a new administration in Kabul. The Taliban would lie low along the Afghan–Pakistan border. President Bush once raised the issue of the Taliban and al-Qaeda operatives retreating to Pakistani border regions with Gen. Musharraf. 'I would be more than willing to send our Special Forces to the border to clear out the areas,' he told the Pakistani leader. But that was a red line for Musharraf. He said to Bush that the American troops crossing the border would violate Pakistani sovereignty. The Islamist sections would revolt. 'My government would probably fall; extremists could take over the country, including our nuclear arsenal,' Musharraf said.[8] Bush bought that argument and instead of sending American troops across the border, he pressed Pakistan to cooperate with the CIA's hunt for al-Qaeda operatives, to which Musharraf agreed.

In March 2002, Pakistani police launched a major operation against several al-Qaeda safe houses in Faisalabad, Pakistan, with help from the CIA and the Federal Bureau of Investigation (FBI). They captured more than two dozen operatives, including Abu Zubayadah, a trusted associate of Osama bin Laden. The intelligence that American and Pakistani officials gathered from the interrogation of Abu Zubayadah led them to Khalid Sheikh Mohammed, al-Qaeda's chief operating officer and the murderer of Daniel Pearl, the *Wall Street Journal* journalist who had been kidnapped and beheaded in Pakistan in February 2002.[9] But even as Pakistan continued close cooperation with the CIA on the ground against al-Qaeda, the ISI continued to be in touch with the Taliban. The ISI opened a special cell, Directorate S, to continue its covert operations with the Taliban. To avoid scrutiny, the agency moved the Directorate out of its Islamabad headquarters to a military facility at Ojhri, near Rawalpindi.[10]

The US, on the other side, was confident it had finished off the Taliban. The period from 2001 to 2003 was relatively calm in Afghanistan. Hamid Karzai, an India-educated Pashtun politician who had spent most of the period of the Afghan civil war in Pakistan raising funds for the anti-communist Mujahideen, was appointed head of the transition government. When the war started, Karzai, Haji Hafizullah, a close companion, and a few others travelled to the Chaman border, bought two motorbikes and rode to Urozgan, where he started mobilizing Pashtun supporters against the Taliban. The CIA had given him satellite phones and cash dollars.[11] The Taliban knew what Karzai was up to and sent troops to kill him. According to one account, a top Taliban commander from Karzai's own Popalzai tribe tipped him off about the attack. The CIA sent a special helicopter to pick him up from Tarin Kot near Kandahar. But Karzai would return to southern Afghanistan later to build an anti-Taliban political coalition, and once the Taliban fell, the tribal leaders would assemble around him. The US thought Karzai could play a critical role in Afghanistan's transition from a religious totalitarian state to a multiparty democracy.[12]

The US had initially deployed some 8000 troops in Afghanistan. They had also set up the International Security

Assistance Force (ISAF), with support from the UN. NATO took over the command of the ISAF and NATO member countries dispatched an additional 5000 troops. In the initial months, it looked as though the US had managed to do what the British empire and the Soviet Union had failed to achieve in the previous two centuries: stabilize an unruly Afghanistan after a foreign invasion. America's confidence was evident in the words of Donald Rumsfeld, the Secretary of Defense, who announced on 1 May 2003 in Kabul that major combat operations in Afghanistan were over. 'President Bush, Central Command Chief Tommy Franks, and Afghan President Hamid Karzai have concluded we're at a point where we clearly have moved from major combat activity to a period of stability and stabilisation and reconstruction activities. The bulk of this country today is permissive, it's secure,' Rumsfeld declared, with Karzai sitting next to him.[13] Karzai shared his optimism, saying that 'many Afghans are now returning to their homeland'. But the war was only beginning.

Call to Jihad

Three months prior to Rumsfeld's declaration of victory, Mullah Omar, the Taliban's emir, had emerged from a long silence. In February 2003, he released a letter urging all Muslims to join the fight against the US. 'Infidels have encroached on Islam and today America is committing atrocities against Muslims so Jihad is absolutely compulsory for all Muslims,' he said. 'Vacate all offices, ministries, provinces so that the distinction between a Muslim and a crusader is made. Anyone of you who helps infidels, or serves them in any manner, deserves to die.'[14]

The letter was the first definite call for action from their leader to the confused and scattered Taliban. After Omar's call, Taliban operations on the Afghanistan–Pakistan border picked up. Police posts and other government buildings on the Afghan side came under attack. Afghanistan also started witnessing suicide bombings, something that was unheard of in the country even during the Mujahideen civil war. By June 2003, the Taliban started distributing leaflets in southern provinces, asking the army and police force to desert the government of Karzai and join them. 'Those who don't join us will be killed,' the pamphlets warned.[15]

In April 2004, amid sporadic attacks on civilians as well as Afghan and coalition troops, Omar gave a phone interview to a Pakistani journalist in which he claimed the suicide attacks 'have been very fruitful by the grace of God'. The Taliban, he said, had dumped their arms and ammunition at various secret locations before they left Kabul. 'We have enough to fight for decades. Moreover, we snatch arms and ammunition from the coalition forces just like we seized it from the Soviet forces.' In the interview, Omar emerged as a leader who was unrepentant about his past decisions and determined about the future war. He called Bin Laden 'the greatest mujahid of the present time', termed Karzai an 'American puppet' and threatened to kill all those who worked with the government. 'We are giving the US and the coalition forces a tough time. We are hunting them down like pigs,' said Omar.[16]

Omar's threats were not hollow. In June 2005, the US troops launched Operation Red Wing in eastern Afghanistan's Kunar province, aimed at disrupting growing Taliban operations in the region. Afghanistan was preparing for a historic parliamentary election in September and Omar had threatened to kill all those who turned up to vote. In the east, the Taliban were being regrouped by a ruthless, ambitious commander, Ahmad Shah. US forces wanted to destroy Shah's network. When a team of four Navy SEALS were conducting surveillance and reconnaissance operations on a mountain named Sawtalo Sar in Kunar, they came under a

Taliban ambush. They had been air-dropped on the mountain to monitor the activities of the Taliban in a village in the valley. US forces quickly sent a Chinook MH-47 with SEAL commandos and other Special Operations personnel on board to extract the team. But the chopper, hit by a rocket-propelled grenade fired by Shah's men, crashed on the slopes of the mountain.[17] Nineteen Americans were killed, including all sixteen on board. The only survivor, Marcus Luttrell, would later write a book to tell the story of the ambush.[18] The Kunar attack was the Taliban's loudest message to the US: the war was not over.

In the following months, Taliban attacks picked up, especially in the southern and eastern provinces of Kandahar, Helmand, Nangarhar and Kunar, the insurgents' traditional base. They carried out roadside bombings using IEDs (improvised explosive devices), ambushes, targeted killings and suicide operations. In September 2006, a Taliban suicide bomber assassinated the governor of Paktia province, which was a major setback for the Karzai administration. Villages in the southern and eastern provinces fell into the control of the Taliban. The repeated attacks and the deteriorating security situation in the countryside revived memories of the civil war, and led many Afghans to doubt Karzai's ability to provide security.

Many factors helped the Taliban regroup during this period. Karzai had successfully organized presidential and parliamentary elections, but he did not want any major challenge to his authority from the old warlords. Most of the Mujahideen commanders and their troops were taken out of the battlefield as part of the Disarmament, Demobilization and Reintegration (DDR) programme.[19] While the DDR's main goal was to disarm the former guerrilla fighters and allow the state to monopolize the right to violence, the move had unintended consequences. By removing the Mujahideen from the battlefield, the Afghan government and the international forces took out the most powerful anti-Taliban force from the ground, leaving a vacuum. The Afghan army and police forces, established after the war, lacked the experience, resources or morale to fill this vacuum. They were also dependent on US forces for operations. But the US focus would shift to Iraq from Afghanistan after the Bush administration invaded the Middle Eastern country in March 2003. This provided the Taliban as well as their patrons some breathing space, and they set out to exploit this vacuum. With violence increasing on a daily basis, Afghans started taking the Taliban threat seriously.

The growing number of attacks prompted the National Directorate of Security (NDS), Afghanistan's spy agency, to dig deeper. In the spring of 2006, Amrullah Saleh, the NDS chief, decided to conduct a field study on the Taliban's advances. Saleh travelled across the country and met with active Taliban commanders and sources to collect intelligence. In May 2006, he completed his classified paper, titled 'Strategy of the Taliban', in which he wrote that the ISI had decided in 2005 to actively support the Taliban with cash and aid. The consolidation of the Hamid Karzai government in Afghanistan and the possibility of a united Afghanistan emerging as an ally of India prompted Pakistan, which he called an 'India-centric country', to support the Taliban. He concluded in the paper that the Taliban would make gains and launch an all-out insurgency that would bog down the international troops.[20]

Saleh presented his findings to President Karzai. The Karzai administration acknowledged the problem. It had earlier blamed 'elements within Pakistan' for the spate of suicide attacks in the country.[21] In February, Karzai had travelled to Pakistan and met Gen. Musharraf and Prime Minister Shaukat Aziz, telling the Pakistani leaders that a stable Afghanistan was also in the interests of Islamabad. While he was aware of the challenge, Karzai still dismissed Saleh's predictions that the Taliban would launch an all-out insurgency in the country. Saleh told his President, 'I hope time will prove me wrong, but this is a product of your intelligence service.'[22] Saleh was proved right. It didn't take much time for Karzai to realize the danger his administration was facing. In 2016 alone, Afghanistan witnessed 119 suicide attacks, nearly one every three days, which shattered public confidence in the Karzai government. Most of these attacks originated from Pakistan.[23]

The US, after having declared a premature victory, was also slowly waking up to the Taliban challenge. In February 2006, after Karzai's visit to Islamabad, Ronald E. Neuman, the American ambassador in Kabul, wrote a cable to the Department of State, warning that the Taliban were regrouping in their sanctuaries in Pakistan. The Taliban's long-term strategy, according to Neuman, 'depends on keeping the [Afghan] government weak in the provinces' outside Kabul's reach. He warned that violence would increase 'as long as they can resupply from their current areas, and if left unaddressed, it will also lead to the re-emergence of the same strategic threat to the United States that prompted our intervention over four years ago'.[24]

Rattled by the Taliban's regrouping and the worsening relations between Afghanistan and Pakistan, America's two allies in the war on extremism, President Bush invited both Gen. Musharraf and President Karzai for a summit in the White House. Bush welcomed them in the Rose Garden of the White House in September. The personal equation between Musharraf and Karzai had deteriorated to such an extent that they did not even shake hands with each other. Later that night, in the Old Family Dining Room of the White House, the leaders blamed each other for the troubles of Afghanistan, while President Bush, Vice President Dick Cheney, National Security Advisor Condoleezza Rice and others looked on. In the heated conversation, Karzai accused Pakistan of harbouring the Taliban.

'Tell me where they are,' Musharraf said.

'You know where they are,' Karzai replied.

'If I did, I would get them,' said Musharraf.

'Go do it,' Karzai shot back.[25]

The White House summit failed to make any breakthrough. Musharraf and Karzai went back to their respective capitals and continued the blame game. Meanwhile, the Taliban became more assertive in south and south-eastern Afghanistan, and attacks jumped manifold. In the following years, more evidence on the double game Pakistan was playing in Afghanistan emerged. According to a discussion paper published by the *London Review of Economics*, whose author interviewed a host of Taliban commanders and operatives, the ISI 'orchestrates, sustains and strongly influences the Taliban'.[26] ISI leaders had even attended the meetings of the Taliban's Shura, the top leadership body that was reconstituted by Mullah Omar months after the 2001 American invasion. It was hardly a secret that the Shura was based in Quetta, the provincial capital of Balochistan that was also emerging as the new base of the Taliban.

American officials, who were initially reluctant to directly blame Pakistan, became more vocal in the following years. Officials would tell the press that they believed the Taliban were getting direct support from the ISI and that some Pakistani officials saw Mullah Omar as 'a valuable asset' should the US leave Afghanistan. Stanley McChrystal, who commanded the NATO troops in Afghanistan, assessed the situation thus: 'Senior leaders of the major Afghan insurgent groups based in Pakistan are linked with al-Qaeda and other violent extremist groups, and are reportedly aided by some elements' of the ISI.[27]

But the US was already in a catch-22 situation. Its invasion of Iraq had gone awfully wrong. Iraq slipped into a sectarian civil war. With violence spreading like wildfire in Iraq, American focus shifted to stabilizing the country, with tens of thousands of troops. In Afghanistan, the US grew more dependent on Pakistan to sustain operations. So even when the military leadership started criticizing Pakistan's role, the US did not want to untangle itself from Pakistan, making its presence in Afghanistan more complicated, at a time when it was bogged down in Iraq. The strategic core of the Pakistan–America partnership had started eroding, but tactical requirements held them together. The alliance was turning into a bitter marriage.

Chasing Peace

One man at the receiving end of all these developments was Hamid Karzai. Sitting in Arg, the presidential palace, he saw more and more territories in the countryside fall into the Taliban's hands. Despite his prodding and pleading, the ISI continued to support the insurgents. The Quetta Shura operated with impunity, almost like a government in exile from Pakistan. Karzai knew that the Americans were aware of Pakistan's dubious policy but were either disinterested or incapable of doing anything to fix the situation. With a military solution beginning to seem remote, Karzai would be more open for talks with the Taliban. Despite resistance from his National Security Council, Karzai would establish secret contacts with the insurgents. The man he reached out to was Mullah Abdul Ghani Baradar, who would later become the Taliban's public face.

Baradar, hailing from the same Popalzai tribe as Karzai, was seen as one of the few relatively moderate voices within the Taliban. Born in 1968 in Urozgan near Kandahar, Baradar had fought the communists along with Mullah Omar during the 1980s. In 1994, he co-founded the Taliban with Omar and had played a key role in their regime as the deputy defence minister. When the Taliban were driven out of power, Baradar, like other top leaders, fled to Pakistan. In 2009, Baradar had issued a handbook to the Taliban supporters and operatives on how to carry out the insurgency. It urged them to avoid civilian casualties and win over the villagers.[28] As Omar largely remained underground, Baradar, as the deputy of the emir, emerged as a powerful voice within the insurgency.

When Pakistan came to know that Baradar was holding secret talks with Karzai, the generals were not happy. Pakistani generals saw Karzai as pro-India. Any direct deal between the Karzai administration and the Taliban would undercut Pakistan's core interests, they feared. They wanted to shut down the talks. And for that, the ISI, with help from CIA officials who at that time were unaware of the ISI's real intentions, carried out a raid in February 2010 at the safe house in Karachi where Baradar was living, and took him into custody. Both Pakistan and the US hailed his arrest as a breakthrough in the fight against terrorism. The real objective of Baradar's arrest, however, emerged months later. Pakistani security officials told the media that Baradar was arrested to shut down the peace talks. 'We picked up Baradar and the others because they were trying to make a deal without us,' a Pakistani security official told *The New York Times*. 'We protect the Taliban. They are dependent on us. We are not going to allow them to make a deal with Karzai and the Indians.'[29]

The Pakistani establishment's position was clear: whether it was a military solution or a political solution, it should have Rawalpindi's stamp on it. Karzai was furious with the collapse of the talks. He, however, was determined to chase peace. In 2010, he called a Peace Jirga in Kabul, aimed at finding a roadmap to a political solution. But the Taliban boycotted the council. Karzai would not be deterred. He was looking for a breakthrough so desperately that in October 2010 his inner circle established contacts with a man who identified himself as Mullah Akhtar Muhammad Mansour, the second in command in the Taliban. The Karzai administration, in collaboration with NATO forces, made all preparations for what were touted as the first direct talks with the Taliban. Mansour and his associates crossed the border from Pakistan into Afghanistan and boarded a special NATO aircraft that took them to Kabul.[30]

NATO troops provided security for the talks between government representatives and Mansour that took place outside the capital. The talks went on for weeks before the Afghan officials involved in the negotiations realized that the man they were holding talks with was not Mullah Mansour of the Taliban. Not only that, he didn't have any direct links with the Taliban's leadership.[31] This episode turned out to be a major embarrassment for Karzai. On the other side, it re-emphasized the vitality of Pakistan in any attempt to find a solution to the Afghan crisis. If Afghanistan and the US wanted to launch peace talks with the Taliban, they needed to find the real Taliban leadership, who were based deep inside Pakistan.

Karzai would exit office in 2014 without seeing any breakthrough in his attempts to find a political solution. The Taliban were now controlling almost one-third of Afghanistan and had demonstrated the capability to strike anywhere in the country. Karzai's successor, Ashraf Ghani, followed his policies of engagement, but with a twist. While Karzai had sought an agreement with the Taliban bypassing the ISI, Ghani reached out to Pakistan first. Pakistan's civilian Prime Minister Nawaz Sharif, already under pressure from the Obama administration, which was carrying out drone strikes inside Pakistan, persuaded his generals to give peace a shot. On 7 July 2015, Pakistan hosted the first official Taliban–Afghan peace talks in Murree, a hill station outside Islamabad. The US and China sent observers to attend the talks. Pakistan's foreign ministry later issued a statement saying, 'Participants recognised the need to develop confidence-building measures to engender trust among all stakeholders.'[32] A second round of talks was scheduled for 31 July.

But the talks never took place. It was after the Murree talks that the world came to know that Mullah Omar had died two years ago. On 29 July, the NDS, Afghanistan's spy agency, announced that Omar had died in a hospital in Karachi in April 2013.[33] The next day, the Taliban confirmed his death. The news threw the Taliban into disarray. The second round of peace talks was postponed. There was confusion among the rank and file about who was in charge of the insurgency. A few days later, the Taliban announced that the real Mullah Akhtar Mansour, Omar's deputy ever since Baradar's arrest by Pakistan, would be the new emir.

It could have been Mansour, as acting leader, who approved the participation in the Murree talks. But after Omar's death was made public, the equations within the Taliban changed. There was reported factionalism within the Taliban top ranks and Mansour, now under pressure over talks with the Afghan government, wanted to quickly mobilize the support of the Taliban behind his leadership.[34] In his first public statement after taking on the Taliban's leadership, Mansour called the peace talks 'enemy's propaganda'. 'This jihad will continue for advancing the word of Allah and until there is an Islamic system in Afghanistan,' he said.[35] The peace process, for now, was over.

The Deal

Mansour's period of leadership was fractious. The Taliban continued attacks in Afghanistan, but his leadership was challenged by different factions within the Taliban and his reign didn't last long. Mansour was killed in May 2016 by an American drone strike as he was returning to Pakistan from Iran. The main challenge of his successor, Hibatullah Akhundzada, was to unify the Taliban factions under his command. Akhundzada, the judicial chief of Mullah Omar's regime in the 1990s, brought in Mullah Yaqoob, Omar's son, who had reportedly challenged Mansour's leadership, and Sirajuddin Haqqani, leader of the Haqqani Network that had been the Taliban's military muscle from its early days. The Haqqanis have also had close ties with the ISI, and their rise to the leadership of the Taliban practically enhanced the ISI's leverage over the Taliban's decision-making.[36]

Under Mullah Akhundzada, the Taliban adopted a talk-and-fight approach. They were ready to hold talks, but only with the US, because they did not see the Afghan government as legitimate. By now the Taliban had clearly established an upper hand in the battlefield. They were controlling almost half of the countryside. The war had reached a stalemate. The Taliban saw that their only hindrance to power in Kabul was the foreign troops' presence. So their strategic goal was to force the Americans, who were looking for a face-saving exit, to leave Afghanistan. To reach that goal, the Taliban were ready to talk.

The US had for years sought to engage with the Taliban indirectly. The Obama administration's decision to send observers to the Murree talks showed, for the first time, America's willingness to engage with the same extremists they had driven away from power in 2001. Under the Trump administration, the US would go a step further and be ready to hold direct talks with the Taliban. In 2018, Trump appointed Zalmay Khalilzad, an Afghan-American diplomat who was the US ambassador in Kabul during the early years of the Karzai administration, as a special presidential representative for Afghan reconciliation.

To begin the talks, the US needed Pakistan's help. Trump adopted a mixed strategy: he heaped pressure on Pakistan to bring the Taliban leadership to the table, while at the same time hinting that his administration would cut a deal with the insurgents. In his 2017 South Asia policy address, Trump blasted Pakistan for giving 'safe haven to agents of chaos, violence, and terror'. He added that he would seek 'a political settlement that includes elements of the Taliban in Afghanistan'.[37] Both the Pakistani generals and the Taliban found an opportunity in Trump's pressure and outreach approach. His opposition to America's 'forever' wars was well known and his transactionalism offered room for diplomatic attempts.

The Americans wanted an 'authoritative and powerful' Taliban leader to hold talks with.[38] They did not want to repeat the mistake of Hamid Karzai. The obvious choice of everyone was Mullah Baradar, who had held secret talks with Karzai before he was arrested by the Pakistani military. Baradar was living in a safe house under the ISI's protective custody. In October 2018, during a visit by Ambassador Khalilzad, Pakistan released Baradar. Soon Baradar would be allowed to join the Taliban's political office in Doha.[39] The Taliban had opened the political office in 2013 but it had largely remained a public relations office run by the group's spokesmen. With Baradar, a co-founder of the Taliban, joining the Doha office, it emerged as the Taliban's most important diplomatic outpost. The stage was set for talks. After seventeen years of war, the Taliban were no longer untouchables for the US.

Before the talks began, the US had agreed to a key Taliban demand. They would keep the Afghan government out of the peace process. The focus of the talks would be on the American withdrawal from Afghanistan, not on finding any political settlement to the Afghan crisis. America's primary concern was the Taliban's ties with transnational terrorist organizations such as al-Qaeda. The Taliban were ready to address this issue. Matters related to peace and stability in Afghanistan became a secondary concern.

Multiple rounds of talks were held between the American and Taliban delegations, led by Ambassador Khalilzad and Mullah Baradar, respectively. The US kept Pakistan in the loop. Khalilzad frequently flew to Pakistan to apprise the generals of the progress of the talks. A Pakistani politician said, 'The military leadership was under the impression that the United States was subletting Afghanistan to them.'[40]

On 29 February 2020, after nine rounds of talks, the US and the Taliban finally signed a peace agreement, announcing the beginning of the end of America's military presence in the country. The deal covered four aspects of the conflict: violence, foreign troops, intra-Afghan peace talks and use of Afghan soil by terrorist groups such as al-Qaeda and the Islamic State. According to the agreement, the Taliban promised to reduce violence, join intra-Afghan peace talks and cut all ties with foreign terrorist groups, while the US pledged to withdraw all its troops, roughly 12,000 at the time of the signing of the agreement, by 1 May 2021.[41] The Taliban, who had been deposed from power by the US in 2001, got what they wanted after nineteen years of war: America's full withdrawal from Afghanistan. President Donald Trump, who had campaigned against America's 'forever wars', also got what he wanted: winding down an unpopular war and rechannelling America's resources and strategic focus to new geopolitical challenges. Pakistan, which joined America's war on terror while at the same time providing sanctuary and aid to the fallen Taliban, saw, once again, its dual strategic bets succeed in Afghanistan.

Clearly, the loser was the Islamic Republic of Afghanistan.

4

The Fall of Kabul

IN MARCH 2021, US SECRETARY OF STATE ANTONY BLINKEN wrote a letter to Afghan President Ashraf Ghani, warning him of what was to come. The Biden administration, which had taken charge in January 2021, hadn't completed its review of the United States' Afghan policy. This was an urgent need considering the Trump administration's withdrawal agreement with the Taliban a year earlier, according to which American troops were scheduled to pull back by 1 May 2021. In the letter, which sounded more like an imperial memorandum than a diplomatic communique, Blinken said that the US was considering sticking to the withdrawal deadline. He asked Ghani to work with the Taliban to 'develop the foundational principles that will guide Afghanistan's future constitutional and governing arrangements, a roadmap to a new inclusive government and the terms of a permanent and comprehensive ceasefire'.[1] He also warned that after the American troops withdrew, the security situation in Afghanistan could worsen and that the Taliban could make 'rapid territorial gains'. 'I am making this clear to you so that you understand the urgency of my tone regarding the collective work outlined in this letter,' said the Secretary of State.

The unwritten but obvious message of the letter was that the US was wrapping up the war in Afghanistan and that Ghani's government could not hold off the Taliban for long. This was not the first time that the US was sending out such a message. In January, when Gen. Austin Miller, who was the commander of the NATO forces in Afghanistan, was asked if the Afghan troops would be able to resist the Taliban, he didn't say they would. He said 'they have to'.[2] President Joe Biden never said the Taliban would be defeated. His repeated comment was that Afghanistan had the resources to resist the Taliban. And then, there were US intelligence assessments that Kabul would fall within months of American withdrawal. In June, while American troops were still in Afghanistan, US intelligence agencies concluded that the Islamic Republic would collapse as soon as six months after the US military withdrawal.[3] In August, in the middle of the Taliban's advances, they revised their estimates, warning the Biden administration that Kabul could fall in ninety days.[4] But President Ghani seemed unmoved.

Immediately after Blinken's letter was made public by Afghan media, Ghani and First Vice President Amrullah Saleh rejected the United States' suggestion of a power-sharing agreement with the Taliban. In February, when the idea of an interim government with the Taliban was floating in the air, Ghani had dismissed it altogether. 'Be assured that as long as I am alive, they will not see the formation of an interim government.'[5] After receiving the Blinken letter, he told US officials he was opposed to 'any transfer of power except through elections'.[6] Ghani said his government would fight on, and blamed Pakistan for Afghanistan's woes. According to him and Saleh, the international community, especially the US, needed to put pressure on Pakistan to rein in the Taliban. In July, while speaking at the Central and South Asia Connectivity Conference in Tashkent, Uzbekistan, Ghani said Pakistan continued to support terrorists inside Afghanistan. With Pakistani Prime Minister Imran Khan sitting a few feet away, Ghani said, 'Over 10,000 jihadi fighters from Pakistan and other places [entered Afghanistan] in the last month and Islamabad had failed to convince the Taliban to participate "seriously" in the peace talks.'[7] When he gave the speech in Tashkent, eighteen of Afghanistan's thirty-four provinces were under Taliban control. He attended the conference, met world leaders and chatted with the press. In an interview, he confidently said, 'The Taliban have won the battles, but we will win the war.'[8] It was Ghani's last foreign conference as the President of the Islamic Republic of Afghanistan.

Theorist-in-Chief

A trained anthropologist, Ghani rose to power in 2014 promising to end corruption and fix Afghanistan's institutions. These had been his favourite themes for decades. In his doctoral thesis at Columbia University, titled 'Production and Domination: Afghanistan, 1747–1901', Ghani studied the country's difficulties in building centralized institutions amid economic backwardness.[9] He was awarded a PhD in 1983. In 2008, a consultancy Ghani co-founded in Washington, DC published a paper titled 'Fixing Failed States: A Framework for Rebuilding a Fractured World', which outlined the measures to be taken to build institutions.[10] In his first presidential campaign in 2009, Ghani blamed a 'double failure' for Afghanistan's miseries: a failure by the international community and a failure by the country's elites in rebuilding the nation.[11] So when he was finally elected President in 2014, it was a chance for

'Afghanistan's theorist-in-chief', as George Packer called him, to put his ideas into practice.[12] But under Ghani's watch, Afghanistan's institutions found their legitimacy further eroded.

Born in 1949, Ghani grew up in Kabul's old city. His paternal grandfather was a military commander under King Nadir, who assumed the throne in 1929. His father was a senior official in the court of King Zahir, Nadir's son. In 1973, the year the Afghan monarchy was overthrown by Mohammed Daoud Khan who became the first President of the republic, Ghani received a degree in political science from the American University of Beirut. In 1977, a year before the communist revolution, Ghani and his family left Afghanistan, and he would not come back to live in the country until 2001.

When the Taliban regime was overthrown by the American invasion in 2001, Ghani travelled to Afghanistan as a UN official. Later he became a special adviser to Hamid Karzai, who headed the transition government, and then went on to become an influential finance minister. But by 2004, Karzai and Ghani had fallen out, with the latter leaving the government. The fall of the Taliban and the formation of a democratic state opened up Afghanistan's polity for the country's elite. Ghani never hid his political ambitions. He quit the government, but stayed active in Afghan civil society. In 2009, he made his first attempt at the presidential election, but lost. In 2014, Ghani was declared the winner after a disputed poll. In the 2019 elections that saw a record low turnout amid surging violence, he was re-elected, only to be deposed by the Taliban two years later.

Both the elections in which Ghani was elected were disputed. On both occasions, the US had to broker a truce between Ghani and Abdullah Abdullah, his main political rival, and put together a united government.[13] Ghani, a specialist in failed states, was expected to build unity, expand his support base and strengthen state institutions that were coming under repeated attacks from the Taliban. But what happened was the opposite. Ghani was mercurial, impulsive and isolated. He projected himself as the rightful Pashtun leader of Afghanistan, alienating other ethnic leaders who made up the erstwhile Northern Alliance that resisted the Taliban in the 1990s. Abdullah, half Pashtun and half Tajik, was seen as a rival. The government was divided between the two. Abdul Rashid Dostum, the Uzbek warlord and Ghani's former Vice President, was living abroad. Atta Muhammad Nur, the Tajik 'strongman' in the North, had publicly challenged the government. He was sacked as the governor of Balkh province by Ghani in January 2018.

Ghani's war on his rivals would have made sense if he had mobilized support under his leadership and built a stable government. But he lacked a strong popular base. He couldn't build an administration that commanded at least all the anti-Taliban forces.[14] Ghani tried to weaken the former warlords in the name of strengthening the national forces, along with shoring up his political base, but in the course of this, he further weakened the anti-Taliban coalition. So, well before the American withdrawal started on 1 May 2021, the Ghani administration looked like a loose confederation of different fiefdoms. What had glued them all together were the American troops. And once it was clear that the Americans were leaving, the cracks in the administration began to widen. All the Taliban had to do, from the outside, was apply a little more pressure.

The Road to Victory

Though the Taliban overran most of the country within days, the road to their final victory started from the agreement they signed with the US in February 2020. In the Trump–Taliban agreement, the US could not extract any concession from the Taliban towards a political settlement in Afghanistan. The Taliban did not even agree to a ceasefire. And the American focus was on getting their troops and diplomats safely out of Afghanistan.

This provided the Taliban a sense of victory, while demoralizing the Afghan troops. Pro-Taliban channels celebrated the Doha deal as their triumph over America. A day before the signing ceremony on 29 February 2020 at the Doha Sheraton Hotel, the Taliban's multimedia chief had described it as a historic landmark, and proclaimed 'the defeat of the arrogance of the White House in the face of the white turban'.[15] They claimed that if they could defeat the US, the world's pre-eminent superpower, the Afghan forces would not be much of a problem. During the war, the Taliban's main challenge was US air power, which had delivered devastating blows to the insurgency. After the Doha agreement, US air strikes went down drastically, in return for the Taliban completely stopping attacks on American forces. This allowed the Taliban to regroup across the country, plan the next offensive and refurbish their supply lines.

Lloyd Austin, Biden's Secretary of Defense, agreed to this narrative while testifying before the House Armed Services Committee in September 2021. The Doha agreement committed the US to ending air strikes against the Taliban, 'so the Taliban got stronger, they increased their offensive operations against the Afghan security forces, and the Afghans were losing a lot of people on a weekly basis', he said.[16] Legitimized by the direct talks and the deal with the US, the Taliban also reached out to regional players such as China, Russia and Iran, who were willing to engage with the insurgents. And then they waited for the Americans to start leaving.

When international troops began withdrawing on 1 May, the Taliban started an offensive in the north, northeast and western districts of Afghanistan. The plan was to consolidate their position in the hinterlands as well as surround the big cities. The Afghan government had the provincial centres under its control, and set up outposts across the rural areas, which were provided supplies by air. America's withdrawal hit this defence deployment hard. Biden withdrew not just American air support but also the intelligence agents and contractors who were serving Afghanistan's war planes and helicopters.[17] This, besides the psychological and political impacts of the withdrawal, debilitated the Afghan air force, the only advantage the Afghan troops had in the war. Knowing this, the Taliban also launched an assassination campaign, targeting Afghan pilots. According to a Reuters special report dated 9 July, seven Afghan pilots were assassinated starting 1 May.[18] As an overstretched and resource-limited air force came under pressure, the supply lines dried up. The Taliban could easily overrun remote government outposts and sweep through the country's north, including Badakhshan and Takhar provinces.

After capturing the northern districts, the Taliban turned their focus to the border crossings. On 22 June, they seized the Sher Khan Bandar crossing with Tajikistan, an important trade gateway between Afghanistan and Central Asia. The US had spent over $40 million to build the border complex, which also included a 38-foot wide and 2204-foot long steel bridge over the Panj river that runs between Afghanistan and Tajikistan.[19] Customs collection at the crossing ran into millions of dollars every year, and was one of the lifelines of Afghanistan's economy which was otherwise dependent heavily on foreign aid. With Sher Khan Bandar under their command, the Taliban took over the entire stretch of the Afghanistan–Tajikistan border, and then seized the Islam Qila crossing with Iran. On 14 July, Taliban fighters took Spin Boldak, the strategic border crossing with Pakistan, the capture of which in 1994 had marked the beginning of the Taliban's territorial victories. With these crossings under their control, the Taliban squeezed the Kabul government out of critical revenues, dealing a crippling financial blow.

The turning point came on 6 August, when the first city, Zaranj, fell to the Taliban. The Taliban allowed the government troops to walk away if they surrendered with their equipment. In some cases, surrendered soldiers, unpaid for months, were even given pocket money by the Taliban.[20] Those who resisted were killed. So Afghan troops, lacking reinforcements, faced two choices: either surrender and save their lives or fight to the death for a government that could not get its act together and was seen to have been abandoned by the US. In most cases, they chose the first. As did several government officials. In Ghazni, which lies along the Kabul–Kandahar highway, the provincial governor, Daud Laghmani, handed the keys to his office to a Taliban commander along with flowers and congratulated him,[21] after which he was escorted out of his office by the Taliban. In several cities, the Taliban overran prisons and recruited prisoners to their ranks. As soldiers surrendered without a fight, city after city fell to the Taliban. Within eight days after Zaranj, more than half of the country's provincial capitals were under the Taliban's control. Kabul became an island in the Taliban sea.

On 14 August, even when the Taliban were at the gates of the city, President Ghani tried to show a brave face, saying his focus was on remobilizing Afghan troops. 'Under the current situation, remobilizing of the security and defense forces is our top priority and required measures are underway for this purpose,' Ghani said in a video message.[22] The President's top military advisers and generals drew up a plan to protect the capital, and it was discussed with Gen. Haibatullah Alizai, the chief of the army staff, and Admiral Peter Vasely, the top US military officer in Afghanistan. The generals also asked Ghani to start negotiations aimed at halting the Taliban at the gates of the city, while at the same time preparing the troops for an eventual fight.[23]

Salam Rahimi, a presidential aide, established back-room contact with the Taliban, seeking a deal. The Taliban agreed they would not attack the city, waiting for an interim power-sharing agreement, something which the US was also pushing for. A period of interim government would allow the US and other countries to evacuate all foreign nationals before the Taliban's eventual takeover of the country. It would also avoid bloodshed in Kabul, Afghanistan's largest metropolis with 4.5 million people. On Sunday, 15 August, the staff at the presidential palace turned up for work as usual. Ghani, accompanied by National Security Advisor Hamdullah Mohib and Chief of Staff Fazel Fazly, two of his closest aides, was deliberating his last act as President of the Islamic Republic.

Even after the Taliban gave assurance that they would not take Kabul by force, Ghani was not convinced. As a wartime President who saw most of his country slip away from his authority, Ghani must have been haunted by what happened when the Taliban took Kabul the last time, when they killed the former communist President Mohammad Najibullah and hanged his body from a lamp post. Ghani feared he would meet with the same fate if he stayed in the city.[24] There was no consensus among the President's inner circle that the troops in Kabul would fight, considering those in other provincial capitals had not resisted the Taliban's advances. Five of the seven army corps of the Afghan National Army had already been taken over by the Taliban. Vice President Amrullah Saleh had left the capital for the Panjshir Valley. Bismillah Khan, the newly appointed defence minister with a mandate of turning around the war, was incommunicado. Ghani knew that the plan to defend Kabul was unravelling.

Three helicopters arrived at the presidential palace. By 3.30 p.m. local time, President Ghani and his close aides, including NSA Mohib and Chief of Staff Fazly, flew out of the country. They stopped over in Termez, Uzbekistan, and then flew onwards to the UAE. By nightfall, the Taliban were in Arg-e-Shahi (Citadel of the King), the presidential palace built by the nineteenth-century emir Abdur Rahman Khan. A group of black-and-white-turbaned Taliban fighters, holding guns, later posed behind Ghani's huge ornate wooden desk deep inside the palace, a book with a marker and a wooden clock – perhaps belonging to the President who had fled – still on the table.[25] Behind them on the wall was an enormous painting, depicting a crowd looking on as a Sufi mystic crowns a kneeling commander. It's the 1747 coronation of Ahmad Shah Durrani, the founder of the modern Afghan state.

Return of the Emirate

Three weeks after they captured Kabul, the Taliban, on 7 September, announced their interim government, ending all speculation on whether the new administration would be different from the previous Islamic Emirate. Despite the Taliban's promises that they would form an 'inclusive government', almost all thirty-three members of the cabinet announced by the group's spokesman Zabihullah Mujahid were from the Taliban's old guard.[26] All but three were Pashtun, while two were from the Tajik ethnic minority and one an Uzbek. The Hazara Shias were totally excluded. In the 1990s, the Hazara Shia minority, who are largely concentrated in Mazar-e-Sharif in northwest Afghanistan, had faced systemic persecution under the Taliban regime. No woman found a place in the cabinet either.

Two days before the government was announced, the Taliban's education ministry issued an extensive document, with instructions to educational institutions and to women attending colleges and universities. All female students, teachers and staff had to wear an abaya robe and niqab covering the hair, body and most of the face, as well as gloves to ensure the hands were covered too, stated the document. It also ordered classes to be segregated by gender or divided by a curtain.[27] Protests broke out in parts of Afghanistan, including in Kabul, where women staged rallies demanding freedoms. The Taliban dispersed them using force, which was followed by Mujahid's night-time press conference in which the announcement about interim government formation was made.

In September 1996, after capturing Kabul, the Taliban immediately issued decrees imposing restrictions on women and announcing new rules and punishments which they claimed were based on the Shariah. On 7 September 2021, after the interim government was announced, Hibatullah Akhundzada, the Taliban's emir, issued a statement, saying: 'Our previous 20 years of struggle and Jihad had had two major goals. Firstly to end foreign occupation and aggression and to liberate the country, and secondly to establish a complete, independent, stable and central Islamic system in the country.' He added, 'Based on this principle, in the future, all matters of governance and life in Afghanistan will be regulated by the laws of the Holy Shariah.'[28]

Akhundzada, the Taliban's spiritual and organizational leader since 2016, became the new Amir ul-Momineen (commander of the faithful) of the country, the title Mullah Omar had previously held. While Akhundzada, who was the judicial chief of the previous regime, would have a final say in all matters related to religion and politics in Afghanistan, Mullah Hassan Akhund would run the day-to-day affairs of the government as acting Prime Minister. Many had speculated that Mullah Abdul Ghani Baradar, the public face of the Taliban, would be the head of the government. But Baradar, a relatively moderate voice among the Taliban's leadership, was given the Deputy Prime Minister's post, while Sirajuddin Haqqani, the leader of the Haqqani Network, got the powerful interior ministry. The Taliban were sending an unmistakable message: the new Islamic Emirate was the continuation of the ancient régime.

Mullah Hassan Akhund's rise was unexpected but not totally surprising. Akhund was one of the co-founders of the Taliban, a close aide of Mullah Omar, a minister in the old regime and a known hardliner. He was also known to be one of the leaders who publicly defended the Taliban's ties with Osama bin Laden. When the UN issued an ultimatum to the Taliban regime in November 1999 to hand over Bin Laden – who was held responsible for the August 2008 bombing of the American embassies in Kenya and Tanzania that killed 244 people – to the US or a third country for trial, Mullah Akhund was the foreign minister. The UN threatened to impose sanctions on the Taliban regime unless Bin Laden was handed over. Akhund dismissed the UN demand, saying: 'We will never give up Osama at any price.'[29] Akhund said a Taliban enquiry had exonerated Bin Laden.

According to the UN, which placed Akhund on its blacklist of terrorists in 2001, he was born in Pashmul village in Kandahar province sometime between 1945 and 1958.[30] He was a governor of Kandahar and a political adviser of Mullah Omar. Akhund studied in various madrassas in Pakistan, and during the anti-Soviet Mujahideen war, he fought alongside Gulbuddin Hekmatyar's Hezb-e-Islami in Kandahar. A December 1997 diplomatic cable from the US embassy in Islamabad stated, 'Hassan Akhund is setting himself up to the champion of those who want a military victory at any cost.'[31] According to a 2001 US intelligence assessment, Akhund, considered 'one of the most ineffective and unreasonable Taliban leaders', held 'prejudices against both the Westerners and the Mujahideen'. 'Extremely committed' to the movement, he sanctioned the destruction of the Bamiyan Buddhas in February 2011, declaring it a 'religious duty'.[32]

When the Taliban lost power, Akhund, with other top leaders, retreated from Kabul. By 2009–10, he had emerged as a top commander of the Taliban, which were trying to strike back and capture territories in Afghanistan. He also became a member of the Rehbari Shura, the Taliban's Supreme Council, which was based in Quetta, Balochistan. So when they captured power again, the Taliban chose an old hardliner who was a comrade of Mullah Omar to run their government.

While the old guard retained most of the seats in the cabinet, the regime also saw the rise of the next-generation Taliban. The oldest son of Mullah Omar, Mullah Yaqoob, was appointed the acting defence minister. Thought to be in his early thirties, Yaqoob's name came to public attention after the Taliban confirmed the death of his father in 2015. He was believed to be one of the contenders to succeed Omar, but the Taliban first chose Mullah Mansour as their emir, and when Mansour was killed in an American air strike inside Pakistan, Akhundzada was chosen. Yaqoob, however, rose steadily in the Taliban's ranks to become, in 2016, the head of military operations in fifteen of Afghanistan's thirty-four provinces. He was also a member of the Rehbari Shura, and after Mansour's death, Yaqoob, along with Sirajuddin Haqqani, became one of Akhundzada's two deputies. After the Taliban captured Kabul on 15 August, they released an audio clip of Yaqoob in which he praised the Taliban's 'martyrdom-seeking force' (suicide bombers). 'All the people of Afghanistan must carry out the duty of jihadi training as much as possible, every citizen must be [a] capable military mujahid and must be ready at any moment to defend independence, land and the Islamic system,' he said.[33]

Most others in the cabinet also came from the Taliban's core leadership. Seventeen of the thirty-three members were UNdesignated terrorists. The Taliban had signalled willingness to engage with the world, but it was now up to the world to decide whether to engage with a government that's run by designated terrorists. On its part, the Taliban has made it clear that they want to establish a totalitarian religious state with exclusive hold on political power. In the 1990s when Mullah Omar tried to do it, the Northern Alliance, commanded by the Tajik warlord Ahmad Shah Massoud, continued to resist the Taliban from the Panjshir Valley. In 2021, the Islamic Republic collapsed, much like the Mujahideen republic in 1996, and President Ghani fled the country along with most of his ministers and parliamentarians. The army, including the highly trained special forces, melted away. Abdullah Abdullah, the former chief executive of the government, Hamid Karzai, the former President, and Hekmatyar, the Islamist warlord, stayed in Kabul for talks with the Taliban. While the remnants of the old regime either fled or tried to make peace with the Taliban, one man vowed to resist them, like Massoud did in the 1990s: First Vice President Amrullah Saleh of Ghani's collapsed government.

The Man Who Defied

Saleh had an illustrious career in Afghanistan's fractious world of politics, intelligence and security. Born in Panjshir in October 1972, Saleh grew up in Kabul. He was the youngest of five brothers. Like many Afghans of his generation, Saleh, a Tajik, grew up witnessing political violence under the Soviet-backed communist regime and suffering personal tragedies. In his early twenties, he joined the militia commanded by Massoud, who sent him to Pakistan in 1992 to do a course on 'post-conflict reconstruction and management'.[34]

Saleh rose to become one of the closest (and youngest) advisers of Massoud. In 1999, Massoud sent him along with seven other senior aides and commanders to the US to attend a CIA training programme. He had already been posted in Dushanbe, Tajikistan, as the Northern Alliance's liaison officer. In that capacity, Saleh coordinated closely with the intelligence networks of the US, Russia, Iran and India. On 9 September 2001, when Massoud was assassinated by al-Qaeda, Saleh was in Dushanbe. He was immediately summoned to Kulyab, a Tajik city close to the Afghan border. In a hospital in Kulyab, Saleh was told the commander was dead. He later recalled a conversation he had with Richard Blee, a CIA operative who was coordinating intelligence operations with the Northern Alliance, immediately after Massoud's killing. 'The decision is that we will fight,' Saleh told him. 'We will not surrender. We will fight to our last man on the ground.'[35] Two days later, al-Qaeda attacked the World Trade Center in New York.

In 2004, after the Islamic Republic of Afghanistan was established, Saleh was appointed the head of the National Directorate of Security by President Karzai. The years he spent as the Northern Alliance's intelligence liaison officer came in handy. Saleh had developed close contacts with the CIA, India's Research and Analysis Wing (RAW) and other regional intelligence agencies. He recruited Pashtun agents and deployed them across Afghanistan and even inside Pakistan to infiltrate Taliban networks. Saleh established a frequent intelligence briefing for the President. The objective was to build a vibrant intelligence network in Afghanistan that could foresee and neutralize threats from the Taliban and al-Qaeda. His relentless pursuit of the jihadists earned him the reputation of being the Taliban's top enemy in Kabul. The insurgents carried out multiple assassination attempts on his life, the most recent of which was in September 2020.

In 2011, after Bin Laden was killed in Pakistan's Abbottabad, Saleh said the NDS had reached the conclusion as early as in 2004 that Bin Laden was in one of Pakistan's residential areas.[36] In 2006, he had brought it to the attention of Ashfaq Parvez Kayani, who was then the ISI chief, at a conference in Bagram. Kayani was angry. 'I don't need to be taught intelligence by someone the age of my son,' he said.[37] But Saleh continued to pursue the thread. In a summit between President Karzai and Pakistan's dictator Gen. Pervez Musharraf, Saleh brought up the Bin Laden issue again. 'Why have you brought this Panjshiri guy to teach me intelligence?' a furious Musharraf told Karzai.[38]

The warm relationship between Karzai and Saleh did not last long. When Karzai started looking for a political dialogue with the Taliban, Saleh fell out with him. In 2010, he resigned as the NDS chief. Saleh believed that the Taliban problem would not be resolved unless the Taliban were disarmed and reintegrated into society. And he remained a strong advocate of the use of force against the Taliban, despite allegations of high casualties from aerial attacks. In a 2011 interview with PBS Frontline, when Saleh was asked if he supported President Obama's drone campaign, he said that 'drones are not enough'. 'I encourage America to use the Air Force, bomb Pakistan and force it to stop supporting the Taliban and al-Qaeda. Period.'[39]

For Saleh, the resignation from the NDS was an opportunity to build a broader support base before an eventual entry into politics. He turned out to be a critic of Karzai's policies. He founded an organization, Basej-e Milli (National Movement), which he called Afghanistan's 'anti-Taliban constituency'.[40] He travelled across the country trying to mobilize supporters in favour of Basej and organized mass rallies in Kabul and elsewhere. In 2018, Saleh returned to the government when President Ghani appointed him interior minister. A few months later, he resigned to join Ghani's election team. In the 2019 presidential election, Ghani, who was seeking re-election, picked Saleh as his running mate, which set the stage for the latter's ascent as the country's First Vice President.

Through a career spanning three decades, Saleh had seen several ups and downs. His views had also evolved. He once quarrelled with Karzai over his efforts to talk with the Taliban. But the administration he was part of sought a political settlement with the Taliban. As an intelligence chief, almost his entire focus was on the Taliban, yet he could not stop their advance. Throughout his career, he remained critical of Pakistan, but he could do practically nothing to stop Islamabad from deepening its influence in Afghanistan through the Taliban. Saleh knew what was coming. In the 2011 PBS interview, when asked whether he was worried about what would happen when the Americans withdrew, he said, 'Yes. If they withdraw and the situation is the way it is, it will be a disaster. Massacre of people. Bloodbath. Disintegration of power and fragmentation of authority.' When the interviewer asked him why America should stay in Afghanistan, he responded, with a smile, 'Why did they come here?'[41] He wanted the Americans to stay and help Afghan troops fight the Taliban.

Valley of Resistance

When the Taliban were closing in on Kabul and Ghani's administration was unravelling, Saleh retreated to Panjshir, the valley of resistance that, under Massoud's command, had kept the Soviets and the Taliban out during the 1980s and 1990s. Panjshir was one of the last provinces standing, where Ahmad Shah Massoud's thirty-two-year-old son, Ahmad Massoud, was commanding a small resistance force, National Resistance Front (NRF). From Panjshir, Saleh declared himself the 'legitimate caretaker President of Afghanistan'. He tweeted on 17 August, 'Clarity: As per d constitution of Afg, in absence, escape, resignation or death of the President the FVP becomes the caretaker President. I am currently inside my country & am the legitimate care taker

President. Am reaching out to all leaders to secure their support & consensus.'[42] Images emerged online showing Saleh and Massoud, Jr, making resistance plans and flying a military helicopter in Panjshir.

The story of Panjshir's defiance goes back decades. When Afghanistan became a republic in 1973, Ahmad Shah Massoud was a twenty-year-old student in Kabul University. Massoud, who was a member of the Muslim Youth, the student wing of the Jamiat-e Islami, started an uprising against President Daoud Khan in Panjshir that was backed by Pakistani intelligence. Initially Daoud Khan's regime put down the protests and Massoud had to flee to Pakistan. But he would return to Panjshir after the communists took over Kabul in 1978. In the Panjshir Valley, Massoud built a guerrilla resistance against the communists. After the Soviets came to Afghanistan in 1979, Panjshir emerged as the hotbed of the anti-Soviet forces.

Located 150 km north of Kabul, the valley is near the Hindu Kush mountain range. It's divided by the Panjshir river and ringed by the Panjshir mountains in the north and the Kuhestan mountains in the south. The mountaintops are covered with snow throughout the year. This difficult terrain makes the valley a nightmare for invaders. It allowed Massoud to keep the valley away from, first, the communist government and then the Taliban regime. Earlier, Panjshir was part of Parwan province. In 2004, the valley and the surrounding region became an independent province. Roughly 150,000 people live in Panjshir, a huge majority of them ethnic Tajiks. When the Taliban started taking province after province in 2021, many from the fallen cities and towns fled to Kabul, escaping the hard-line Islamists. Some others fled to Panjshir, hoping that the valley, the traditional capital of the Tajik Mujahideen, would hold off the Taliban onslaught.

In Panjshir, Saleh and Massoud vowed to continue fighting the Taliban, and sought external help. In an article in *The Washington*

Post on 18 August, Ahmad Massoud said he was 'ready to follow my father's footsteps'. 'But we need more weapons, more ammunition and more supplies,' he wrote, in a direct call for help.[43] It was Panjshir's declaration of war on the Taliban. But this time, the odds were against them from the very beginning.

In their second coming, the Taliban seemed to be aware of the challenges that could emanate from the north, and they adopted a two-pronged strategy. When the Taliban launched their offensive of 1 May – the day the remaining US-led international troops started withdrawing – their focus was on the northern provinces. They took Badakhshan province, which shares a long border with Tajikistan. The Taliban did not attack Panjshir, but seized all provinces around it. So by the time provincial capitals started falling on 6 August, Panjshir had already become an island surrounded by the Taliban with no direct access by land to Tajikistan. Also, the Taliban had started a charm offensive to win over Afghanistan's neighbours, who had backed anti-Taliban forces in the past. The Taliban delegations had visited Moscow many times starting in 2018. Mullah Mansour, the former Taliban leader, was killed in a US strike in 2015 when he was travelling from Iran to Pakistan, suggesting that Tehran had also established contacts with the Taliban leadership.[44] China was one of the first countries that declared willingness to work with the Taliban after the fall of Kabul. What the Taliban did in all these cases was to turn their biggest weakness – ties with transnational terrorist organizations – into an opportunity. They promised Iran, Russia and China that they would not host or aid terrorist groups that were opposed to those countries' interests. In return, the Taliban wanted those countries not to help any resistance forces within Afghanistan.

So when Saleh and Massoud, Jr, started their resistance against the Taliban from an isolated Panjshir after the fall of Kabul, they were on their own. They had neither direct access to a friendly border (say, Tajikistan) nor direct military assistance from regional players. The Taliban held talks with Panjshir representatives but did not make any concessions; they wanted total surrender. Immediately after the US troops were out of the country on 31 August, the Taliban launched the Panjshir offensive aimed at taking over the valley.

Within days, the Taliban claimed they had the control of the entire Panjshir province. Their supporters posted photos of the Taliban's white flag raised at the provincial headquarters at Bazarak. Taliban fighters carrying guns posed for photos before administrative buildings with Massoud's murals on them. The NRF dismissed the Taliban claims. 'Taliban's claim of occupying Panjshir is false. The NRF forces are present in all strategic positions across the valley to continue the fight. We assure the ppl of Afghanistan that the struggle against the Taliban & their partners will continue until justice & freedom prevails,' the NRF tweeted on 6 September. But the Taliban got what they wanted for now – the administrative headquarters of Panjshir – which allowed them to claim control over the whole of Afghanistan for the first time ever. The next day, the Taliban announced their government. Saleh and Massoud, Jr, are believed to be in Tajikistan. Any NRF plan to regroup and counter-attack the Taliban would depend on regional support, which, in turn, depends on whether the Taliban can establish a stable government in Afghanistan and can keep the promises they made to regional powers.

The New Jihadist Challenge

The NRF is not the only armed opposition the Taliban faced towards the end of 2021. While the Taliban claim they have an advantage over the NRF for now, the former are facing growing challenges from another front, where the Islamic State-Khorasan

(IS-K), the Afghan branch of the Middle East-based terrorist outfit, have begun unleashing a reign of terror.

The Taliban's troubles with the IS-K went back to the rise of the latter six years ago in Afghanistan. In June 2015, a few months after the IS announced its Wilayat Khorasan (Khorasan Province), the Taliban wrote a letter to the then IS chief, Abu Bakr al-Baghdadi, asking him to stop recruiting jihadists in Afghanistan. The letter, signed by the then political committee chief of the Taliban, Mullah Akhtar Mansour, said there was room for 'only one flag and one leadership' in the fight to re-establish Islamic rule in Afghanistan.[45] But the IS faction, which came to be known as the Islamic State-Khorasan, did not stop recruiting disgruntled Taliban fighters. Nor did it stop launching terror attacks across Afghanistan.

On 26 August, eleven days after the Taliban captured Kabul, the IS-K carried out one of its biggest attacks in Afghanistan, killing about 200 people in the capital, including thirteen American service members. This was the first major security threat for Afghanistan's new rulers, no strangers to terror tactics themselves. It was the deadliest day for the US military in Afghanistan since 2011. The day also saw the first American fatalities in Afghanistan since the US–Taliban agreement was signed in February 2020 under the Trump administration. The IS-K carried out more attacks in the following weeks, mainly targeting Shias. On 3 October, they attacked a mosque in Kabul where a memorial service for the mother of Taliban spokesperson Zabihullah Mujahid was being held, killing five. On 8 October, a Shia mosque in the northern city of Kunduz was attacked in which at least fifty people were killed. Another Shia mosque in Kandahar, the Taliban's stronghold as well as its spiritual headquarters, came under IS-K attack on 15 October, killing at least forty people.

In the past six years, the IS-K have built an organizational network in Afghanistan from the eastern Nangarhar province, attracting followers from across South, West and Central Asia, and killed hundreds. When the IS announced the formation of the Khorasan Province, referring to an area encompassing Afghanistan, Pakistan and Central Asia, in January 2015, the group's immediate strategy was to exploit the divisions within the main jihadist groups operating in the region. It appointed Tehrik-i-Taliban Pakistan (TTP) commander Hafiz Saeed Khan as its leader and former Afghan Taliban commander Abdul Rauf Aliza as his deputy (both were killed in US strikes).[46] The group attracted members from different militant organizations such as Lashkar-e-Taiba, Jamaat-ud-Dawa, the Haqqani Network and the Islamic Movement of Uzbekistan into its fold.[47]

The IS-K have declared its allegiance to the Islamic State core. In operational tactics and ideology, it follows its parental organization. The key goal is to establish 'Islamic rule' in the 'province' and for that they are ready to wage jihad. 'There is no doubt that Allah the Almighty has blessed us with jihad in the land of Khorasan since a long time ago, and it is from the grace of Allah that we fought any disbeliever who entered the land of Khorasan. All of this is for the sake of establishing the Shariah,' the IS-K said in a video message in 2015.[48]

When the IS in Iraq and Syria came under pressure in 2015 and 2016, the core organization shifted its focus to Afghanistan. The IS was losing territories to Kurdish militias in Syria and to government forces and Shia militias in Iraq. In Afghanistan, a divided country with the government's writ hardly reaching its hinterlands, the IS saw an opportunity to rebuild its organization. Having built its base in eastern Afghanistan, the IS-K issued propaganda messages, calling on Muslim youth across Asia to join the group. Many radicalized youth, including dozens from India, travelled to Afghanistan to either join the IS or live an 'Islamic life' under the caliphate's rule.[49] But the IS came under pressure in Afghanistan as well. The Taliban did not like its monopoly over violent jihad being challenged by another organization. Also, the

Taliban are a tribal, nationalist, militant force, backed by Pakistan, whereas the IS-K do not believe in national borders and stands for a pan-Islamic caliphate.

'The leadership of Daesh [IS] is independent, the goals of Daesh are independent,' Omar Khorasani, who was the IS-K's top leader, said in an interview from prison in August 2021. 'We have a global agenda and so when people ask who can really represent Islam and the whole Islamic community, of course we're more attractive.'[50] The ideological and operational differences led to open clashes between the IS-K and the Taliban. When the Taliban seized Kabul in August 2021 and took over prisons, they freed several of their members, but not IS-K members. They executed Khorasani and other IS-K jihadists. Shahab al-Muhajir has been leading the terrorist group since Khorasani was arrested in April 2020.[51]

The US had carried out a number of targeted attacks, killing several of the IS-K's leaders. In April 2017, US President Donald Trump ordered troops to drop the 'Mother of all Bombs', the most powerful non-nuclear bomb, on IS caves in eastern Afghanistan. But despite the United States' targeted bombings and the Taliban's counter-attacks on the ground, the IS-K have continued to expand its operations. As much of Afghanistan remains lawless, the conditions favour the IS-K to grow, like their mothership grew in crisis-hit Iraq and Syria in 2013–14. And the host of suicide attacks they have carried out in the immediate aftermath of the Taliban takeover – Kunduz in the north, Kandahar, also the Taliban's birthplace, in the south and Kabul in the east (all in October 2021) – suggest that the IS-K are no longer confined to Nangarhar and Kunar. Their operational capability has been spreading across the country.

While the Taliban have started to rule Afghanistan, it would appear that the IS-K now want to be the new Taliban.

5

Return of the Silk Road

IT TAKES LESS THAN FIVE HOURS FROM THE OLD SILK ROAD oasis city of Kashgar, driving south on the well-paved G314 expressway that runs all along China's western border, to reach the town of Tashkurgan, which means 'stone fortress'. Needless to say, the journey took a lot longer for the caravans on the old Silk Road. Travellers journeying from the west, from Badakhshan and beyond, would stop for the night in this town that served as an unofficial entry point to the prosperous hinterlands and the trading towns of Khotan and Kashgar.

The stone fortress, which still stands today perched on a hill, can be seen from miles away across the barren Taklamakan desert. The sight would have offered respite for weary travellers as they broke their journey. If the state of the expressway that runs past the fort today offers a reminder of how much has changed, Tashkurgan's main market, where farmers still usher in sheep and goats to sell every Sunday, is a postcard of things that haven't.

Tashkurgan is as far south as an Indian reporter can go. If you're an Indian traveller, it is perhaps as sensitive as a town in China can possibly get. Continue southward, and the G314 national highway, a few kilometres on, winds its way into PoK towards Gilgit, the route traversed daily by Chinese and Pakistani traders. Head west, and you are a stone's throw from the Wakhan Corridor, the narrow piece of land sandwiched between Tajikistan to the north and Pakistan and PoK to the south, where Afghanistan meets China.

It was only by chance that Afghanistan and China came to share a border. It was a result, like most of the borders in this part of Asia, of colonial machinations – an 1895 agreement between the great powers in London and St Petersburg that wanted a buffer to keep their two empires geographically separated. Thus was born the Wakhan Corridor.[1] But even a thousand years before that agreement, in an age where boundaries were fluid and regions such as this passed in and out of the extremities of kingdoms that rose and fell, this passage bound China's empires to the lands beyond its western mountains.

The Bamiyan Connect

Among those who travelled this road, as far back as the seventh century, was the legendary Chinese traveller-monk Xuan Zang. He would stop in Tashkurgan as he journeyed east from Badakhshan to Khotan, on his triumphant journey home carrying the scriptures from India that would bring Buddhism to China and change the course of its history.

When Xuan Zang arrived in the town of Bamiyan in what is today central Afghanistan, Buddhism was thriving and had already taken hold there, having come to Afghanistan during the time of Ashoka in the third century BCE.[2] According to one interpretation,

Bamiyan's name itself, which comes from a combination of words meaning cliffs and terraces, owes its etymology to the towering idols of the Buddha that were carved into its cliffs.[3]

The Chinese monk's writings of what he saw in Bamiyan, then both a booming trading point and a cultural meeting ground on the Silk Road that connected West and East, still contain some of the most important insights into its history. The two most significant works that were Xuan Zang's great legacy, *The Great Tang Record of the Western Regions*, authored by him, and *The Life of Xuan Zang: The Tripitaka Master of the Great Tzu En Monastery*, written by his disciple Hui Li, offer 'the most important oldest accounts of the Bamiyan site'. Xuan Zang, who visited in 632 CE, through his records helped establish the age of the two colossal Bamiyan Buddhas, with the oldest going back to the fourth century and the second to the second half of the fifth century.[4]

Xuan Zang wrote of Bamiyan:

> Fan-hsing-na (Bamiyan) country is 2,000 li east to west (about 700 miles) and 300 li north to south (about 100 miles) … The monasteries number several tens. The monks and followers number 1,000 persons … Northeast of the king's city, the mountain slope has a standing stone Buddha image. Its height is 140 or 150 feet. The golden colour is dazzling and glorious and the precious ornaments are lustrous and glistening.

The monks, he added, were 'very courteous' and 'were surprised that China had such a monk' as himself, apparently unaware that Buddhism had found its way to China.[5]

Bamiyan's influence, carried through Xuan Zang's records, made its presence felt hundreds of kilometres away to the east in China. As the scholar Marylin Rhie writes, Chinese art 'may at first sight not appear to have much in common with the art of Bamiyan, but in certain features, motifs of general technical and stylistic approaches, it does to a certain degree'. In Dunhuang, China's most famed Silk Road site in what is today Gansu province, the spectacular grottoes carry figures that have 'a Gandharan or western representation' which are 'more closely comparable to the Bamiyan paintings'.[6]

Xuan Zang arrived during central Afghanistan's Buddhist peak. This golden age of Buddhism did not last forever. While many of the monasteries remained undisturbed after the decline of the Kusanas and during the Zoroastrian Sassanian rule, by mid-seventh century, the Arab entry to Kandahar brought this period to an end, as the people turned to Islam.[7] But regardless of those changes, the influence from China's west and southwest remained etched in the Chinese consciousness, the 'long trail of Buddhist sites, inscriptions, sculptures, documentational hoards and paintings extending from north-west India round or through the western Himalaya and then from Parthia, Afghanistan and Sogdiana (Samarkand) to Xinjiang, Gansu and Luoyang' all seen as a continuum of the same tradition – one that deeply shaped China's philosophical and cultural history.[8]

Fading Relevance

The Bamiyan Buddhas offer a useful snapshot of the ebbs and flows of a relationship that, for all its cultural significance, gradually drifted into irrelevance. Centuries later, the destruction of the grand Buddhas, which had survived so much change, by the latest new rulers of Afghanistan deeply shocked people in China and incited wide revulsion there, and of course, around the world.

Despite the undeniable importance of the western regions to China's political, cultural and religious history, it was also the case that these distant frontier lands that connected China with the West were not settled conclusively by any great power, passing in and out of the control of various competing kingdoms. Nor were they directly incorporated into the empires ruled from China's hinterlands. Indeed, until the mid-eighteenth-century conquests, the Qing empire, in fact, had little contact with regions beyond the Karakoram and the western mountain ranges.[9]

The Qing conquest over the Zunghar Mongols between 1755 and 1757 would bring into their fold important trading centres in Xinjiang such as Yarkand which had ties 'reaching across the Pamir and Karakoram Mountains to India, Afghanistan and Central Asia'. The most direct route to the west ran from Yarkand through the Karakoram to Leh, while another ran west through the Pamirs, through Afghanistan, and entered Punjab and Sindh from the west. This conquest brought the Qing and the Mughals in close proximity. The Mughals at their height claimed their empire's territory ran up to Badakhshan but with 'tenuous' authority. The Zunghars controlled this region until the Qing expansion which 'coincided with a decline in Mughal unity and power'.[10]

If the Qing conquest did bring Xinjiang into the fold of the empire – and the western regions ever closer – in truth, Xinjiang was not under the empire's direct administration even after the conquest. The Qing presence was 'in essence nothing more than a huge garrison under the command of the military governor'. Qing officials there 'neither respected nor learned much about the languages and customs', and learned 'even less about the … lands beyond'.[11]

Forging Connections

With the slow decline of the Qing in the nineteenth century, and the events that would follow the First Opium War (1839–42) and mark what would come to be known in China as its 'Century of Humiliation' that saw the carving up of much of China's eastern seaboard by foreign powers, the western frontiers went out of the spotlight. The end of the Chinese Civil War (1927–49), the Communist Party coming to power and the establishment of the People's Republic of China (PRC) in 1949 presented a fresh opportunity to reassess the western regions, from the perspective of both the Party bringing Tibet and Xinjiang under its direct control and negotiating the unresolved boundaries that the PRC inherited.

Afghanistan, in fact, would be among the first countries to recognize the PRC in 1950, with diplomatic relations between the two nations established in 1955. The most significant development in the early years was a border agreement to settle the China–Afghan boundary. When the Kingdom of Afghanistan proposed holding boundary negotiations in December 1962, China agreed. The talks moved quickly. On 2 March 1963, the same day China signed a provisional border agreement with Pakistan, China and Afghanistan said they would enter formal talks.

From China's view, the main issue was determining the Afghan–Soviet–Chinese trijunction, which was linked to China's claim to the Pamir mountains, controlled by the Soviet Union; the settling of this would also help China in moving towards agreeing its border with the Soviets. Afghanistan, on the other hand, wanted China to recognize its sovereignty over the Wakhan Corridor, which some Chinese maps had shown as China's territory. The agreement was reached in double quick time, with both countries announcing a draft treaty on 1 August 1963. On 22 November of that year, a boundary treaty was signed in Beijing, which 'overall favoured Afghanistan'. It largely followed the boundary of the 1895 agreement between Britain and Russia, and saw China give up claims to the Wakhan Corridor and recognize Soviet control of the Pamirs. A boundary protocol was signed in March 1965 after the demarcation process was completed.[12]

In 1964, Mao Zedong hosted Afghanistan's King Mohammed Zahir Shah in Beijing. He began the meeting expressing his admiration for Afghans, telling the king, 'Afghanistan is a heroic country and has never surrendered.'[13] But the Soviet occupation of Afghanistan, fifteen years later amid strained Sino-Soviet relations, would be a transformative event in Beijing's calculus and one with great implications for the security of its western borders. So concerned was Beijing by the Soviet invasion that it feared Pakistan might be next, with Vice Premier Geng Biao lamenting, 'If the Soviets' barbarous aggression goes unchecked, the next target is Pakistan.'[14]

These concerns weren't empty words. Beijing decided to jump into the efforts to support the Mujahideen against the Soviets, with the People's Liberation Army (PLA) even helping train Mujahideen fighters in Xinjiang, a prospect that, today, seems unthinkable given Chinese concerns over separatism and extremism in Xinjiang. Indeed, Beijing became 'the arms-supplier-in-chief for the guerrilla war against the Soviet Union', offering everything from AK-47s to RPGs (rocket-propelled grenades). Its ally Pakistan was the main facilitator of the shipments. One curious element in the Beijing–Mujahideen relationship was China's cultivation of what was a small Maoist faction, Shola-e Jawed or Eternal Flame, though by no means was Chinese support limited to them. Among the many direct recipients of Chinese military aid was Ahmad Shah Massoud of the Northern Alliance.[15] In 1993, four years after the Soviet occupation ended, and with the country plunged into civil war, China would evacuate its embassy in Kabul.

The Taliban coming to power in 1996 hardly inspired Beijing's confidence, with the outfit viewed with suspicion for its links with extremist groups, including those that China believed were active in Xinjiang. As the scholar Andrew Small has noted, Beijing's initial outreach to the group was motivated primarily by that concern. As would be the case twenty-five years later when the Taliban regained power, the group's biggest challenge was gaining international legitimacy, which it needed in order to access financial aid from abroad. The West not wanting to step in, then as now, opened the doors for China. China would make its first tentative outreach to the Taliban in the year 2000, after a visit to Kandahar by experts from the China Institutes of Contemporary International Relations (CICIR), a Beijing-based think tank affiliated to the Ministry of State Security. That was followed by a visit from Lu Shulin, China's envoy in Islamabad and a career diplomat with expertise in Pakistan (and fluent in Urdu) going to Kabul to meet Mullah Akhund (then Vice President of the Council of Ministers, he would be appointed head of the interim government that came to power in 2021). Lu then flew to Kandahar where he became, as the scholar Small observed, 'the first senior representative of a non-Muslim country to meet the Taliban's amir' Mullah Omar, and 'one of only a tiny handful of non-Muslims that Omar ever dealt with'. The meeting, however, did not have the most ideal beginning. In a reminder of the vast gulf between the communist visitor and his mullah host, a gift of a camel statue was received as if it was 'a piece of red hot coal', because of the Taliban view of idols and statues, made known to the world in the barbaric destruction of the Bamiyan Buddhas.[16]

Mullah Omar went to great lengths to assure China, just as Mullah Baradar would do two decades later, that the Taliban would not allow Afghan territory to be used against China. Those assurances would lead to opening the door for Chinese companies, though in a very limited way. Huawei and ZTE, the two Chinese telecom giants already established in next-door Pakistan, for the first time started offering services in Afghanistan. Infrastructure and mining companies followed, eyeing the country's massive untapped mineral wealth.

The Taliban regime, of course, barely survived a year into this tentative Chinese outreach. The 11 September 2001 attacks and the US invasion would bring down the Taliban by the end of the year. In the decade of US occupation that followed, Chinese companies had a largely fruitless experience. Their broad conclusion was that the political instability was not worth their while. Much celebrated projects, such as the Aynak copper mine, never materialized.

Attacks on Chinese personnel didn't inspire confidence either, such as the June 2004 killing of eleven Chinese workers working on the World Bank-supported highway construction in Kunduz. Reports at the time said the attackers were linked with Gulbuddin Hekmatyar's Hezb-e-Islami outfit – one of the groups China had reached out to, and by some accounts, even offered material support in exchange for cooperation. Hekmatyar denied the accusations, blaming the Americans for using the attack 'to malign jihad and jihadis'. The experience, needless to say, was chastening for China.[17]

Two events that followed a decade of US occupation would change China's geopolitical calculus. Afghanistan would gradually shift in that calculus from a country that was, to put it simply, too much trouble for China, to one where Beijing saw both economic interests, and for the first time, a larger geopolitical stake that its mandarins believed was coming into play.

The first was the killing of Osama bin Laden, found hiding in a safe house in the Pakistani military town of Abbottabad, in 2011, which further deepened the impulse within the Barack Obama administration to push for an exit strategy from the region. If Obama, who opposed the Iraq war, came to see Afghanistan as America's 'good war', he was aware that patience at home for endless wars was wearing thin. In 2014, the US-led International

Security Assistance Force began the process of ending operations and transferring greater responsibility to the Afghan army.

The second big event, coinciding with these first steps towards an inexorable Western exit, was the launch of China's Belt and Road Initiative in 2013. The launch of the BRI, which had an explicit focus on China's neighbourhood, dovetailed with Ashraf Ghani coming to power in Kabul and beginning his administration with a push for infrastructure projects. It was no surprise that Ghani chose China as his first overseas visit, sending a strong signal about his investment in ties with Beijing. Welcomed by Xi Jinping in Beijing, Ghani declared that Afghanistan viewed China 'as a strategic partner, in the short term, medium term, long term and very long term'. Xi, in return, said China was prepared to work towards 'a new era of co-operation' and 'to take development to a new depth'.[18]

With Ghani coming to power, and the US looking at exit doors, China was entering a geopolitical sweet spot as arguably 'the only country to have good working relations with virtually every party that has a stake in the conflict', from the Afghan government and the Taliban, to Iran, Russia and particularly its 'all-weather' ally Pakistan.[19] China and India had even begun discussing coordinating their approaches to Afghanistan, later launching a joint programme to train Afghan diplomats when Xi and Indian Prime Minister Narendra Modi met in Wuhan in 2018.

For Ghani, China offered two things: investment, particularly with the launch of the BRI, and, the prospect of securing cooperation with Pakistan, which had continued to shelter and back Taliban forces and in the view of many in Kabul was undermining any reconciliation effort. The latter would, perhaps, turn out to be a rather naïve expectation given how things would turn out in 2021. China, in turn, began to insert itself more confidently in discussions on Afghanistan's future, in 2014 hosting the Heart of

Asia Conference. The following year, there would be more visits from China in twelve months than there had been in the past decade.[20] Things were changing quickly, and driving this change, more than anything else, were the ambitions of China's new leader at the helm and his mission of expanding China's footprint around the world.

Project of the Century

Dubbed 'the project of the century' by Xi, the Belt and Road Initiative is aimed at establishing China's global ascendancy.[21] The BRI, and Xi's new emphasis on neighbourhood diplomacy, significantly changed how China viewed its periphery, ushering in a transition from what could broadly be termed a defensive approach, geared towards primarily securing China's interests especially on core issues and guarding Chinese territory, to an active approach, where Beijing began to be less averse about inserting itself into the internal affairs of its neighbours in order to shape events to suit its interests. To get a sense of how Afghanistan figures in China's geopolitical and geo-economic calculus today, it is important to first understand that calculus, and how dramatically it has shifted in the past decade.

In one sense, this change was a natural evolution – one seen in the behaviour of all rising powers. As China's economic stakes grew rapidly around its periphery, it was inevitable that Beijing would be more involved in the politics that determined the future of its investments. The BRI did not bring about this change overnight. But what it did, in the years since its launch in 2013, was bring out into the open China's new ambitions in its neighbourhood, and create a narrative – that would work powerfully for some of Beijing's neighbours – of the inevitability of Beijing's ascendancy and Western decline. This was a theme that China's diplomats began to articulate more forcefully. And in Afghanistan, where a Western exit literally loomed, it had particular resonance.

The Chinese narrative also smartly played on China's old Silk Road links which, as we have seen, had a special significance as far as Afghanistan and Central Asia were concerned. The BRI, as the name suggests, refers to a belt and a road. (In Mandarin, it's still known as the 'One Belt, One Road', or *yi dai yi lu*, which was the plan's original name in English before it was rechristened. One theory suggests the name change was to connote a more democratic, open approach rather than 'one' belt and 'one' road, though somewhat tellingly, the name remained the same in Mandarin.)

The 'road' part of the plan, somewhat confusingly, refers to the seas. The focus of the Maritime Silk Road is to China's east and south, drawing on old maritime links that bound the seafaring communities on China's eastern seaboard to Southeast Asia. The other part of the plan is the Silk Road Economic Belt, which runs to China's west. Central and South Asia are the focus, with corridors planned to Pakistan (China Pakistan Economic Corridor [CPEC]); Bangladesh, Myanmar and India (Bangladesh China India Myanmar Economic Corridor [BCIM]); the Trans-Himalayan Multi-dimensional Connectivity Network to Nepal; and several corridors through Central Asia, all the way to Europe. Afghanistan lies right where many of these planned corridors converge, with Chinese officials, early on, speaking of wanting to extend the CPEC to Afghanistan and all the way to Iran.

Politics of the BRI

The BRI also underlined a momentous shift in China's diplomacy, one that Xi Jinping took forward soon after coming to power.

After taking over as Communist Party General Secretary in 2012, Xi emphasized 'the Chinese dream' – improving the lives of people at home – and the 'great rejuvenation of the Chinese nation' – returning China to what many of its people see as its rightful place in the centre of the world – as two key campaigns.[22] Pursuing these goals also meant essentially abandoning the maxim that had governed China's foreign policy for decades, described by former paramount leader Deng Xiaoping as '*taoguang yanghui*', or 'biding time, hiding brightness'. The new maxim favoured by the leadership was '*fenfa youwei*', meaning 'striving for achievement'.

Accompanying this change was a newfound confidence about the China model. If Chinese officials in the past were generally defensive about their one-party authoritarian state and issues such as human rights, now they were actually prescribing China's model as the solution for the world, especially developing countries. This was a sentiment that began to take hold starting with the global financial crisis in 2008 – a turning point seen by many in China as marking the start of Western decline – and deepened with the anti-globalization wave and populist movements that would roil Western countries, seen in Donald Trump's victory in the US and Brexit in Britain. These developments marked a profound shift in how Chinese thinkers saw the world, and also gave them the chance to offer their model as a counterpoint to the West.

Indeed, Xi Jinping did what no other leader since Mao was prepared to do: speak of the Chinese experience as a lesson for those abroad. For Mao, it was his communist revolution that offered a template for others. For Xi, it is China's one party-led development model. As he put it in the 2017 National Congress that marked the start of his second five-year term in charge of the Party, China was 'moving to the centre stage of the world', having 'blazed a new trail for other developing countries to achieve modernization'. The China model, he said, provided 'a new option for other countries and nations who want to speed up their development' and 'offers Chinese wisdom and a Chinese approach to solving the problems facing mankind'.[23]

This theme of Western decline and a Chinese alternative would be prominently highlighted by the Chinese state media in the summer of 2021, amid the chaos of Kabul, a hasty US exit and the return of the Taliban. The fall of Kabul was being compared, not just in China but globally, to the fall of Saigon. The intense US–China rivalry that was taking shape, after four turbulent years and amid a trade war launched by the Trump administration, was another factor behind Beijing missing no opportunity to take a shot at the US. Beijing offered itself to Afghanistan as the antithesis of the West, adopting a 'transactional, flexible approach' and 'implying an alternative to the Western development model'. Its aid may have paled in comparison, but the difference was that it came 'without preconditions'.[24]

Indeed, this all-consuming rivalry with the US was, in a sense, the broader canvas on which the BRI was being drawn. What would distinguish Chinese power from US hegemony, Chinese strategic thinkers argued, was a new demonstration of authority. This was one that would invoke China's past, the idea of *tianxia* or all united under an interconnected heaven, which was an example of what the leading strategist Yan Xuetong called 'humane authority'. Thinkers like Yan were offering intellectual heft to the BRI by drawing on China's past, in this case, pre-Qin era (221 BC) thought. As he put it, this was quintessentially different from US power – backed by military might, with disastrous consequences for countries ranging from Vietnam to Afghanistan and Iraq, as Chinese thinkers never fail to point out.

'Only when the international community accepts that China is a more responsible state than the United States,' Yan believes, 'that China will be able to replace the United States as the world's leading state.' Doing so, he says, requires China to distinguish itself from the US when it comes to promoting its values abroad. China, in his view, should reverse the US approach and 'not impose a single standard on international society'.[25]

The BRI and Afghanistan's Riches

Politics aside, there is of course, a strong economic rationale driving the BRI. The BRI did not arise out of a vacuum. It was, in fact, merely a continuation of a more than decade-long global geo-economic strategy, as the leading Chinese thinker Zheng Bijian, regarded by many as one of the BRI's architects, explains in his 2018 book, *Economic Globalization and China's Future*. Zheng, in the book, recalls how as far back as 2004, he was asked to prepare a report for the government on China's geo-economic future. In the report, he identified nineteen key strategic questions confronting China. Most were tied to China's economic health and ensuring its continuing importance to the world economy. The first, and most important, question for him, was whether China would always be able to maintain the impetus for economic reform and ensure its economy would continue to expand. The next seven challenges concerned China's ability to handle various domestic challenges while it continued on the path of economic globalization, while the following eleven challenges dealt with China's external environment, such as the Taiwan question, relations with major powers and its dealings with neighbours.

The last question emphasized the need to ensure 'a strategic resource passage network', pointing out that China was then the world's second largest oil importer with 50 per cent of its supply from the Middle East and 80 per cent through the Malacca Strait, which China termed its 'Malacca Dilemma'. What was needed, the report argued, was a web of channels to ensure the free flow of resources through strategic passages. making the exact case for a BRI-like project a good ten years before it was actually unveiled.[26]

Countries along China's western borders would assume particular importance in this quest for resources. One principal motivation of the BRI is to secure China's access to external sources of resources and energy in the long term, through pipelines for oil and gas from Central Asia as well as long-term energy deals with oil companies from Russia, Central Asia and the Middle East. A second motivation is to address the internal challenge posed by the transformation of China's own domestic economy and finding avenues to export the excess capacity of waning industries.[27]

Both motivations are apparent in China's decades-long engagement with its Central Asian neighbours that pre-dated the BRI. But what remains an open question is whether what has been called China's 'Central Asian playbook' will work in Afghanistan, and how far China will be prepared to go to tolerate the risk there after a decade of unrest and instability. As far back as 1994, the then Premier Li Peng spoke of developing connectivity and reviving the Silk Road to Central Asia. A decade later, China and Kazakhstan would open an oil pipeline. Another pipeline to Turkmenistan would follow four years later. For Central Asian countries, the deals offered the promise of Chinese investment as well as diversification from their reliance on Russia. China also invested in refurbishing old railway lines for cargo, with China–Europe trains now criss-crossing Central Asia. Since the launch of the BRI, new routes and more trains have followed. Chinese state-owned enterprises have also invested in renewing old Soviet infrastructure projects in these countries.[28]

In Afghanistan, on the other hand, the decade-long presence of Chinese companies represents a promise unfulfilled. Since 2014, however, Beijing has made new, albeit calibrated, forays to test the waters. These included policy moves such as tax-free entry for products from Afghanistan starting in 2015, which saw Afghan exports increase from a paltry $12 million to an only slightly less paltry $52 million in five years, with a new demand in China for goods such as Afghan pine nuts. In 2016, Kabul and Beijing signed a memorandum of understanding to formally include Afghanistan in the BRI.

In the first three months of 2019, Afghanistan exported $15 million worth of pine nuts, greater than what its entire trade was just a few years previously. A China–Afghanistan air corridor followed in 2018, and the following year, a more ambitious rail route from China to Afghanistan via Kazakhstan and Uzbekistan. Pine nuts are not, however, the riches of Afghanistan that China's companies have in mind. It has been slow going for more ambitious infrastructure projects that Chinese companies are working on, which have largely been suspended, including an oil and gas project in northern Afghanistan and, of course, the famed Aynak mine.[29]

Beginning a New Chapter

It is thus no surprise that when the Taliban seized power in 2021, many of their first statements about China invoked the BRI. Just as was the case twenty years earlier, the new regime was aware it faced a real problem of legitimacy in the West, and would badly need funds to survive. The legitimacy problem was even more acute at the start of their second innings, given how rapidly they seized power, even while a number of countries proclaimed they would not recognize a new government that took power by force; further, they had quickly backtracked on promises made of building an 'inclusive government' by reverting to type and excluding women and minorities from their cabinet.

Even as they seized power, the Taliban was making all the right noises to China. Abdul Salam Hanafi, deputy director of the Taliban's office in Doha, described China in a phone call with the

Chinese assistant foreign minister Wu Jianghao as 'a trustworthy friend' and said, just as Mullah Omar had promised years ago, that the Taliban 'will never allow any force to use Afghan territory to threaten China's interests'. He pledged protection to Chinese investments and praised the BRI, saying it was 'conducive to the development and prosperity of Afghanistan and the region' and Afghanistan 'hopes to continue to actively support and participate in it'.[30]

The Taliban spokesman Zabihullah Mujahid went so far as to describe China as 'our most important partner', saying Beijing's cooperation represented 'a fundamental and extraordinary opportunity for us, because it is ready to invest and rebuild our country.' There were 'rich copper mines', which, he said, 'thanks to the Chinese, can be put back into operation and modernised'. 'China,' he added, 'is our pass to markets all over the world.'[31]

Sentiments of support and statements of cooperation are, of course, all very well. But if there was anything China had learned from a decade of engaging with Afghanistan, the proof of the pudding would be in the eating. Every Chinese move, whether it was hosting the Heart of Asia Conference in 2014, signing a deal on the BRI two years later, or its outreach to the Taliban in 2021, would be met in the world's press with breathless headlines of China tapping the country's extraordinary mineral wealth. Yet a decade on, not one piece of mineral had been extracted.

If access to external resources and exporting excess Chinese capacity were two principal motivations of the BRI, a third involved security. And considering Beijing's long-held concerns about Tibet and Xinjiang, security, for the Communist Party, is in one sense paramount. The idea was it could bring development to the troubled regions of Xinjiang and Tibet, while at the same time securing those regions by incentivizing neighbouring states, usually through economic deals, to cooperate on the security front.

Chinese officials saw the BRI as offering the chance to address these potential sources of instability from outside China that could spill over, most notably from Afghanistan and Pakistan as far as Xinjiang was concerned, and Nepal when it came to Tibet.[32]

China views Pakistan and Afghanistan, and the presence of jihadist groups in both countries, as key to dealing with its terrorism problems in Xinjiang. It also sees both Kyrgyzstan and Tajikistan 'as transit states for the narcotics trade from Afghanistan'. China and Pakistan share a border only through PoK, claimed by India, while China and Afghanistan share a rather narrow border in the Wakhan Corridor. With the initiation of the BRI came reports that Beijing had quietly begun carrying out joint patrols with security forces in both regions. This was, in one sense, a modest effort at securing the borders. But it was also, in fact, a momentous development for a country that had never stationed forces on the ground overseas except as part of UN peacekeeping operations. After images of joint patrols by the PLA and Afghan forces surfaced online, so did reports that China was helping Afghanistan build a base in the Wakhan Corridor in Badakhshan. China denied those reports.[33]

However, the big unanswered question would remain: how far would China be willing to go to protect its interests? And how chastened was Beijing by its experience over more than a decade? Indeed, its very high-profile entry into Afghanistan at Aynak had, in one sense, served as a warning sign. If it symbolized anything, it was that 'for China, Afghanistan remains largely a land of threats, real, potential and imagined, rather than one of opportunities'.[34] Despite all those concerns, what was beginning to become clear was that under Xi, and with the BRI, Beijing's tolerance for risks was growing. And the best way to manage these risks, Beijing would come to believe, would be by betting on the Taliban.

6

Betting on the Taliban

THE PHOTOGRAPHS CAPTURED THE ABSURDITY OF THE moment. On the right stood Wang Yi, China's suave foreign minister, dressed as he usually is in a sharp suit. On the left was Mullah Abdul Ghani Baradar, head of the Taliban's political office in Doha and one of the group's founders. The date was 28 July 2021. The location was Tianjin, the booming Chinese port city an hour from Beijing. In the photo, both Wang and Baradar have their arms outstretched, palms open and facing downward, as if to say, 'How did we get here?'

That meeting in Tianjin was by no means the first time China played host to the Taliban. But it was, without question, the most significant. The fate of Afghanistan hung in the balance. The US was hurtling towards a hastily managed withdrawal: three weeks before that meeting, American forces had abandoned the Bagram airfield, the symbol of US military power in Afghanistan, by 'slipping away in the night' and not notifying the Afghan commander that they were leaving.[1] Talks on a political reconciliation had stalled, while city after city in the provinces was falling to the Taliban.

Kabul was firmly in the Taliban's sights, but even the most conservative estimates at the time expected the Ghani government to hold on for at least a few months, if not weeks. A power-sharing agreement appeared to be on the cards. That is, before the spectacular overnight fall of Kabul on 14 August. And amid this perilous state of flux, here was China making a statement that would reverberate around the world. The message was simple: China saw the Taliban as a legitimate stakeholder in Afghanistan's future, and when it came to power, Beijing would have its back.

That message was certainly apparent reading between the lines of what Wang told Baradar. China, as Afghanistan's largest neighbour, he said, 'has always respected Afghanistan's sovereignty, independence and territorial integrity, adhered to non-interference in Afghanistan's internal affairs and pursued a friendly policy toward the entire Afghan people'. 'Afghanistan belongs to the Afghan people, and its future should be in the hands of its own people,' he said, and in China's view, that certainly included the Taliban. Wang went as far as to say 'the Afghan Taliban is an important military and political force in Afghanistan and is expected to play an important role in the country's peace, reconciliation and reconstruction process', the first time China had said so.[2]

The statement of support did come with clear expectations from Beijing on the Taliban's behaviour. Wang said China hoped the Taliban 'will make a clean break with all terrorist organizations including the East Turkestan Islamic Movement and resolutely and effectively combat them to remove obstacles, play a positive role and create enabling conditions for security, stability, development and cooperation in the region'. Baradar, for his part, made all the right noises, saying China had 'always been a reliable friend of the Afghan people' and expressing the Taliban's commitment to 'never allow any force to use the Afghan territory to engage in acts detrimental to China'. 'The Afghan Taliban believes that Afghanistan should develop friendly relations with neighbouring countries and the international community,' he said, adding that the group 'hopes that China will be more involved in Afghanistan's peace and reconciliation process and play a bigger role in future reconstruction and economic development'.[3]

Wary Welcome

For all the bonhomie of 28 July, the Taliban's rapid seizure of power barely two weeks later would spark a range of reactions in China. For many Chinese, memories of Taliban 1.0 – the destruction of Bamiyan's Buddhas, the public executions – remained ingrained, as also a wariness of extreme Islamist groups. Truth be told, there was a wariness of any kind of Islam, as viewed in the attitudes of many in China towards the country's own Muslims in Xinjiang and elsewhere. That did not, however, stop the state media from doing its best to paint the return of the Taliban as a big win for China, and just as importantly, a humiliation for America.

This was a theme emphasized by Chinese nationalists in particular, some of whom even compared the Taliban's victory to that of Mao's communist rebels in 1949. Sinologist Geremie Barmé noted, 'They praised its army as a fraternal force akin to the PLA, one similarly dedicated to the interests of the broad masses of Afghans, a people long oppressed by a venal administration propped up by the American Imperium and its myrmidons.' Among them was Wang Yiwei, professor of international relations at Renmin University in Beijing and a regular presence in the media, who claimed some among the Taliban were reading Mao's series of lectures, *On Protracted War*. 'It's stunning to think that among the Taliban today studying Mao Zedong Thought takes precedence over reciting the Quran,' he wrote on China's Twitter equivalent Sina Weibo, asserting that 'the Taliban have been demonized by America but they are really Afghanistan's People's Liberation Army'. 'What's more,' he added, 'they are true buddies of China.' The PLA comparison, for China's censors, might have been a bridge too far; the Weibo post was later removed, either by Wang himself or by the censors. When Wang's comparison of the Taliban with the PLA caused some amount of outcry, other nationalist writers came to his defence. Sima Nan defended Wang, saying he was 'making a legitimate comparison'.[4]

While it was true that China was somewhat ahead of the curve in betting on the Taliban's return, the embrace was, in many senses, wary and reluctant, despite the professed enthusiasm of state propaganda. As strategic affairs expert Yun Sun wrote in the aftermath of the Tianjin meeting, there were 'questions about how moderate the Taliban will ever be, which has a tremendous impact on Chinese officials' perception of, and policy toward, the organization'. She noted China's past experience of being badly burned in Afghanistan and its many stalled projects, and suggested that the outreach to the Taliban was as much a way of hedging as it was a bet on them.[5]

China continued its contact with the Ghani government till its last days. Indeed, even as Wang Yi hosted the Taliban, Xi Jinping would, a few days prior, make a phone call to Ghani, which did not garner as much attention. In the call, Xi told Ghani that China 'always believes that political dialogue is the fundamental way to achieve national reconciliation and lasting peace in Afghanistan' and will 'continue to support the "Afghan-led, Afghan-owned" principle, the peace and reconciliation process in Afghanistan'. No matter that even as they were speaking, city after city was falling to the Taliban's attacks. Ghani, for his part, praised China, saying it 'has always been an important and positive force in maintaining regional security and stability'. He told Xi he hoped China would 'continue to play an important role in pushing for a political settlement of the Afghan issue'.[6]

China was betting on the Taliban, to be sure. But it was also hedging its bets.

Security, Not Conquest

As Yun, the strategic expert, notes, China had over the years gradually built up relations with the Taliban, taking off on the contacts it had established, as we have seen, during the regime's first innings. This outreach was stepped up in the post-2014 period, coinciding with the accelerating Western exit strategy and Xi Jinping's new neighbourhood diplomacy. In 2015, China hosted secret talks between Taliban representatives and the Afghan government in Urumqi, reported to have been brokered by Pakistan, while the following year, a Taliban delegation led by Mohammad Abbas Stanikzai visited Beijing. Baradar, who led the July 2021 visit, would visit China in 2019.[7]

If every Chinese engagement with the Taliban, particularly amid the US exit, was framed by breathless headlines in the world's media as the latest Chinese attempt to take over Afghanistan and all its mineral wealth, China's motivations, in truth, were a lot more pragmatic. A deteriorating security environment, one that could spill over into Pakistan and affect Chinese projects there, or worse, impact Xinjiang, was the chief concern.

Beyond the optics of the Wang–Baradar meet, two suicide bombings in the months of July and August 2021 would arguably be of greater consequence for Chinese companies. In one of the worst attacks on Chinese personnel abroad, nine Chinese workers, along with four Pakistanis, were killed in July by a bomb attack near the Dasu hydropower project in Pakistan, part of the CPEC.

The following month, a motorcade carrying Chinese workers for the East Bay Expressway project in Gwadar, the Arabian Sea port where the CPEC ends, was attacked by a suicide bomber, with two local children killed and one Chinese worker injured. The attacks prompted an unusual statement from Chinese authorities 'demanding Pakistan ... properly treat the wounded, conduct a thorough investigation on the attack, and severely punish the perpetrators'.[8]

The attacks underlined the fragile security situation in Pakistan, and what might lie in store in Afghanistan where the political situation was in even greater flux. Workers at the Dasu project said they were 'on tenterhooks and fearful of another terrorist attack', and expressed concern about the security situation, saying that 'without consistent army protection at the worksites, senior executives of the Chinese firms have reportedly refused to put their staff at risk and ordered a go-slow'. The Dasu attack was claimed by the Pakistani Taliban, or TTP, though Pakistan would try to deflect criticism by blaming India for the attack, with no less than the foreign minister claiming the attacker had 'received support from Indian and Afghan intelligence agencies'. The Chinese, however, did not seem to make much of the claims, choosing to not repeat them, and these were dismissed by India as 'absurd' and 'yet another attempt by Pakistan to malign India in a bid to deflect international attention from its role as ... a safe haven for proscribed terrorists'.[9]

The hope for China was that the sweeping Taliban victory would, despite the group's well-known links to extremist groups, at the very least bring an end to the civil war and some measure of stability to the country. This was, to be sure, more hope than expectation. In the days after the Taliban claimed Kabul, Chinese companies would express cautious optimism that long-stalled projects would resume, amidst all the positive noises made by

Taliban leaders about China's importance and the need for investment. 'While some Chinese companies are involved in several major projects in Afghanistan, including the Aynak Copper Mine project, which is the second-largest copper mine in the world, many have been stalled or seen slow progress due to political instability in the country,' the Communist Party-run *Global Times* reported three days after the fall of Kabul. 'With a major political shift, some believe that there could be a chance for those projects to resume.'

The newspaper quoted a source at the China Metallurgical Group Corporation, which won the right to mine Aynak for thirty years in 2008 but was yet to start actual work, as saying they 'would consider reopening [the copper mine] after the situation is stabilised, and international recognition, including the Chinese government's recognition of the Taliban regime, takes place'. Those were two very significant caveats, and a far more cautious assessment than the unbridled glee voiced by some nationalists about the Taliban return being a huge victory for China and the green signal for Chinese companies to go all in.[10]

After all, despite all the rhetoric post-2014, with Ghani's visit to Beijing and Xi's promotion of the BRI, there was little to show for this in Afghanistan. In 2020, the total Chinese foreign direct investment in Afghanistan was a paltry $4.4 million, or 'less than 3 percent of that type of Chinese investment in Pakistan, which was $110 million for the same year'. The two biggest projects, Aynak and the oil basin at Amu Darya, remained dormant. And this was despite American troop presence there that lent a measure of stability that 'Chinese companies had benefited from'. Now, all bets were off.[11]

This state of play as the Taliban returned reflected the curious dichotomy in China–Afghanistan relations. Both sides had their own reasons to trumpet the start of a new era: for the Taliban,

China represented an important source of international legitimacy when its friends were few and far between; for China, the chaos of the US exit was a propaganda point to be milked at home, framed as a victory and yet another point of evidence of the inexorable decline of the West. Yet, for all the grandstanding, the truth was that there had been, after close to a decade, very little to show for China's endeavours in Afghanistan.

China's Man in Kabul

Yue Xiaoyong would be the man tasked with changing this situation. In late July 2021, as the US exit drew near and a few days before Baradar's visit to Tianjin, Beijing announced Yue as its new special envoy for Afghanistan. He would be tasked with outreach to the Taliban, engaging with the new regime that would take shape in Kabul, whatever its hue. Yue's mission would be to ensure, first and foremost, China's security interests, and also, of course, that its companies' economic interests were protected in the new Afghanistan. Yue would also have to assess how best China could navigate this new environment, and exploit its special relations with the Taliban, at least relative to the West, to break the cycle of low-level engagement that ties had been stuck in for the past decade.

Yue's appointment was widely seen in Beijing as an indicator that China was indeed ready for a new chapter and a new approach, and as 'a signal that Beijing was willing to play a greater role in the country following the US troop withdrawal'. Announcing his appointment, the Chinese foreign ministry described him as 'a seasoned diplomat' and said 'he will establish contacts with all sides as soon as possible'. Yue has had a long career in the foreign service, serving as ambassador to Qatar and Jordan, as well as a stint as the head of the political section at the Chinese embassy in Washington, DC. In 2019, he joined Renmin University in Beijing to head its

Centre for Global Studies. Two years later, he would be pulled out of retirement for this new role. Li Weijian, a leading Chinese scholar on the Middle East, observed that amid the growing chaos of the US exit, 'China sending an experienced diplomat to Afghanistan shows that China is a responsible power and also sends a signal to the world that China will play a greater role on the Afghanistan issue along with the international community following the US withdrawal.'[12]

Two weeks into the Taliban takeover, Yue gave an extraordinarily wide-ranging interview with the Chinese intellectual and venture capitalist Li Shimo – also known as Eric X. Li – published in Guancha, the popular news and opinion website founded by Li. In it, Yue provided by far the most detailed insights from anyone in Beijing into how China saw its relations with the Taliban and its role in the new Afghanistan. The interview was published in Mandarin and so largely flew under the radar of most international media barring a cursory report in some of the English-language Hong Kong press.[13] Yue was speaking from Islamabad, which was, in a sense, significant in itself. It underlined how much China had come to rely on Pakistan, not only in its outreach to the Taliban, which counted Rawalpindi as its chief backer, but in navigating the fast-changing and complicated terrain in the last stages of the fight between the Taliban and government forces.

Li asked Yue how the Taliban, with 75,000 fighters, was able to so easily defeat the 300,000-strong Afghan army, and if this reflected, as many like Wang Yiwei among the Chinese nationalists had been saying, their strong support among the grassroots in Afghanistan. Yue responded that the question was 'a very good description of the situation in Afghanistan', and right off the bat, slammed the US for the state of events:

> Let me put it this way. The irresponsible withdrawal of the US and NATO troops is the main cause of this disaster and crisis, and the emergence of this chaotic situation in Afghanistan. This is indeed a good lesson that the US should learn from the last 20 years. They have invested a lot of resources in Afghanistan, spent over two trillion dollars, had thousands of casualties, and now there is such a chaotic situation. This is not just a military failure. This is also a failure of international politics and American credibility.

When Li pressed Yue to offer a view on the Taliban and the question of its grassroots support, and whether the Western criticism of the group, its human rights record and its past was valid, he responded:

> I have a feeling about that. I met with them in Tianjin [the 28 July 2021 meeting] and after that, I also had the opportunity to meet with them at the 6+2 meeting in Doha and the 3+1 meeting [with China, Russia, US and Pakistan]. In all these multilateral dialogues, I had the opportunity to meet them and see if they changed. As you said, there was a lot of commentary and criticism of them, and there were also some reports that made positive comments about their changes, as well as some that raised questions about their behaviour. Whether they have actually changed or not, it seems to me that the Taliban have become an important political and military force in this country.

He continued:

> Now that the Taliban are in power, and there are other stakeholders in Afghanistan too, the best thing for us to do is to engage in dialogue with them and to work with them

> to bring about peaceful reconciliation in Afghanistan ... From what we are seeing now, the Taliban have committed that they will work with the region, their neighbours and the international community to facilitate this process ... Of course, we don't just listen to what they say, we are more concerned about what they are doing and what they will do in the future. So far, we have seen some positive trends as the Taliban have moved into Kabul and taken over many cities and almost the whole country, except for a few places. There are positive developments for the Taliban and other stakeholders. At the same time, we are mindful of the negative elements emerging.

Cutting through the diplomat-speak, Yue summed up China's view as follows: the Taliban weren't perfect but in China's view, they were a legitimate part of Afghan society, and being the quintessential pragmatists that they are, the Chinese would deal with them and engage with them as needed to protect their own interests.

Remaking the Taliban

Yue described the Afghanistan situation as both 'a crisis and an opportunity'. 'The biggest opportunity,' he said, 'is to see that for the first time in the last 20 years, even in the last 40 or 70 years, Afghanistan has a chance to take control of its own destiny.' China saw this as a hugely significant moment, and Yue said Beijing would, both 'as a major power' and 'Afghanistan's largest, long-standing and friendly neighbour', stand with them in this new era. This would include, he said, offering China's development experience, which he revealed the Taliban had expressed interest in:

> Certainly from my contacts with their political office in Doha and others, they are very keen to learn from the experience of their neighbours and other successful countries, and from China. But we always say that you should find the right path for your own development, achieve stability and peace in your country and rebuild your country. But we are ready to help.

Part of the goal of the interview, it appeared, was to slowly but surely refashion the image of the Taliban for the Chinese public. This was, after all, the same group that had demolished the Bamiyan Buddhas, carried out public executions and was seen by most in China as a bunch of backward Islamist radicals. Now, the Taliban were being presented as folks of the grassroots – kindred spirits to Mao's revolutionaries, as Wang Yiwei put it – and far less threatening than their popular perception. Li asked Yue, 'What are the Taliban like? Are they as scary as we see them on CNN or BBC? Are they ordinary people like you and me?' Yue replied:

> From my contact with them, my feeling is that they are like other Afghans, like the people of this region, they are very friendly, they like to exchange ideas with me, to talk to other people, they listen to other people's ideas and to explain things. Of course, they like to show what they stand for.

Describing the Taliban as 'friendly' and open to 'listen[ing] to other people's ideas' was extraordinary in itself. What was all the more striking, given the Taliban's long history of dalliances with extremist groups, was Yue's framing of the Taliban as an ally in China's war on terror. Referring to the East Turkestan Islamic Movement (ETIM) and its attacks on Xinjiang, Yue said the Taliban 'pledged to continue to follow the situation effectively and to completely cut off any links with the terrorist organizations'. The Chinese envoy was bullish about the future, suggesting the Taliban was 'actively considering' whether the China Pakistan Economic Corridor could be extended to Afghanistan.

Li finally asked Yue what his message would be to the Afghan people. He responded:

> I will say that China is a friend of Afghanistan. China and Afghanistan have always maintained traditional friendly relations, and we established diplomatic relations back in the 1950s. Historically, we have had thousands of years of traditional friendship along the ancient Silk Road. Now we have the opportunity, on the basis of all these friendly relations and on the principle of mutual respect for national sovereignty and independence, to achieve peaceful reconstruction and reconciliation in Afghanistan, to share China's path of peaceful diplomacy, and to share the same future.[14]

A few days after Yue's interview, and seemingly part of this concerted effort at giving the Taliban an image makeover at home, the Communist Party-run *Global Times* published a lengthy interview with Suhail Shaheen, the Taliban's spokesman. The interview was published days after the Taliban announced its interim government, which had belied promises – and expectations from many, including China – of a more inclusive government than the previous Taliban regime. The interim cabinet had not a single woman or minority representative, and several of its members were on UN sanctions lists. The focus of the interview was, however, on China's security concerns, the ETIM in particular, and on the Taliban's interest in Chinese investment. The *Global Times* wrote, 'Regarding the question of the ETIM, the spokesperson made it clear in the interview that after the Doha agreement, many members of this organization had left Afghanistan because they were told no one can use Afghanistan against other countries.' Shaheen went on to make three commitments: 'First, we will not allow any training on our territory. Second, we will not allow any fundraising for those who intend to carry out a foreign agenda. Third, we will not allow the establishment of any recruitment centre in Afghanistan. These are the main things.'[15]

China's deep-rooted concerns about the Taliban's links to extremist groups certainly didn't dissipate overnight, yet Beijing's actions did appear to show a newfound confidence in the fundamentalist organization. This was evinced in China being among only four countries to keep its embassy open when Kabul fell to the Taliban (the others were Russia, Pakistan and Iran). In the *Global Times* interview, Shaheen assured the Chinese the Taliban 'security force will be there to provide security around the clock'. He also revealed that when the Taliban entered Kabul, they 'were in contact with your embassy, and your diplomats were in contact with us around the clock'.[16]

Keeping the Chinese embassy open was certainly a symbolic statement, just as significant as Wang Yi's hosting of Mullah Baradar in the days before Kabul fell. For outside observers, this was further evidence of China 'quietly attempting to secure its interests in post-US Afghanistan'.[17] Reports would note Beijing's interest in exploring new and ambitious infrastructure projects, such as a motorway from Peshawar in Pakistan to Kabul, part of the wider conversation on bringing Afghanistan into the CPEC. Reports would also suggest Beijing was building 'a major road through the Wakhan Corridor', which borders Xinjiang, and onward to Pakistan and Central Asia. And, of course, as with every development on the China–Afghanistan front, the familiar invocation of Afghanistan's 'trillion dollars' worth' of mineral wealth being ready for exploitation by China would increasingly reappear in the world's media, regardless of the fact that this now familiar hyperbole had not been reflected on the ground with mines remaining idle and no infrastructure in place.[18]

As has always been the case with China and Afghanistan, some of this hype is to be treated with a grain of salt. It is true that a majority of China's state media was encouraging this hype, which, for many external observers, meant the leadership was making a policy statement. That wasn't exactly a correct reading: much of state media coverage was driven more by impulses of point-scoring with the US and celebrating American humiliation than declaring Chinese policy. In China, propaganda is not always policy.

What was interesting is that amid the cheering of the US exit and heralding of a new era in China–Afghan ties, even within China there were calls urging Beijing to continue exercising caution, as it generally had done, rather than start believing the hype. Among those calling for restraint was Mei Xinyu, a scholar at a think tank run by China's Ministry of Commerce, called the Chinese Academy of International Trade and Economic Cooperation. Mei wrote a forthright article that deviated from much of the coverage, saying it was not a time for 'blind revelry' about the economic opportunities in Afghanistan. 'China must not indulge in a dream-like revelry,' he wrote, which 'thinks Afghanistan will develop peacefully and steadily from now on, that there will be unlimited business opportunities immediately, that Afghanistan is extremely important to the Belt and Road … Wake up! Learn about the history of this country!'[19]

First, Mei cautioned, it was by no means a given that the Taliban would remain in power and unite the country given its history of a highly fragmented polity. Further, he added, the roots of Afghanistan's turmoil lay in a 'predatory' political economy that failed to build a sustainable economic and industrial base. Food, he reminded his readers, remained the first and abiding priority for a country still reliant on international aid. And with the US and the West unlikely to continue the levels of aid of the past decade and more, the Taliban regime was facing a pressing economic crisis.

As for Afghanistan's much celebrated mineral resources, on which, Mei noted, many had 'pinned their hopes', he warned they 'should not expect too much' and they should consider the security needed to develop such industries, not to mention the required transport infrastructure. For those pointing to Aynak and its record resources, he suggested observers look at Zambia and other large copper mining countries for the limited transformative impact of mineral wealth on a broader economy. Mei was also bearish on Afghanistan's future in the BRI, rejecting the argument of its geography at 'the crossroads of civilization' as 'nothing more than fantasy'.

Caution, Mei concluded, should determine China's continuing approach, no matter what assurances it may or may not have received from the new regime. He noted China's past economic commitments, from a pledge of 500 million RMB (around $80 million) to the Ghani government in 2014 to another 1.5 billion RMB (around $240 million) in the three years that followed. In 2020, he noted, bilateral trade was only a little more than half a billion dollars, and was down 11 per cent year on year. That same year, Chinese enterprises signed contracts for construction work amounting to $110 million, a 158 per cent jump. 'After the change of regime,' he warned, 'a considerable part of the above-mentioned projects may fail.' China, he said, could step in with aid and consumer goods, but needed to go slow on large-scale investments. 'We need to be calm and objective,' he concluded, 'and not revel blindly.'[20]

A Strategic Trap

So then where on the spectrum of celebration to caution – amid the cheering of the fall of America and the remaking of the Taliban's image on the one hand, and the notes of warning from informed observers like Mei on the other – are we likely to find China's approach to Afghanistan in the new era? Somewhere in the middle: that is the view of those closely following Beijing's policymaking. China will not repeat the mistakes of the West and pour in billions, let alone set boots on the ground. It is, on the other hand, increasingly inserting itself as a power player, willing to step in to mediate and use its deep pockets to influence outcomes more than previously, such as the Taliban's behaviour when it comes to its dealings with extremist groups. As we have seen, security, and not conquest, is China's priority, and securing its western frontier will remain the abiding objective. Whatever economic benefits may accrue in the new era will be a bonus.

Andrew Small, a leading scholar on China's relations with Pakistan and Afghanistan and author of *The China Pakistan Axis*, says that 'there is an obsessive focus on the Chinese side on "the graveyard of empires", that this is a strategic trap'.[21] He believes they do not want to be 'sucked into a serious role' in the country:

> The question on the economic side is, what kind of economic involvement would China want? If you look at three kinds of issues – mineral extraction, the Belt and Road Initiative, and then the kind of short-term dimensions of a new government coming to power and needing outright aid and handouts – one of the things China is going to be concerned about is, what level of legitimacy is a new government able to establish? They're not going to get the

> same kind of financial backing that the last government was able to get from the West.
>
> This is a government that's highly dependent on external revenues and external financing. How are they going to finance themselves as a state? There's a version in which you have a kind of criminal drug economy, which, of course, China would not be very comfortable with seeing in its backyard. If it's going to be economically viable, then you're going to need some of these larger-scale investments, which are long term, require a lot of infrastructure to be economically viable, and a commitment from the investors that they're going to follow this through for a period of many years. How will the security context be? Will political power really be consolidated? Will this be another round of kind of fictitious calm for a while that gets reversed and you have civil war some x number of years down the line? All of these are going to be questions that China has.

For a start, Small says, China could certainly 'come in with some direct, quick fix assistance', which Beijing already announced in early September to the modest tune of $31 million. He added:

> China can give some small sums of assistance and there would be a certain kind of more modest projects that they could move ahead with. I think they want to be able to dangle the promise of larger-scale investments. But I would focus very heavily on what actually happens in practice, because it will suit both a new government and the Chinese to pretend that there's a lot going on there but in practice, we'll have to wait and see. China sees this as stability first, investment later. With the Belt and Road, how comfortable China really is going to be with putting in

> place an expanded set of infrastructure connections, when they're very worried about this becoming a militant hub in the region, is another major question. There is a reason that China has not constructed serious direct infrastructure links across the border through the Wakhan Corridor. They're quite happy to see Afghanistan kind of contained, and quite happy to see buffers there. I don't think they're going to be moving with such alacrity to build deeper infrastructure connections across the region and make sure that Afghanistan is deeply connected again, until they're confident about the situation that's emerging there. I think we will also get a lot of speculation about Afghanistan and the Belt and Road, but there'll be a level of caution on China's part. They'll give this a bit of time before they're really willing to make these commitments on the ground.

What China has been doing, however, is more confident signalling and propaganda, but as we have seen, propaganda does not necessarily mean policy. Small says they used the Tianjin meeting 'to send some kind of positive political signals', but actions on the ground needed to closely follow this. 'The political signalling around this is strong, but the execution on the ground often lags very, very significantly behind,' he noted.

> The political relations are obviously going to be stronger than they were in the past on this. But there will be continued reasons for the Chinese to be a little tentative. China wants to have a benign relationship with the Taliban. This is something that at this stage they can offer – this kind of diplomatic signalling. But I don't think it changes a lot of the apprehensions that are there. The Chinese had

> been preparing for the US withdrawal for some time. I don't think they had anticipated it would be conducted in such a disastrous manner. There's a certain amount of hay that they can make with this, but they didn't want to see this happen. That is very clear – they did not want to see the US withdraw in advance of some kind of a political settlement in Afghanistan.

For all the cheering of the US exit in the Chinese press, the fact is, as Small notes, China would have preferred a government in Kabul that saw power being shared by different factions, which would have constrained the behaviour of all parties, especially the Taliban. As we have seen, Beijing courted Ghani too, and perhaps would have preferred a scenario where it had leverage with all parties rather than end up beholden to one, as is the case now. Small says China 'wanted to see the Taliban somewhat constrained by the need to reach political agreement with other parties' in Afghanistan and to some extent 'being a little bit more beholden to other international actors' as well:

> They wanted to see them a little bit hemmed in, so that on the issues that China is most concerned about, there would be a bit more leverage over them. The concern now is they're taking power in a maximally emboldened fashion, that the Taliban think they don't really have to make particularly serious moves and concessions on a lot of the issues that China is concerned about. This is why China had been talking for a while about responsible withdrawals, and it's now talking about an irresponsible withdrawal. They genuinely did not want to see this happen in the manner that it did. Now, they have to make the best of it.

Pragmatism First

Can China make the best of this situation? No one in Beijing expects an immediate answer. China will wait and watch. But if there is one clear message emerging from the early days of China's Taliban diplomacy, it is that there is a new-found confidence in Beijing in its own ability to influence outcomes beyond its borders. That was evident in Wang Yi deciding to host Baradar, in China keeping its embassy open in Kabul while others shuttered theirs, the aid China announced, however paltry, and the increasingly frenzied diplomatic activity being led by Beijing, in cahoots with the Pakistanis and Russians.

Two questions will give Beijing pause as it crafts its approach in this new era: how much legitimacy will the Taliban gain internationally, and will they indeed, as Wang Yi urged them, make a clean break from extremist groups – at least the groups that Beijing has reservations about? China's expectations on both questions will be pragmatic. The first question is, of course, tied to the Taliban regime's behaviour at home. China has generally stuck to its guns, even when it comes to distasteful regimes, of not getting into their 'internal' affairs and looking the other way as long as Chinese interests are protected. Here, however, having an isolated and pariah government next door will hardly suit Chinese interests.

Small argues:

> China cares about this from the perspective of 'Do you have a government there that's able to establish some kind of international legitimacy?' They don't necessarily care about the substance of what the Taliban have been doing. They may find it distasteful, I know that Chinese officials do, but as in so many other contexts, this is something that they

> would tend to keep out of. But they do know that on a certain scale, it affects the way the rest of the world treats the government there, and so that certainly matters.

He continues:

> They're not going to kick up a fuss about anything specific that the Taliban do, unless there's some really direct effect on Chinese interests. But I think they do want to see something that looks quite different from the Taliban's rule last time, even if just for pragmatic reasons.
>
> If you go back to the turn of the millennium, it was actually the destruction of the Bamiyan Buddhas that set the relationship between China and the Taliban back by some time. They leaned on them quite hard on that issue and lobbied very actively on this question. You had instances then of the Taliban sending delegations to Beijing and finding all their meetings have been cancelled. It's still a fundamental concern that you have, in the Taliban, a regime that is in some fundamental way ideologically hostile. They know that the Taliban, also for pragmatic reasons, need to develop a decent working relationship with them. But I think plenty of actors on the Chinese side think that in the end, when it comes to the agenda for Xinjiang, when it comes to the level of support for Islamic militants around the world, they're quite deeply and fundamentally at odds on some of these questions.

'Ruthless pragmatism' is how Small describes China's likely approach to Taliban 2.0. There is perhaps no better description of China's mindset as it crafts its new Afghan diplomacy. Indeed, it is ruthless pragmatism that explains the glaring contradiction of China's state media rebranding the Taliban – once widely reviled as extreme Islamist radicals and now being praised as 'grassroots' fighters – even as Beijing was, at home, launching an all-out crackdown on Muslims in Xinjiang, sending hundreds of thousands to internment camps for 're-education' for no crime other than practising their faith.

For Beijing's mandarins, consumed in their all-encompassing rivalry with the US which has become the lens to view every development in the world, the Taliban were now the good guys, throwing off the yoke of foreign interference in Afghanistan. No matter their extreme views, treatment of women and minorities, and embracing of violence. And no matter that back at home, the Communist Party was, at the very same time, taking an altogether different view towards China's own Muslims in an extraordinary crackdown that would upend the lives of hundreds of thousands of its Muslim citizens.

7

Good Terrorists, Bad Terrorists

As the sun sets on a Friday evening, it is almost prayer time. The faithful, silently and patiently, gather outside the Xiguan mosque, located at the heart of Yinchuan's old district in Ningxia, a province in China's far west. Among them is Hai Ming Tang, who hasn't missed a prayer at Xiguan in three decades. The last time, he says for the record, was during the Cultural Revolution (1966–76), when Mao Zedong's Red Guards were running amok, decrying the 'four olds': customs, culture, habits and ideas. The mosque then had to close its doors to save itself from the rampaging mobs.

Hai Ming is one of China's 10 million Hui Muslims, the country's second biggest minority Muslim group. Huis have lived in China for more than ten centuries: they are the descendants of the first Arab traders the Silk Road brought to China. Over a millennium, they assimilated into Chinese culture, marrying with the local Han, China's majority ethnic group, and setting up their own communities.

Hai Ming looks 'Chinese'; he even dresses in the dull blue workman's uniform that is still a common sight in small-town China, a legacy from the days of Mao. The only clues to his faith are his square grey hat and a small white beard that protrudes from his wrinkled chin. As the light dims, the call to prayer finally sounds, diffusing through the stillness of the hot desert evening. Hai Ming briskly jogs up the steps of the grand mosque and disappears into the darkness of the prayer hall.

It is also prayer time some 2500 km to the west, on another hot Friday evening. Mahsum, in his early thirties, relaxes with his friends at the sprawling square that is the centre of life in Kashgar, the ancient Silk Road city in China's western frontier Xinjiang region. Young women in brightly coloured headscarves stroll around the square, children in tow. Old men sit side by side on a rickety wooden bench, silently watching the proceedings, their weathered faces shaded by the intricately designed hats that are unique to the Uighurs, the ethnic Turkic-speaking people for whom Xinjiang is home. The grand 550-year-old Id Kah mosque, freshly painted in a jarring yellow, glistens in the fading evening light, casting a shadow over the square.

Mahsum waits for the call to prayer, but in Kashgar, it will not come. A ban on the use of loudspeakers means his wristwatch is his only guide. The only sound comes from a nearby police van: a recorded message urging all ethnic groups 'to maintain harmony, support the Communist Party and serve the motherland'. A battalion of armed police, with guns at the ready, watch over the square. Mahsum heads towards the Id Kah's bronze gates in silence.[1]

Islam in China

Prayer time at the two mosques presents two snapshots of Islam's complicated, and continuing, encounter with China. There are more than 22 million Muslims in China, including the Hui, Uighur and Kazakh minorities, all of whom are among the 55 minority ethnic groups recognized officially by the Chinese government. The Hui make up a little less than half with around 10 million, concentrated mainly in Ningxia and in China's northwest. The Uighurs, an ethnic Turkic minority mainly residing in Xinjiang, are the biggest Muslim minority in China, with around 12 million.[2] The majority Han account for 92 per cent of China's population.[3]

China's Muslims are likely the country's third-biggest religious group, behind Buddhists and Christians. There are no official religious surveys in Communist Party-ruled China, but it's safe to say that those practising the variety of traditions that could fall within the broad umbrella of Buddhism would constitute the biggest group. There are close to 15 million who pray in state-sanctioned churches, but there is a huge underground following for Christianity with millions more who pray in what are called 'house churches'. Islam would probably be the third biggest faith, not far behind Christianity.

Islam has a long history in China. In Ningxia, the Huis have flourished and thrived for centuries, developing their own unique brand of Islam and assimilating into Chinese culture. Xinjiang has had a more troubled relationship, in part because of a very different history. Unlike the slow assimilation of the Hui, Xinjiang's integration was abrupt and rough. The Uighurs have a distinct identity they are proud of, which includes their own language. Indeed, they are distinct even in appearance, more resembling the people of Central Asia than of China. Xinjiang has a long history of proud kingdoms whose reach, in moments of time, extended as far west as Ladakh and east into China's hinterlands. As noted earlier, even after the Qing conquest that brought parts of Xinjiang nominally into the empire's folds, China's imperial presence remained thin and distant. In the early 1940s, an independent

East Turkestan republic briefly existed as a satellite of the Soviets, before it was brought under the control of the People's Republic of China in 1949.

A decade of horrors, violence and turmoil was unleashed during Mao's Cultural Revolution, which saw mosques burned in Xinjiang and monasteries razed to the ground in Tibet. A brief period of moderation followed in the 1980s, when the liberal Party leader Hu Yaobang supported a progressive law on ethnic autonomy that guaranteed, at least in theory, some degree of autonomy for minority regions. The law, unfortunately, would largely only exist on paper, with the Party's focus firmly on control, particularly in the wake of the break-up of the Soviet Union which reinforced for Beijing the need for centralized control.

While China's minority policies, in the reform era, broadly reflected a push and pull between recognizing autonomy and greater centralization, the Party would move decisively towards the latter in the Xi Jinping era. Starting around 2012, the year Xi took over as Party General Secretary, senior leaders in the Party began speaking of the need for what was being called 'second-generation ethnic policies'. If the first-generation policies, rooted in the ethnic autonomy law of the 1980s, recognized the need for a degree of autonomy, the thinking in the Party had taken a harder turn, with some viewing autonomy as leading inevitably to what the Party calls 'splittism'. This would mean a change in focus from autonomy to assimilation, and would be reflected in hardline policies in Tibet and Xinjiang, before spreading elsewhere too, including Ningxia.[4]

This hardening of policy would coincide with China's stepped-up diplomacy to the Middle East and Afghanistan. This turn, for some observers, would mark a serious missed opportunity for Beijing just as it was trying to present itself as a credible interlocutor and offer an alternative to the West as a country that was sympathetic to the developing world and one that wouldn't go bombing others to solve problems – an argument, as we have seen, that was repeated ad nauseam as America left Afghanistan. That argument would be all that much harder to make if China was locking up Muslims and banning religious practices at home.

Indeed, China, in theory, could have presented an altogether different story given the unique history of its Muslim communities. The Hui, for instance, through a centuries-long process of 'cultural accommodation', had created a unique space among Muslim communities in the world with their own brand of Islam. Not only that, the community had, as M.A. Aldrich and Lukas Nikol point out, made 'extraordinary efforts' to integrate, from translating Islamic texts to Mandarin to fighting against the Japanese occupation.[5] The Hui story, they argue, could have turned out to be 'an extraordinary resource for China's foreign diplomacy', but only 'if the state can throw off the blinkered views such as those expressed by Han Islamophobes'. China, then, could 'rightfully boast that it has been a home and haven' for a unique Islamic community and thus could be 'an honest and effective broker especially if China can show that its own Muslims are in positions of authority and trust'.[6]

But it was not to be. The Islamophobic undercurrents in China were not only gaining wider currency but finding themselves translated into extraordinary policies that would upend the lives of China's Muslims. For China, this posed a tricky dilemma amid its growing outreach to its western neighbours and its narrative of being the new 'good power'. For Muslim countries that began to fall deeper into China's economic embrace, it presented an equally challenging balancing act as they weighed whether to speak out about China's treatment of its Muslims, or hold their silence.[7]

A War on Religion

If 2012 and Xi's ascension can be seen as a landmark for China's minority policies, three key events around Xi's coming to power shaped how the Communist Party would rule Xinjiang, and usher in a broader change that made itself felt beyond the region, including in Ningxia. First, riots in July 2009 in Urumqi, Xinjiang's provincial capital, between Uighurs and Han would leave close to 200 people dead. Second, the riots would be followed, five years later, by a terror attack by a group of Uighurs on a railway station in Kunming that killed twenty-nine people. While Xinjiang had seen a series of attacks over the years, the fact that this took place in faraway Yunnan, along with the high death toll, made this different. Third, starting in 2013, reports would confirm that 'thousands of Uighurs' had left Xinjiang for Syria, amid the unrest there, to take up arms, fight against al-Qaeda and join groups such as the Turkistan Islamic Party (TIP), as the East Turkestan Islamic Movement (ETIM) had rechristened itself.[8]

In the Party's language, a 'war' needed to be fought, though how much of this terrorism threat facing Xinjiang – including that of thousands of Uighur fighters abroad returning to wreak havoc (as Party officials warned) – was rooted in hard evidence is a matter of debate. After all, as the following chapter discusses, many of Xinjiang's problems were rooted in ethnic, social and economic issues, and the sporadic acts of violence were often crude knife and home-made bomb attacks, not sophisticated terror assaults carried out by fighters from overseas jihadist camps.

This war would, however, turn out to be as much a war on Islam as on any sort of terror. The man tasked with waging the war was Chen Quanguo, the Communist Party official who had made a name for himself in Tibet with strict policing and sweeping clampdowns that all but ended major protests, including a wave of self-immolations carried out to protest Chinese policies. In 2016, Xi sent Chen to Xinjiang with a mandate to launch an all-out assault to end the continuing series of attacks and bring the region to heel.

Chen's policies would culminate in the setting up of a massive network of 're-education' centres across Xinjiang, dubbed 'vocational training' institutes by the Party. Up to a million Uighurs would be sent to the centres, meaning one out of every eight Uighurs, leaving out children and the elderly, has likely been taken forcibly into one of these centres. The crackdown has focused on young Uighur men, so if you were a male and between the age of twenty and forty, the odds were you would find yourself locked up in a centre.

The scale of Xinjiang's 're-education' was extraordinary. Government procurement bids alone would detail as many as seventy-three construction bids 'valued at around RMB 680 million (approximately $108 million)' to build sprawling centres to house the detainees, most held without trial or prosecution. The majority in the centres were Uighurs, but other minority Muslims living in Xinjiang were also detained, such as Kazakhs and Huis.[9]

When news of the centres brought global criticism, the Communist Party insisted to the world that the centres were merely for 'vocational training' and those inside had gone there 'voluntarily'. But official Party language on Xinjiang, and Islam in particular, had taken a darker turn, even likening religious beliefs to a 'mental illness'. The Party was ostensibly talking about 'extreme beliefs', but it is to be remembered that 'extreme' in the view of Party officials included normal Islamic practices such as fasting during Ramadan, which students and government officials were banned from doing, or for that matter wearing veils, growing beards or abstaining from alcohol.

'There is always a risk that the illness will manifest itself at any moment, which would cause serious harm to the public,' said one statement. 'That is why they must be admitted to a re-education hospital in time to treat and cleanse the virus from their brain and restore their normal mind.' Those involved in the 'de-radicalization' campaign spoke of 'eradicating tumours'. One government document in Khotan described the re-education as 'a free hospital treatment for the masses with sick thinking'.[10]

In Xinjiang, the re-education campaign would drastically change the practice of Islam, as the next chapter details. Even in Ningxia, once a model of ethnic harmony, policies began to take a much darker turn amid the push from 'autonomy' to 'assimilation'. Ningxia, as we have seen, had a Muslim community with a long and unique history, whose roots in both China and the Arab world could have, at least in theory, offered a platform to Beijing to engage with Muslim countries and present itself as different from the West.

Indeed, there was evidence of Beijing seeking to do precisely that, choosing Yinchuan to host a major China–Arab states trade expo, first launched in 2013, that is held every two years, and establishing Yinchuan as China's centre of halal food exports, with an eye on the markets of the Middle East. The local government poured in money to build a halal food processing zone, with as many as 10,000 companies involved in an industry that the Ningxia government estimated, in 2011, was worth close to $4 billion – one that they wanted to dominate.[11]

The Chinese government's argument was that the Hui offered a natural, historical and cultural link with the Arab world and could become a reason for a bond as China's westward outreach was deepening. A decade ago, that case could have been argued with some merit. Huis made up 36 per cent of the Ningxia population, with Han making up most of the rest. Ningxia has 3760 registered mosques, mostly run on government support. On a visit in 2011 to one of the biggest of those mosques, the Xiguan mosque in Yinchuan, its soft-spoken and professorial imam Lou Zhan Jun said, 'We are largely left to pray as we wish, and they don't interfere' – referring to the authorities. The imams, however, have to be registered with the government's ethnic affairs department. Back then, Lou's fears were less about government intervention than waning interest in religion among younger Hui and the fading away of Arabic as one of the languages spoken in Ningxia. One reason for that dwindling interest is, however, government regulations that forbid teaching of religion during the first nine years of free and compulsory primary education. Lou said children would start coming for lessons on religion when they turned ten, but by then they were either too old or too busy with school work to take on Arabic. At the time, he was optimistic about the community's future, saying it had 'survived for 500 years so it will continue'. 'This,' he added, 'is a model for the rest of China.'

At the Ningxia Islamic College not far from Xiguan, religion coexists with Party propaganda, even if uneasily – emblematic, indeed, of the many uneasy compromises that defined the 'first-generation' ethnic autonomy policy. 'Love the country, love religion' is the sign on its front gate. 'The country comes first, and then your religion. That is our message,' says Ma Ming Xian, the vice dean. Getting the equation right in the curriculum is just one of many balancing acts that Islamic schools in China face. The Quran in the morning, Xi Jinping Thought in the afternoon. The five state-run Islamic colleges are something of an exception in giving space to religious studies in the curriculum. Most of the college's 3400 graduates try to find work in Ningxia's mosques, but because of an 'oversupply' of religious teachers, some end up taking up jobs as translators in West Asia or Africa where Chinese investments have been growing.

Even this controlled space would, however, diminish rapidly with the Party's turn to assimilation. Ningxia wouldn't see the system of mass re-education that was deployed in more troubled Xinjiang, but it wouldn't escape the war on Islam. The battle began with targeting of the mosques, including Xiguan. Following a campaign, now 'virtually every mosque in Ningxia's countryside has been denuded of its domes', which the Party saw as an Islamic symbol that had no place in China. Since April 2018, Hui mosques have been 'forcibly renovated or shuttered, schools demolished, and religious community leaders imprisoned'. Hui who have travelled internationally 'are increasingly detained or sent to re-education facilities in Xinjiang'. In August 2018, authorities in the Ningxia county of Tongxin tried to demolish the Weizhou Grand Mosque which led to residents staging a protest. The demolition was stopped after the uproar, but the authorities returned with another plan, 'pressuring residents to sign letters stating their acquiescence to "renovate" the mosque by removing its main dome and domed minarets'. 'Of course we are afraid we will become the next Xinjiang,' one Hui man told a visiting foreign reporter.[12]

Glaring Contradictions

The new emphasis on assimilation would coincide with China's growing international influence and economic ties with the Middle East. The economic relationship, in particular, explains why there has been little outcry about China's persecution of Muslims. Even the Organisation of Islamic Cooperation (OIC) comprising fifty countries – which considers itself the representative of Muslim interests and regularly criticizes Israel's actions in Palestine and India's in Kashmir – in a March 2019 resolution said it 'commends the efforts of the People's Republic of China in providing care to its Muslim citizens' after China hosted an OIC delegation. This prompted a group of Muslim organizations in the US to issue a statement on Xinjiang, with one scholar and activist saying, 'It's very clear that China has an economic chokehold on the Muslim world and has been able to isolate every Muslim country into fear of even paying lip service to the Uighur cause.'[13]

Pakistan, China's close 'all-weather' ally, is emblematic of this glaring contradiction. Its Prime Minister Imran Khan, who frequently criticizes India for alleged human rights violations in Kashmir, stayed mum on the Xinjiang issue despite repeated questions from both the Pakistani and foreign media. Khan went so far as to tell reporters in 2021 that 'because we have a very strong relationship with China, and because we have a relationship based on trust, so we actually accept the Chinese version' on Xinjiang. 'What they say about the programs in Xinjiang,' he said, 'we accept it.'[14]

In return for Pakistan's support on Xinjiang, China would emerge as the strongest defender of Pakistan on its abysmal record of dealing with terrorism. This would lead to another, perhaps even more glaring, contradiction in China's diplomacy. While positioning itself as a victim of terrorism to justify its crackdown in Xinjiang, China would simultaneously become the sole defender of Pakistani terrorists abroad, as India would discover time and again at the United Nations Security Council where repeated attempts to sanction Pakistani terrorists and organizations would run into a Chinese wall.

Barely a month after Indian Prime Minister Narendra Modi returned from a visit to China in 2015, marking the highest point in the often-strained bilateral ties in several years, with President Xi Jinping even breaking protocol to receive Modi in his home province, Indian diplomats approached China and fourteen other members of the UNSC. Pakistani terrorist Zaki-ur-Rehman Lakhvi had been released from jail in Rawalpindi, contravening UNSC sanctions, after payment of a hefty bond to secure his release. India's request before the UNSC 1267 sanctions committee, which facilitates listing of terrorists and groups with links to al-Qaeda, the Taliban and ISIS, was to investigate how the sanctions were violated and ask Pakistan who paid for Lakhvi's release.

India's earlier attempts to list Pakistan-based terrorists – entailing arms embargoes, travel bans, and most importantly, the freezing of financial assets – had run into Chinese opposition. According to the UNSC committee's arcane rules, any of its fifteen members can place a 'technical hold' if they find something amiss with an application. Not only can this be done without informing countries outside the UNSC which country had placed the hold, but members can also choose not to explain why they had done so. China would prevent the listing by asking for more information, and months later, in March 2016, Beijing would place yet another technical hold on listing Jaish-e-Mohammed chief Masood Azhar as a terrorist. The move strained relations with India, erasing much of the goodwill from Modi's visit to China, and served as a reminder of both how crucial Pakistan had become to Chinese interests, in Xinjiang and beyond, and the hypocrisies of China's stand on terrorism.

Indian officials, at various levels, conveyed to China that if it wanted to be a part of the global effort to eradicate terror, as Beijing had claimed on numerous occasions, it needed to stop differentiating between good terrorists and bad terrorists. Perhaps to prove its point, India for the first time issued an electronic visa to exiled Uighur leader Dolkun Isa, to enable him to attend the first ever meeting of leading Chinese dissidents and activists to be held in Dharamshala in 2016. Isa had fled Xinjiang and become a German citizen in 2006. While Beijing says he is a 'terrorist' responsible for bombings in the 1990s, he denies the charges. The visa was cancelled on 25 April, nine days after it was issued, with the home ministry citing an Interpol red corner notice placed on Isa at China's behest.[15]

To get China to sign off on the UNSC's listing of Masood Azhar, India had to play hardball, going through long and tortuous negotiations and enlisting the support of other UNSC permanent members to isolate Beijing. When Beijing placed a hold and then a block, India, with the help of the US and UK, returned with a second application. The move to isolate Beijing worked, suggesting that even for the new China, which was less bothered about its international reputation as actions in Xinjiang would show, its image in the eyes of the world still mattered to some degree.

Finally, Beijing conveyed 'five pre-conditions' from Pakistan in negotiations that ran through the spring of 2019, underlying how openly China was now batting for Pakistani interests and abandoning any pretence of de-hyphenation in how it dealt with India and Pakistan. Among the demands was to not link the Pulwama terror attack, that had taken place in February 2019 in Kashmir, to Azhar's listing and for India to not push, along with the US, for more listings of Pakistani groups. India was aware from past experience that it could reach an agreement with Beijing, as it had done in 2018 to secure its support to 'grey list' Pakistan at the Financial Action Task Force; Beijing had agreed to this after India backed its campaign to become the vice chair of the financial watchdog. India also agreed to not issue any statement on an upcoming Belt and Road Forum that was to be held in China. Ahead of the first forum in 2017, New Delhi had issued a statement criticizing the BRI for its lack of transparency and respect for territorial sovereignty. Finally, 'China decided that it was a good deal' and its hold on the sanctioning was lifted. The listing, eventually, did not link Azhar to Pulwama.[16]

If China's moves to block the listing of terrorists caused bewilderment – and revulsion, for these were after all terrorists with the blood of many on their hands – it is, again, 'ruthless pragmatism' that best explains Chinese actions. As much as Pakistan has dragged its feet in dealing with terror groups that target India, the Chinese believed the Pakistani army has moved rapidly and effectively to bring to heel anti-China groups and disrupt camps of the banned ETIM that were near the Afghan border in Pakistan. For China, shielding its ally from international criticism, no matter the hypocrisy, was a price worth paying. India had finally got China to relent on sanctioning Masood Azhar by appealing not to its voice of reason but, again, to pragmatism.

The Acceptable Extremists

The question of China's views on Islam certainly casts a shadow as Beijing prepares for a greater role in Afghanistan and beyond. Amid all the celebration in Beijing of the US exit and the careful outreach to the Taliban, there were indeed many voices expressing caution, and asking how Beijing would engage with an outfit that, despite the media's rebranding of them, was still very much a religious extremist organization with which the Communist Party had little in common.

Dangling the promise of investment, and helped by its 'all-weather' friend in Pakistan, China not only secured the Taliban's silence on matters such as Xinjiang and its treatment of Muslims, but also a commitment from the group to cut all ties with the ETIM. This was, however, on paper. Many Chinese officials were well aware of their experience two decades ago, when these commitments did not necessarily translate into actions; also, within the broad umbrella of different factions that made up the Taliban, there were groups ready to make trouble for Chinese investors and their projects. After all, despite all the efforts at rebranding, after twenty years, the essence of the Taliban in many respects remained the same.

This was the argument made by one of China's leading Middle East and counterterrorism experts, Pan Guang, in the days after the fall of Kabul and the resultant glee in Chinese state media. Pan, who heads the Shanghai Cooperation Organisation Research Centre in Shanghai, dealing with China's relations with the Eurasian security grouping, and is also an expert at the National Counterterrorism Office, gave a wide-ranging interview to the Chinese website Guancha, where he spoke on what's changed and what hasn't with the Taliban, offering a counterpoint to much of the media coverage. He observed:

> We should acknowledge that over the years the Taliban have changed with the times, even the Taliban leader has recently been interviewed by a female presenter on TV, which was unthinkable 20 years ago … but at the same time we must not forget the point that the Taliban are Sunni Muslims and their religious claims are ultra-orthodox. One might even say they are religious extremist forces, and this essence will not change.[17]

Pan said what many in the Chinese media weren't saying: 'The measures taken at the moment are only temporary,' he said, 'and it is possible that after a while the ultra-orthodox Sunni nature will gradually emerge.' Considering how quickly, in the days that followed the fall of Kabul, the promises of an 'inclusive' government were belied, Pan was spot on. He continued:

> In fact, if we pay a little attention, we can see that, for example, Taliban fighters still have beards, unlike the regular

> forces of the state; the treatment of women, some of the advertisements of female portraits on the streets of Kabul have been painted off. So you can say that the Taliban is not the same as it was more than 20 years ago, but its essence has not changed.

This, he suggested, posed a challenge for Chinese engagement. China had to 'get a handle on this', and acknowledge that 'some things are not likely to change'. Rather than agree with what some Chinese papers were suggesting – that this new era would usher in Chinese investment and stalled projects would resume – Pan offered a more cautious take. 'I am afraid the Taliban's policy is still in flux,' he said, adding that factionalism, a mainstay of Afghan politics, hadn't gone anywhere.

Asked 'how long' the Taliban would stay in power, Pan replied:

> This is a question that we are all concerned about as well. My view is that the Taliban are generally united at the moment, mainly because of the ultra-orthodox Sunni religious ideology that keeps them together. But there are some internal factions, such as the Haqqani Network, that are a more independent faction and will engage in external terrorist activities ... There are places where commanders still adopt old extreme policies, and there are still local wars in some places.

The situation, Pan concluded, was far more in flux than many of his colleagues appeared to realize.

This was also the point made by Qian Feng, who heads the National Institute for Strategic Studies at Tsinghua University and is a leading South Asian affairs specialist in China. Qian was speaking to the Chinese edition of the *Global Times* – a more widely read and influential newspaper than its well-known English version, which is largely aimed at a foreign audience. The English version, by contrast, appeared largely bullish on the return of the Taliban, presenting it as a win for China. In this interview, Qian offered a more nuanced take, warning that 'even 25 years ago, the Taliban failed to unify the whole of Afghanistan' which reflected its divided polity and long history of 'ethnic and tribal feuds', and a 'complicated situation' with 'many variables'.[18]

Asked what the chances were 'of another extremist fundamentalist regime' like Taliban 1.0 returning, Qian said it 'would be almost impossible to re-establish a fundamentalist regime like the one that existed in the Islamic Emirate for more than two decades and to restore sharia rule' because Afghan society and people had changed while the international community remained consistent on its views on the Taliban. He drew a difference between the Afghan Taliban and the Pakistani Taliban, which had targeted the Chinese in several attacks in Pakistan.

China, Qian said, 'has never identified the Afghan Taliban as a terrorist organization' but 'sees it as a more fundamentalist, religiously radical organization that once held national power in Afghanistan and represented the political ideas and interests of a section of the Pashtuns, the largest ethnic group in Afghanistan'. In other words, the Chinese had to accept them, even if they found them disagreeable.

For Qian, the Xinjiang question was the most crucial when it came to framing China's interests and concerns. He noted that before the fall of Taliban 1.0 in 2001, there were elements of the ETIM which had 'engaged in anti-Chinese activities in Afghanistan under the patronage of Al Qaeda'. Since the start of the war, he noted, some of these elements had fled to the Afghanistan–Pakistan border, where China was leaning heavily on the Pakistani military to carry out air strikes on ETIM camps.

The Taliban had pledged repeatedly to China that it would, as Wang Yi had asked Baradar in Tianjin, 'make a clean break' from terror groups and particularly the ETIM. Qian warned that those pledges did not necessarily mean that would happen. 'The Taliban,' he said, 'had no policy to host the ETIM against China, but there is some sympathy and support for the ETIM within the Taliban due to its continued smearing of the situation in Xinjiang.' He cautioned further that 'some tribes have taken in some of the ETIM elements because of the centuries-old tradition that "as long as an outsider comes and takes refuge with you, you must accept them unconditionally"'.

Qian saw two threats to Xinjiang from the Afghan turmoil: terrorism and the spread of drugs, with elements in Taliban relying on narcotics to finance themselves. China could secure itself, he said, as it 'would not be technically difficult to "close the door"' as the Wakhan Corridor's border with China was less than 100 km long. As Qian put it, the main priority for China should be security, and guarding Xinjiang. Even if it could prevent a direct spillover from Afghanistan, it also had to contend with, in his view, the likelihood of an indirect spillover that would see instability spread to Pakistan and Central Asia, and then find its way to China's west.

According to Qian, Beijing needed to tread carefully and cautiously, and there was, for him, 'no immediate need for China to send military personnel to fill the so-called "vacuum" left by the US military or to start investing in the country on a large scale now'. Both those prospects, he said, were 'unrealistic'. In his view, the Afghan situation and the return of the Taliban called for caution and care, not delusions of grandeur about China stepping in. This was the path the Chinese leadership should follow, remembering above all else that China's interests lay at home and in guarding its sprawling western territory – which had no shortage of problems of its own.

8

The Xinjiang Factor

'AFTER THE UNITED STATES PULLS TROOPS OUT OF Afghanistan,' China's President and Communist Party General Secretary Xi Jinping warned in a 2014 speech, 'terrorist organizations positioned on the frontiers of Afghanistan and Pakistan may quickly infiltrate into Central Asia.' He continued, 'East Turkestan's terrorists who have received real-war training in Syria and Afghanistan could at any time launch terrorist attacks in Xinjiang.' This explicit warning from Xi was delivered to top officials of the Communist Party in secret: China's leader hasn't ever publicly spoken so directly about the terrorist threat from abroad, let alone mentioned China's 'all-weather' friend Pakistan as among the homes of terror organizations.

During a 2014 visit to Xinjiang, and a later 'work conference' in Beijing to flesh out the Party's new Xinjiang policy, Xi would hold forth in great detail on the Xinjiang question in four speeches. The speeches were never made public – they were leaked by an insider to *The New York Times* – and would herald a transformative change in how the Party governed Xinjiang, with the move from autonomy to assimilation culminating in the extraordinary internment of close to 1 million Uighurs in 're-education' camps.[1]

Those concerns of Xi, of Afghanistan and Central Asia emerging as the new terror battleground with enormous security implications for China's western frontiers, would in the months ahead lead to China taking small but significant steps to secure its borders. In a region close to the Wakhan Corridor, which borders Xinjiang, and the Afghan–Tajik border, Chinese security forces quietly moved into an old abandoned Soviet outpost, the first ever overseas base with officers from the People's Liberation Army and the People's Armed Police Force (PAPF).

What is particularly striking is the presence in Tajikistan of the PAPF – a security agency that is tasked with China's internal security. The focus, clearly, is on Xinjiang. While both China and Tajikistan have denied the existence of this post, foreign reporters visiting the compound interviewed locals who described 'regular sightings of military drones flying overhead and the presence of surveillance equipment'. Two locals said the site, in a region adjoining the China, Afghanistan and Tajikistan trijunction north of the Wakhan Corridor, consisted of 'Chinese, Afghan, and Tajik personnel'. A Tajik official said that under the agreement, 'Chinese personnel are replacing their Tajik counterparts along lengthy sections of the Tajik–Afghan border where they patrol on their own.'[2] In 2021, both countries would strike a deal to transfer full control over the base to the Chinese side, making it a full-fledged overseas Chinese facility, only the second such foreign base maintained by China anywhere in the world. The only other overseas base we know of is a naval support base in Djibouti near the Horn of Africa, that was put to use by the PLA Navy in 2017. As part of the 2021 deal with Tajikistan, China's Public Security Bureau, or police authority, also agreed to build a new base for Tajikistan's special forces to keep an eye on Afghanistan and carry out counterterrorism operations. The Chinese side would invest $10 million, and the new China-constructed base would be operated by Tajikistan.[3]

China has in place a similar arrangement on the Xinjiang–Pakistan-occupied Kashmir border, launching joint patrols with the Pakistani military.[4] Both arrangements reflect Beijing's growing security concerns in Xinjiang. Even as China's western neighbours were entering a period of unprecedented flux, amid the impending US exit from Afghanistan and continuing turmoil within Pakistan that would see repeated attacks on Chinese interests, dramatic changes were unfolding within China. A month before Xi's all-important Xinjiang visit, an extraordinary terror attack in Kunming would bring Xinjiang, and the terror issue, front and centre for China's Communist Party.

For the Party, domestic stability (including regime preservation) matters more than anything else. Indeed, it is not possible to make sense of China's global geopolitical ambitions without viewing them through the prism of domestic politics. Understanding the Party's domestic motivations offers the clearest picture of the impulses driving China's external actions. And as far as China's deepening relations with Pakistan and growing engagement with Afghanistan are concerned, one domestic consideration looms large above all others: the Xinjiang factor.

Settling the Border

Xinjiang is a sprawling land of black deserts, with territory larger than France, Spain and Germany combined. Nestled between mountains of the Karakoram and the Tibetan plateau, Xinjiang has historically been a gateway to China's hinterlands, a key point on the Silk Road that bridged China and the western regions beyond the Karakoram and Pamir mountains. As we have seen, Xinjiang was through the centuries never fully integrated with the hinterlands. In fact, Xinjiang had its own proud kingdoms. It was only in the mid-eighteenth century that the conquests of the Qing brought the imperial presence to this region, but even the Qing conquests didn't bring direct control, leaving behind a faint imperial footprint.[5]

Through history, various Chinese kingdoms, dating back to the Han dynasty in the second century BCE to the later Tang and Qing rulers, sought to bring this frontier land under their control; they met with varying degrees of success. In the 1940s, an independent Soviet-backed republic called East Turkestan briefly existed, until the Communists brought Xinjiang within the control of the People's Republic of China in 1949.

It isn't difficult to understand Mao's keenness to bring the region known previously as East Turkestan, called Xinjiang by the Chinese (meaning 'new frontier'), under Beijing's control. It offered an important buffer, bordering India (and Pakistan-occupied Kashmir, which is the only connect between China and Pakistan), Afghanistan, Tajikistan, Kyrgyzstan, Kazakhstan, Russia and Mongolia. From the early days of the PRC, the military would have a leading role in managing Xinjiang. Mao's strategy was to send in Han Chinese settlers by the thousands.

Most of the initial Han settlers were demobilized soldiers and their families who worked for an organization called the Bingtuan, which is unique in China's history. Known in English as the Xinjiang Production and Construction Corps, the Bingtuan, which still functions in Xinjiang, was a vast paramilitary organization that was given massive tracts of land, farms and towns to manage. The Bingtuan would come to run its own cities, administering everything from the courts to education. A 'state-within-a-state', it was the Party's key vehicle in its efforts to acquire a firm grip on Xinjiang. The Bingtuan employs more than 12 per cent of the workforce in Xinjiang, most of them Han.[6]

It is for this reason that Xinjiang has been described as 'an internal settler colony' within China. As the scholar Darren Byler writes, the 'dispossession' of land and resources was 'not just about a lack of compensation' but about 'a process of illegalizing traditions and turning sacred land into property'. The highways, pipelines and industries that would follow – owned by the state and, for the most part, built and managed by those from outside Xinjiang – were symbols of the change. As Byler puts it: 'Three elements – material dispossession, institutional domination, and settler occupation – are what established Xinjiang as a contemporary settler colony that was internal to the Chinese state.'[7]

After the turmoil of the Cultural Revolution (1966–76) that saw Mao's Red Guards ransack mosques in Xinjiang and monasteries in Tibet, the reforms of the 1980s brought relative calm, including with the passing, as noted previously, of the ethnic autonomy law (even if its implementation was, to put it mildly, patchy). This brief period of moderation, Byler writes, 'threatened to flower into a full-throated movement for self-determination' as Uighurs began to rediscover their identity after decades of suppression. Connections and trade with neighbouring Central Asian countries, such as Kyrgyzstan and Kazakhstan, blossomed. But with Chinese authorities 'increasingly concerned that Uyghurs would begin to demand the autonomy they had been promised in the 1950s', the Chinese state invested in shoring up ties with its neighbours, including through massive deals to purchase resources; these were aimed in part at securing their cooperation on the Xinjiang question and ensuring 'an intentional isolation of the Uyghurs'.[8]

A Widening Chasm

The Party adopted a dual-track approach of, on the one hand, rapidly integrating Xinjiang's economy into the hinterland and, on the other, maintaining a tight grip on security to ensure its control. The consequences of this would exacerbate Xinjiang's political and social tensions. One major consequence was the demographic change. In 1949, Han Chinese made up roughly 6 per cent of the population. According to the 2010 census, this number had risen to just under 40 per cent of Xinjiang's population – more than other ethnic groups like the Kazakhs and Huis, and second only to the Uighurs. The numbers do not account for the substantial floating Han population in major cities, where they constitute much of the migrant workforce, which would become a driving factor behind worsening Han–Uighur tensions. Between 1990 and 2000, the 'population of Han settlers grew at twice the rate of the Uighur population' and 'by the late-2000s, it was almost the same size as the Uighur population'.[9]

The other consequence of the Party's tight grip was a gradual narrowing of the moderate spaces for Uighur expression. In 1997, the Party's move to crack down on a widely popular Uighur traditional practice known as Meshrep, which involved performances of music and dance and poetry recitals, led to widespread protests, culminating in the city of Ghulja in what would become 'the most severe street violence since the Cultural Revolution'.[10] What came to be known as the Ghulja Incident would mark a profound change in how the Party began to portray incidents of unrest in Xinjiang. Initially described as 'a case of beating, smashing and looting by drug addicts, looters and social garbage', it would be described by a Party White Paper published five years later 'as a serious riot perpetrated by the East Turkestan Islamic Movement'. An act of terrorism that took place two weeks after Ghulja – when three bombs detonated on a bus in Urumqi killing nine people – led the authorities to describe the Meshrep protests as 'terrorism' as well.[11]

This would become the norm for subsequent protests in Xinjiang, with 'the new representation of Xinjiang as a battleground in the "global war on terror"', which was just taking off in the early 2000s, marking a departure from previous PRC practice. It would also mark, as the scholar James Millward writes, the start of a long period of disjuncture between Xinjiang and the rest of China, with 'the correspondence of a crackdown in Xinjiang with modest expansion of free expression elsewhere in China' throughout the first decade of the twenty-first century. If Xinjiang and its people were already beginning to become isolated from their neighbours to the west, with links to Central Asia all but disconnected, they were also growing further apart from those to their east in China's hinterlands.[12]

Within Xinjiang, the net effect of the Party's new policies would be a widening chasm between its Uighur and Han residents. Even as Han migration was bringing with it social tensions, the 'terrorism' narrative would further result in the 'othering' of Uighurs within China, feeding into already existent stereotypes about Muslims. For Uighurs, renting apartments in major Chinese cities, or even finding hotel rooms, became extraordinarily difficult. As did finding jobs, even in Xinjiang, where the competition was against Han settlers. A common gripe heard in Urumqi was the systemic discrimination imposed by this system. For Uighur graduates who do not read or write Chinese, few well-paying jobs are on offer. They are faced with three choices: attend bilingual government schools where Chinese is the main language of instruction barring a Uighur language class, settle for a low-paying job that doesn't require language skills, or leave Xinjiang to find work in another Chinese province.[13]

The chasm was widening not only between Xinjiang's communities, but between its booming urban centres and Uighur-dominated countryside. At the heart of the Urumqi oasis, Chinese construction cranes busily hover, day and night, adding an impressive new skyscraper to the skyline every other month. Sprawling shopping malls, selling the wares of high-end Chinese designers, line the city's downtown streets. On one main street stands a five-star Sheraton hotel, frequented by wealthy tourists and Chinese government officials. Xinjiang's only Pizza Hut outlet sits right opposite. Nightclubs and karaoke bars dot the city's main boulevards.

In small towns like Turkul, farming and religion are the mainstays of daily life. Even up until the 2016 crackdown, Islam was at the centre of everyday life, from daily prayers to weekend lessons from the local imam. For the atheist Communist Party, the role of imams in Xinjiang has historically been a source of tension. Crackdowns, from time to time, would ensnare unregistered teachers and ban private and informal religious classes, while the Party routinely appointed government-backed imams to positions of authority to manage Xinjiang's religious affairs. Government schools in Xinjiang, for their part, were gradually phasing out religious education – a reason behind the popularity of informal local religious schools. The 'bilingual education' programme, in theory designed to teach both Mandarin and Uighur, prioritized Mandarin as the medium of instruction. The sidelining of religion was particularly evident in universities and government jobs, where Uighurs are not allowed to fast during the holy month of Ramadan and are discouraged from going to mosques.[14]

A rural education has also left students at a serious disadvantage. In universities and the job market, they were competing against Han Chinese, and were expected to have the same level of fluency in a language that many would only begin learning in their teens.

Under a state programme for high-achieving students, Uighurs would be sent for two years of intensive language training to faraway cities such as Beijing or Shanghai, where students would be alarmed to find that classes did not stop for daily prayers. Eventually, the move from autonomy to assimilation would make itself felt in the countryside too, which would not be immune to the sweeping changes that began to unfold across Xinjiang.

Riots of 2009

Many of those changes were precipitated by the events of 5 July 2009, which marked a turning point in Xinjiang's politics. That evening, hundreds of students had gathered at Urumqi's People's Square. The fact that they could assemble there reflected the moderate space that existed then for dissent; it would be unthinkable in the security state that is today's Xinjiang. The students were protesting the death of two Uighurs in a factory brawl in southern China. The soaring unemployment among Uighurs in Xinjiang had pushed many to find low-paying factory jobs elsewhere in China. In factories, Uighurs worked side by side with Han Chinese; their presence wasn't always welcome, reflecting the mistrust between the two groups and the negative stereotypes that determined how Uighurs were seen by Chinese outside Xinjiang.

What happened in that factory, in Dongguan in the southern Guangdong province, remains a mystery to this day. Rumours spread on social media that a Han Chinese female employee had been raped by Uighur workers. Police officials said the rumours were untrue and spread by a laid-off worker. Whether the police statement was meant to douse the flames, or was indeed accurate, was anyone's guess.

What was clear is the Han workers didn't believe the police, reflecting another strand in communal relations in China, where many Han believe minorities are coddled by the state, for instance by not having to follow the same family planning rules and being allowed separate cut-offs in college exams. The great irony, of course, was that the Uighurs in Guangdong were there because they couldn't find jobs in their own home towns amid the influx of Han residents. A massive brawl ensued, with Han workers attacking the Uighur dormitory. Images of the attack quickly spread on social media and sparked anger back in Xinjiang. It led to the protest that afternoon. Hours later, Urumqi was in flames.

Those events would have numerous consequences, including the banning of Twitter, YouTube and Facebook across China, some of the platforms where the images were shared. The bans continue to remain in place until today. For Xinjiang, it would also lead to the securitization of policies that would culminate, less than a decade later, in the extraordinary internment campaign that would see hundreds of thousands locked up without trial.

By the evening of 5 July, armed Uighur mobs were seen rampaging on the streets of Urumqi, setting fire to Han Chinese-owned business and brutally attacking Chinese residents of the city, including women and children. As with the Ghulja Incident, the Chinese government said the mob violence was premeditated and organized by exiled groups with links to terrorist organizations. Many Uighurs have questioned that narrative, blaming heavy-handed policing of the protests for sparking the violence. The scale of the violence – official reports said 197 people, mostly Han, were killed and more than 1700 people injured – indicated that the government was grossly unprepared.

For three days, the city was torn apart by mob violence. On 6 July, organized mobs of Han Chinese attacked the city's Uighur neighbourhoods in revenge for the killings of the previous evening. Uighurs abroad accused the government of not reporting the number of revenge killings. Amid the chaos, as the PLA and

PAPF were deployed in Urumqi in their thousands to restore order, China's President Hu Jintao had to leave an ongoing G8 summit in Italy and rush back to China, in what was certainly an embarrassment for the Chinese leadership.[15] Especially so since it was barely a year after their policies in Tibet had, with the 2008 protests there, brought on global scrutiny.

The July riots left Urumqi a city divided. Han moved out of Uighur neighbourhoods, and the divides in an already segregated city became further entrenched. Security clampdowns became more severe. In the years that followed, a series of attacks, some targeting police and others at locations popular with Han residents in Urumqi, Kashgar and Hotan, further widened the Han–Uighur split, and the state responded in the only way it knew: with even stricter clampdowns.

China's 9/11

Two years after the riots in Urumqi, the old Silk Road city of Kashgar, which had also seen protests break out in 2009, was reeling from fresh violence as it prepared for the holy month of Ramadan. The city was bustling, as always during Ramadan after the sun set, and outside the Id Kah mosque which represents the heart of Kashgar's religious and cultural life – alleys were abuzz with the carts of shopkeepers selling naan and dried fruit. But the prominent security presence in front of the Id Kah was a telling clue of the troubles that were brewing.

In the days leading up to Ramadan, violence had left at least twenty people dead in two separate attacks. Explosions had been set off in minivans in a crowded street of food stalls in the heart of the city. At the same time, two attackers hijacked a van and rammed it into a crowd of pedestrians, leaving at least eight people dead. Then, the following afternoon, attackers targeted a restaurant in a commercial food street in downtown Kashgar that is frequented by Han Chinese tourists, killing its owner and at least four others. Four attackers were reportedly shot dead by the police.

Along with more expansive security deployments came restrictions on the practise of religion. The number of worshippers at the Id Kah was limited. The government also put in place new policies calling for all religious texts, even those used in local schools, to be submitted for government approval. It expanded regular inspections of religious sites. 'Religious teachers are strictly prohibited from using non-approved texts, and no person may conduct religious activities outside of pre-approved religious sites, or face investigation as an unapproved Imam,' read one regulation. Informal schools were closed down. Imams were arrested. The making of a security state had begun.[16]

The violence in Kashgar in 2011 would be followed by other such incidents at regular intervals, many in Xinjiang's Uighur-dominated southern heartland, where Kashgar and Hotan are located. In August 2013, twenty-one people were killed in a clash with six people in a town in Bachu county in Kashgar prefecture. The six were identified by state media as members of a group that was 'planning to launch terrorist activities'. And in the worst violence since the Urumqi riots, at least fifty were killed in Hotan, after authorities said forty 'rioters' had been killed in clashes along with six civilians and four police officers.[17]

Since most of these attacks were carried out in Xinjiang – many in remote towns and counties in the far south – they did not receive prominent attention in the Chinese media, barring a 2013 attempted attack in Beijing that saw a group of Uighurs drive a van into a crowd right near Tiananmen Square. The van, filled with gasoline, crashed into a railing and apparently failed to detonate. Two tourists were killed, though the damage, in a crowded pedestrian area filled with tourists, could have been far worse. Xinjiang had appeared to settle into a restive equilibrium marked by repeated small-scale attacks, followed by clampdowns, in an endless cycle. This status quo would be shattered in the spring of 2014, prompting a massive overhaul in how the Party ruled Xinjiang.

In 2014, on the morning of 1 March, as commuters were preparing to board their trains in Kunming, the provincial capital of southern Yunnan province – more than 3500 km away from Urumqi – a group of masked Uighur attackers, armed with knives, began a brutal rampage. Eight attackers, CCTV footage would later reveal, caused panic and chaos, moving quickly and stabbing at will. They appeared to have had some level of training given the devastation they caused, killing thirty-one people and injuring 150 before four of them were killed by police. The attackers, reports in the media said, remained unfazed when police were deployed, marching into a shower of bullets. They appeared to have come prepared to die and inflict as much damage as they could.

The Kunming attack shocked the Party and the entire nation, and was dubbed China's 9/11. The provincial party leader of Yunnan told the media the attackers had earlier attempted to leave China to carry out 'jihad', but unable to leave, set on a plan to attack Kunming. Kunming brought renewed attention in China to the series of attacks since 2009, from Kashgar to Hotan, that had largely gone unnoticed.

'The frequency and expansion of attacks has demonstrated that terrorism is no longer a casual problem but a regular issue in Xinjiang,' Li Wei, a leading Chinese expert on counterterrorism at the China Institutes of Contemporary International Relations, an influential think tank linked to the Ministry of State Security, told the *Global Times*. Li observed:

> It also signals and sets alarm for the rest of China, especially large cities, that terrorism has already crept in. This new tendency pushes China's anti-terrorism efforts into a much more severe and demanding situation. Xinjiang is not dealing with this issue alone any more. Chinese citizens, no matter where they live and who they are, need to build the awareness that terrorism is not far away from anyone.[18]

Others slammed US 'hypocrisy' for not recognizing Xinjiang's growing terrorism problem and instead only pointing to human rights issues in the province. 'The terrorist attacks in Beijing and Kunming are a mirror of Western hypocrisy,' wrote scholar Zhou Zunyou. 'For many politicians, academics and journalists in the West, the word "terrorism" is only reserved for those they disapprove of, but not for those they sympathize with.'[19] Calls were growing for the Communist Party to take stronger action. There was no clarity on what that precisely was, but the consensus was that something needed to be done.

Defining Terrorism

How much of the 'terrorism' threat in Xinjiang that Chinese officials cited was based on evidence, and how much of it was merely a narrative that justified a harsh security crackdown that ultimately ensnared not terrorists but tens of thousands of ordinary Uighurs?

It is true that China has long been concerned by what it calls the 'three evils' of 'terrorism, separatism and religious extremism'. Yet the rather broad definition of 'three evils', in truth, led to a blurring of what all three terms meant in reality. For instance, in Xinjiang, going to an unofficial Quran study session, seen by the Party as 'extremist' behaviour, could get one charged with terrorism or separatism. The Urumqi riots, which resembled more communal violence than terror attack, were quickly blamed on 'terrorists' and 'separatists'.

One factor that enabled China to make a strong case to the world about the situation in Xinjiang was the evolving global narrative on a 'war on terror'. Indeed, China's language on terrorism neatly dovetailed with the US war on terror as it was taking off, and thus allowed Beijing to quickly gain international legitimacy for many of its actions in Xinjiang, at least until the mass internment of Uighurs which evoked widespread condemnation in the West. India, too, was among the countries happy to go along with this narrative, viewing it as an opportunity to make common cause with China on an issue that, as we have seen, both had not seen eye to eye on because of India's concerns about the role of Pakistan.

This was despite the fact that the nature of violence in Xinjiang was largely a very different beast from, say, Jammu and Kashmir, where there was ample evidence of cross-border infiltrators, often heavily armed with automatic rifles and hand grenades, coming in and causing attacks. Here, most attacks were carried out by locals, usually using knives and swords, as was the case in Kunming, or low-grade home-made bombs – far less sophisticated attacks than what jihadists in Kashmir were carrying out. The presence of Uighurs in Syria, however, did bolster the Chinese government's argument that it was facing the prospect of armed fighters returning, a point that no less than Xi Jinping had emphasized. In the Chinese government's view, the emergence of evidence of Uighur fighters abroad was alarming enough to warrant a crackdown.

It was a different matter that the government's prescription to deal with Xinjiang's problems targeted thousands of ordinary Uighurs. That alone suggested the authorities too were more than aware, despite their public claims to the contrary, that the problem wasn't only about a small group of overseas terrorists or radicals destabilizing China. If that was the case, there would have been no reason for the mass internment. The government's actions indicated the problem wasn't about terrorism, but about far broader social issues and deep grievances that disenfranchised Uighurs had towards Chinese rule. Those grievances were being crushed with an iron fist.

The Security State

A month after the Kunming attack, President Xi Jinping would tour Xinjiang, giving a series of speeches that called for a drastic and new approach to deal with the terror problem. Xi installed a new Party chief for Xinjiang, as we have seen, transferring in Chen Quanguo from Tibet. Chen had won praise from the Party leadership for putting in place iron-fisted policies in Tibet and stamping out any signs of protest. He had taken over after a series of more than a hundred self-immolation protests against Chinese policies had roiled China's Tibetan regions. Chen made a name for himself within the Party by putting in place a so-called 'grid-based' security system in Lhasa, where each part of the city was divided into small grids, each of which was tasked to maintain security within its limits. This required a massive expansion of the police force, roping in of citizen volunteers and a huge expansion of surveillance.

Like Chen, the Party bosses of Xinjiang were always Han Chinese, while Uighurs could never rise above the position of governor, which was largely ceremonial. In Xinjiang, Chen would use Xi's speeches as a platform to launch an extraordinary campaign. Cities were blanketed with surveillance while thousands were rounded up on a chilling principle outlined by him, which simply was 'round up everyone who should be rounded up'. Housing the detainees required infrastructure. Chen ordered the construction of a vast network of detention camps, which would, through 2017 and 2018, come to house up to one million people. The Chinese government dubbed them 'vocational training' centres.[20]

The detention camps marked the denouement of a decade-long gradual securitization of Xinjiang, culminating in the unprecedented internment of hundreds of thousands of ordinary people. The rare accounts from detainees who left the camps portrayed a chilling picture, aimed not at what the authorities claimed to be 'deradicalization', but more broadly 'de-Islamification'. One Kazakh national who was swept up into one such centre at the height of the campaign in March 2017 – he was accused of running a travel agency that the government said allowed people to leave illegally, but never faced a trial or any form of due process – revealed after he returned to Kazakhstan that he couldn't call his parents or a lawyer, and was held in a tiny cell for months. So much for a 'voluntary vocational training' programme – one that doesn't allow its participants to call their families, let alone go home.

The detainee said he was strapped into a 'tiger chair', a device that clamped down his wrists and ankles, and 'hung by his wrists against a barred wall, just high enough so he would feel excruciating pressure in his shoulder unless he stood on the balls of his bare feet.' Before every meal, inmates were forced to chant: 'Thank the Party! Thank the Motherland! Thank President Xi!' Daily brainwashing sessions were held 'about the dangers of Islam'. 'Do you obey Chinese law or Shar'iah?' instructors asked. 'Do you understand why religion is dangerous?' Other prisoners 'were forced to apologize for wearing long clothes in the traditional Uighur Islamic style, praying, teaching the Quran to their children and asking imams to name their children'. For the authorities, 'praying at a mosque on any day other than Friday was a sign of extremism; so was attending Friday prayers outside their village or having Quranic verses or graphics on their phones'.[21]

Testimonies of those who left the camps and of relatives of inmates who were abroad painted a picture of prison-like conditions, where Uighurs were made to denounce their religion and ethnic identity. The Party's own internal documents list out the criteria for authorities to select people for internment. Signs of 'extremism' for the Party included 'wearing long beards, giving up smoking or drinking, studying Arabic and praying outside mosques'.[22]

The Communist Party rejected criticism of the camps, claiming they were 'job training' centres and entirely voluntary. But the Party's own propaganda belied those claims. Videos on state media showed classrooms where the 'students' all sat in precise rows, all sporting the exact same haircuts, while each classroom had several security cameras. Moreover, hundreds of Xinjiang's most renowned intellectuals – professors, writers, musicians – were among those detained. They were hardly in need of 'vocational education'.

By the end of 2020, China started releasing many of the detainees, several of whom had spent up to three years in the camps. Some of the camps were refashioned into factories. Officially, Chinese authorities maintained that those detained had 'graduated'. Why they were released remained a matter of debate: some experts speculated that the global outcry – mainly from the West since much of the Muslim world remained silent – may have pushed Beijing to wind up the centres. Western media reports documented the abuses in detail, while the US, the European Union, Britain and Canada for the first time imposed joint sanctions on several Chinese officials for human rights abuses in Xinjiang.[23] Others argued – perhaps more convincingly given Beijing's global swagger that was marked by growing disregard for Western criticism – that the reason was more chilling: Beijing felt it had broken the back of what little Uighur resistance remained, and those who had been locked up would not dare challenge the government lest they were sent back to detention camps.[24]

The five-year campaign under Chen's rule would dramatically alter Xinjiang. What little space had existed for Uighur expression was firmly extinguished. So was the practise of Islam beyond Potemkin mosques run under the close scrutiny of the Party. Foreign reporters visiting in the autumn of 2021 found that in many cities 'historic centers have been bulldozed and the Islamic call to prayer no longer rings out'. In Kashgar, 'one mosque was converted into a café, and a section of another has been turned into a tourist toilet'. Deep in the villages, in counties like Turkul, local mosques were shuttered while Han Chinese Party officials, some from other provinces, had been sent to run the villages.[25]

The Troubled Frontier

The Xinjiang question – and how the Party chooses to manage it – is key to unravelling how Beijing views both the opportunities and challenges in its engagement with the lands to China's west. Historically, Xinjiang was a bridge between East and West, a stopping point on the Silk Road. Today, there is a firm Chinese wall that Beijing is building to protect its frontiers. And assessing the trajectory of China's policies in Xinjiang, it is apparent that for all the talk about rebuilding the Silk Road, Beijing hardly envisages a corridor of openness and business linking its western regions to Central Asia, Pakistan and Afghanistan.

That ensuring Xinjiang's security is China's abiding objective as it connects with its western neighbours is the clear message from Xi's 2014 secret speeches, which, until date, are the only instances where the Chinese leader has so explicitly warned of the security threat to China's west from the political unrest that many of China's neighbours were grappling with. For all the effort to rebrand the Taliban as friends of China, Xi's views underline the deep-seated concerns of the Communist Party as it tried to figure out how to deal with its western periphery. In his 2014 speeches, Xi also held forth on the dangers of extremism, warning that 'the psychological impact of extremist religious thought on people must never be underestimated'. The speeches revealed that the language of Party officials – which described religious thought even as a mental illness, as we have seen – came right from the top: 'People who are captured by religious extremism – male or female, old or young – have their consciences destroyed, lose their humanity and murder without blinking an eye,' Xi said, warning of its 'toxicity'. 'It's like taking a drug, and you lose your sense, go crazy and will do anything,' he warned. Visiting a counterterrorism unit, he called for 'no mercy'. 'The methods that our comrades have at hand are too primitive,' he said. 'None of these weapons is any answer for their big machete blades, axe heads and cold steel weapons. We must be as harsh as them, and show absolutely no mercy.'[26]

Publicly, Xi had spoken about the economic opportunities of the Silk Road. Privately, he warned of 'terrorist organizations positioned on the frontiers of Afghanistan and Pakistan' that 'may quickly infiltrate into Central Asia' after the US exit.[27] Just as the Party was waging this war on extremism at home, the return of the Taliban in Afghanistan would certainly only deepen those concerns, as well as pose new questions for China's diplomacy in the region and how it planned to deal with the possible spillover that Xi warned of. As Beijing began seeking those answers, and crafting its relations with the new Afghanistan, it would come to the conclusion that one country would be key to securing Chinese interests in this state of flux: the one that Beijing's mandarins liked to call China's 'Iron Brother'.

9

Iron Brothers

FOUR DAYS BEFORE CHINA'S FOREIGN MINISTER WANG YI hosted Mullah Baradar and the Taliban delegation in Tianjin on 28 July 2021, a meeting that made headlines around the world, Wang was playing host to another important guest. This meeting, held in Chengdu, the picturesque capital of south-western Sichuan province famed for its teahouses, went under the radar of the world's media. It was, however, arguably just as significant.

Days before Mullah Baradar's delegation landed, Pakistan's foreign minister Shah Mahmood Qureshi boarded a plane for China. Over two days, Qureshi held intense consultations with Wang. Ostensibly, the meeting was for the third round of a foreign ministers' strategic dialogue, usually held annually. Reading between the lines of the lengthy communiques that followed, it was clear that this was no ordinary meeting. For, a lot more was at stake now than ever before.

In the meeting, Wang waxed eloquent about the state of China–Pakistan relations, saying both countries had 'forged an ironclad friendship and established an all-weather strategic partnership of cooperation'. He said 'facts had proven' that 'China and Pakistan are the most reliable good neighbours, friends, brothers and partners to each other, and the friendship between the two countries is unbreakable'. Qureshi responded that 'strengthening the ironclad Pakistan–China friendship is the common understanding of the whole country and the basis of Pakistan's foreign policies'.[1]

Wang did add a less pleasant footnote, though, to his flowery appraisal of the state of China–Pakistan relations. Two weeks before the meeting, the attack at the Dasu hydropower project killing nine Chinese workers – the biggest such terror attack targeting Chinese interests abroad – had made headlines in China. Wang revealed that China's response to the attack had gone all the way up the chain of command to President Xi, telling Qureshi that Xi 'made important instructions immediately after the incident, and put forward clear requests'.

Wang delivered a carefully calibrated message. On the one hand, he noted that 'both China and Pakistan are victims of this terrorist attack' and called for the two allies 'to strengthen cooperation, bring the perpetrators to justice at an early date, give the people of the two countries an explanation, and prevent similar incidents from happening again'. He offered China's 'assistance and cooperation' in the investigation. (China would, for the first time, send its own team to investigate the attack on the ground in Pakistan – not exactly a vote of confidence from Beijing on Islamabad's competence to investigate the matter adequately.) And finally, and somewhat cryptically, Wang said that 'the perpetrators must be thoroughly investigated and punished without leniency no matter for what intentions, at any place, and protected by what forces'.[2]

A Shared Strategy

The most important takeaway from Chengdu, however, was what Wang and Qureshi announced to the press after their dialogue concluded. Afghanistan, Wang said, was 'one important agenda' for the visit, and with the changes there, it was 'necessary for the two countries to strengthen cooperation and respond to changes'. Wang delivered a few withering criticisms of the US, saying that 'without eliminating terrorism or bringing peace to Afghanistan, the US suddenly withdrew its troops from Afghanistan, which has resulted in a new security black hole'.

To deal with the new situation – and the increasingly likely return of the Taliban in some form, which China too was clearly preparing for as it would host Mullah Baradar days later – China and Pakistan said they would 'launch joint actions', outlining five pillars of a shared Afghan strategy. The first of those was to cooperate 'to prevent Afghanistan from spiralling into a full-scale civil war'. Both also agreed 'to take substantive steps towards political reconciliation'. The third step focused on terrorism and China's particular concerns on the ETIM, with both saying they would 'work together to combat terrorism and push all major forces in Afghanistan to draw a clear line against terrorism, firmly combat the East Turkestan Islamic Movement and other terrorist forces, and resolutely stop Afghanistan from becoming a hotbed of terrorism'. Fourth, they pledged to work together to 'promote coordination and cooperation among Afghanistan's neighbouring countries'.[3]

The last point called for both to lead the effort to 'pool the strengths of the international community' to promote the coordination of 'Afghanistan-related regional and multilateral mechanisms'. This point included a reference to 'urge the United States to earnestly fulfill its responsibilities for the peace and reconstruction of Afghanistan', yet another reminder of how, for Beijing, the Afghan question had become a useful stick to beat Washington with. It also underlined how closely China and Pakistan were coordinating diplomatically.

As part of this diplomatic effort, three weeks after the fall of Kabul, Pakistan would convene what was called the 'First Foreign Ministers' Meeting on the Afghan Issue Among the Neighbouring Countries of Afghanistan', a new platform that China was actively backing. The virtual meeting was hosted by Qureshi, and attended by Wang and the foreign ministers of Iran, Tajikistan, Uzbekistan and Turkmenistan. At the meeting, Wang announced China's first humanitarian assistance to the new Kabul government, saying Beijing had 'decided to urgently provide food, materials for winter, COVID-19 vaccines, and medicines worth 200 million yuan (around $30 million)'. 'When security and other conditions are available,' Wang added, 'China is willing to help Afghanistan build projects that will contribute to improving people's livelihood, and support peace, reconstruction and economic development of Afghanistan within its capacity.'[4]

The exchanges in Chengdu served as a reminder of the curious dichotomy that has characterized the China–Pakistan relationship for years: repeated pledges reaffirming the unbreakable bonds and the strength of ties, punctured occasionally by serious Chinese concerns over security and Pakistan's ability to ensure it, which came to the fore after the Dasu attack. They also underlined how China was now dealing with this familiar dichotomy. While China's long-persisting concerns over security – and Pakistan's capacity (or lack thereof) to address them – certainly remained an inherent tension in the relationship, it was becoming apparent that Beijing had decided the best way to address that tension was to go even deeper in its embrace of Pakistan. By doing so, Beijing reasoned, it would not only come to hold ever greater sway over the developments next door, but also garner a firmer foothold amid the changing situation in Afghanistan, where Pakistan had become an important player with the return of the Taliban. For Beijing, the road to Kabul ran through Islamabad.

The New New Frontier

'*Chun chi xiang yi*', or 'as close as lips and teeth', was how Mao Zedong once described China's close relationship with North Korea. For decades, the North was China's only ally, but in Beijing today, the epithet that is currently the flavour of the moment is '*ba tie*', meaning 'iron brother' Pakistan. When Mao's People's Liberation Army marched into Xinjiang in 1949, the Chairman had christened the People's Republic's newest province 'Xinjiang', literally, 'new frontier' – a historical name used intermittently for China's borderlands. Today, Pakistan is, in a way, China's new 'new frontier'. A relationship that had its roots in close ties between the two militaries is rapidly deepening in every sphere, leaving China with deep stakes in Pakistan's future.

The close ties are not new, going back to the early 1960s, forged in their mutual animosity towards India. Both fought wars with India during that decade, and signed a border agreement a year after the India–China war in 1962. Over the years, China offered Pakistan its missiles and aircraft, and both helped each other's nuclear programmes.

Yet for all the rhetoric of the relationship being, as Chinese and Pakistani officials like to say, 'higher than the Himalayas, deeper than the oceans, sweeter than honey', Beijing remained calibrated in pursuing relations with Pakistan. This was particularly the case after the normalization of ties with India in 1988, which would see a rapid improvement in India–China relations most notably expressed in booming trade ties. China kept one eye on India as it developed relations with Pakistan, for instance staying out of Kashmir and insisting it was a 'bilateral' issue for India and Pakistan to solve despite constant Pakistani appeals to internationalize it. Pakistan also remained a key US military partner, playing a crucial role for Washington especially after 2001 and the resultant 'war on terror' when the US would become Pakistan's biggest military supplier and financial donor.

China's ties with Pakistan – and the balancing act with India – underwent a profound transformation with the launch of the Belt and Road Initiative. China decided to make the China Pakistan Economic Corridor, which runs from Xinjiang, through Pakistan-occupied Kashmir, all the way to Gwadar port on the Arabian Sea, a 'flagship' project of the BRI, underlining Pakistan's primacy in Xi's new pet initiative.

For India, the CPEC also underlined something more troubling: a growing pattern of Beijing more openly siding with Pakistani interests at the expense of India's. The announcement of the CPEC, which runs through PoK, essentially forced India to boycott the BRI, a development that would presage an alarming slide in India–China relations. Though Indian officials had made it clear to China that having a 'flagship' BRI project running through Kashmir would leave India little option but to stay out of the plan, Beijing went ahead with it. India's decision to abstain from the BRI, boycott the first BRI forum in Beijing in 2017, and publicly question the plan's respect for others' sovereignty and debt sustainability became yet another thorny point of discord, adding to a growing list of differences between the neighbours.

Growing Stakes

The CPEC, to put it bluntly, was China's twenty-year bet on Pakistan. Indeed, both sides prepared an extraordinarily ambitious two-decade-long blueprint. If that blueprint comes to fruition – which remains a big 'if' in light of China's continuing concerns over terror attacks targeting its projects and personnel in Pakistan – it will mean a dramatic expansion of China's presence and stake across literally every sector of the Pakistani economy. A leaked draft CPEC masterplan brought home the extent to which China plans to involve itself in almost every aspect of Pakistan's economy. Besides roads, power projects and dams, which make up most of the investment, Chinese firms will even take up agricultural land in Pakistan as well as build tourism and cultural projects.[5]

Today, Chinese companies are already building and managing the country's key transport networks, from national highways to Lahore's metro rail. China has bought a stake in Pakistan's stock exchange. Chinese state-run energy companies are building Pakistan's power sector, coal plant by coal plant, and will eventually, some experts believe, have a say in how much Pakistani citizens pay their government for electricity. In the BRI era, China has replaced the US as Pakistan's biggest benefactor. China's trade with Pakistan jumped to $13.7 billion in 2016, up from just $4 billion in 2007. In 2020, China accounted for 40 per cent of Pakistan's foreign direct investment, which is around $2 billion.[6]

Under the CPEC, thousands of acres of Pakistani land will be transferred to Chinese companies to grow crops, build meat processing plants and develop free trade zones. Chinese garment factories will be transferred to Pakistan, while China will manage and run tourism projects and special economic zones along the southern coast, with rather ambitious plans for ventures such as yacht clubs and hot spring hotels to develop an unlikely tourism hub in the restive Balochistan province, of all places. S. Akbar Zaidi, a leading Pakistani political economist, has written that the CPEC would reduce Pakistan to 'a vassal state', describing it as 'a Chinese project, for Chinese interests, and Pakistan just happens to be part of the geographical terrain'.[7]

In Gwadar, a dusty town on the Arabian Sea in Balochistan, China has already built a port that it is managing. China Overseas Port Holdings Limited had acquired the rights to operate what was a languishing port from the Singapore Port Authority in February 2013. Since then, a first shipping route was opened by the Chinese state-run Shipping Ocean Company (COSCO) in May 2015 exporting local seafood to Dubai. The first Chinese CPEC export, a convoy carrying sixty containers of a range of Chinese goods, from machinery to appliances, to be exported to Africa and the Middle East, arrived in Gwadar after travelling 3000 km from Xinjiang along the Karakoram highway through PoK. Beyond the port, which will give China access to the Indian Ocean, it envisages a free trade zone and manufacturing hub that could serve as a launch pad for Chinese and Pakistani exports to Africa and the Middle East. China has secured a tax-free deal for twenty-three years for its companies that will operate out of Gwadar.

Risks and Rewards

There are, however, enormous risks involved in the engagement with Pakistan on the security front, as repeated attacks on Chinese citizens and projects show. In 2013, Renmin University in Beijing quietly sent a team of researchers to assess those risks. The findings were sobering.[8]

Security is one major concern, highlighted by the kidnapping and reported killing of two young Chinese in Quetta, Balochistan, in May 2017. The Renmin study cited a number of other incidents that had targeted its citizens in 2016. In May 2016, a Chinese engineer at the Kazmu project was targeted by a bomb attack claimed by an outfit called the Sindh Revolutionary Force. Two months later, a bomb attack in Quetta killed seventy-four people, while in November of that year, a team from a Chinese oil and natural gas exploration company was targeted in an attack by a group called the Baloch Revolutionary Army in which two Pakistani security personnel were killed.

The wider concern was because of security. Chinese staff in Gwadar, for instance, will have to be 'cloistered within the Chinese zone as the situation around the city is not stable'. The Chinese report worried this would alienate the local population because 'Chinese personnel are carrying out work under the protection of armed forces and this inhibits improving relations with local people to the extent that it could lead to opposition and lack of people's support'. The Pakistan army has deployed a special security division of 15,000 troops to protect Chinese personnel and assets, but the report argued that 'a troop size of 15,000 can hardly guarantee the safety of projects around the country … And considering that Pakistan needs to deploy a large number of troops in its eastern borders adjoining India and now needs to deploy troops in Afghan border, allocating 15,000 is the largest capacity.'[9]

The report came to a striking final conclusion that the only way for China to guarantee success was to assume even more sweeping control. 'Neither China nor Pakistan can afford the consequences of the failure of constructing the corridor,' it advised. 'If the current uncertainty was to continue, it would not only delay the opening of the flagship project but CPEC would end up becoming a burden on China and have a great negative impact.' The Chinese study was still optimistic about the long-term scenario. For Gwadar, it forecast an ambitious annual cargo throughput of 300–400 million tonnes, more than ten times that of Pakistan's current biggest port, Karachi, and – the study pointedly added – almost equivalent to India's total current throughput.

Reports in Pakistan estimate China will invest as much as $62 billion in the CPEC. That amount might not, however, materialize for some time. In the first four years of the CPEC, the estimated total investment was around $5 billion. The lion's share went to energy projects, aimed at bridging Pakistan's huge energy deficit, while the rest went to road projects such as widening of the Karakoram highway and work on sections of the Karachi–Peshawar expressway. In fact, the CPEC draft masterplan from China's planning agency noted that 'Pakistan's economy cannot absorb FDI much above $2 billion per year without giving rise to stresses in its economy', and 'recommended that China's maximum annual direct investment in Pakistan should be around $1 billion', suggesting that the many breathless media reports of China putting $62 billion need to be qualified with a few large tubs of salt.[10]

The Road to Kabul

Sums of money, however, do not convey the transformative impact of the CPEC on the China–Pakistan relationship. The project is not just about economics: it is a strategic commitment by China to Pakistan, one that has dramatically altered Beijing's calculus in how it approached relations with Pakistan and India. Indeed, since its launch India has been alarmed by the extent to which China has once again begun deferring to Pakistan's interests on key bilateral issues: the protection of Masood Azhar at the UN Security Council, as we have seen, is a case in point. This was a reversal of a two-decade trend that saw Beijing attempt to more carefully strike a balance between its historical ties with Islamabad on the one hand, and a sensitive but growing relationship with Delhi on the other.

China's overriding strategic concern at the moment is not India. It is more preoccupied with the growing challenge posed by the US and its partners on its periphery. As one Party academic puts it, Beijing's 'biggest fear is India becoming a Japan or South Korea'.[11] China was facing 'a Pakistan dilemma' as it weighed its ambition to build a regional counterweight to India against its fears of an India–US alliance.

That dilemma now appears to have been resolved unequivocally, likely because of a combination of factors. The CPEC certainly increased China's stakes in Pakistan. Beijing's continuing concerns in Xinjiang, too, led to an ever greater dependence on Pakistan to clamp down on Uighur groups along the Pakistan–Afghanistan border. Beijing's security agencies see Pakistan as key to ensuring stability not only in the western Xinjiang region, where Beijing is dealing with a jihadist threat, but also in Afghanistan. This explains why Beijing is often prepared to tolerate Pakistan's fostering of anti-India terrorists. Beijing's rationale is that as long as Islamabad demonstrates willingness to crack down on groups that target China, such as the East Turkestan Islamic Movement – which in China's view it has done – it has no reason to complain about other Pakistani misdemeanours. In fact, it would go as far as enabling them, as its UNSC actions demonstrated.[12]

The prevailing view in Beijing is that Pakistan needs to be at the centre of China's plans in dealing with the rising Islamist threat it is grappling with in its western Xinjiang region. Cooperation between both countries has worked well and satisfied Beijing, says South Asia scholar Han Hua of Peking University. So far, Beijing's approach has been twofold: in the short term, it has leaned on Pakistan's army and ISI to crack down on Uighur terror camps along the Pakistan–Afghanistan border, and in the longer term, it hopes its investments in the CPEC will bring greater stability to Pakistan.[13]

In the days after Kabul fell in 2021, Yue Xiaoyong, China's newly appointed special envoy to Afghanistan, was asked if the return of the Taliban was a major victory for Pakistan, and hence, a positive development for China too. Yue replied as a diplomat would, carefully weighing his words, but didn't deny this was the case. 'As you know,' he said, 'we have an all-weather strategic partnership between China and Pakistan, which provides a very good basis for communication, exchange of views and cooperation on the situation in Afghanistan. I believe that this cooperation will in turn strengthen this all-weather strategic partnership.'[14]

Reading between the lines of Yue's careful answer, one can assess that in Beijing's view, the new situation in Afghanistan could, in one sense, be mutually reinforcing for the already close China–Pakistan relationship. Yue, who was speaking from Islamabad, continued:

> Indeed, Pakistan, as an important regional country and a neighbour of Afghanistan, has a very important role to play in resolving the Afghan issue. People here, both the government and the public, are very concerned about the changes and the crisis in Afghanistan and they are very interested in the situation in Afghanistan. They have really contributed a lot to the peace and reconciliation process in Afghanistan before and now, as well as to the negotiations within Afghanistan.[15]

Hailing Pakistan's 'contribution' to the peace and reconciliation process was an extraordinary comment. It was, of course, an open secret to anyone in Kabul, New Delhi and Washington that Pakistan had, from the get-go, undermined the process through its open advocacy for the Taliban (the US, of course, was equally responsible, in the way it carried forward its talks with the Taliban).

What Yue's comments underlined was a growing Chinese reliance on Pakistan on the Afghan question. Beijing had, for better or for worse, cast in its lot with Islamabad, viewing this approach as its best bet to secure its interests. 'These contexts where China becomes quite reliant on Pakistan – they are not on the Chinese side hugely capable of analysing and making judgments on all the subtleties of what's going on within the Taliban, in intra-Afghan politics, etc.,' says Andrew Small, author of *The China Pakistan Axis*. He notes:

> Even if you look back at their involvement in the reconciliation process, China was not an actor that was able to play a very kind of direct mediating role. In terms of its involvement in the minutiae, this is not their comfort zone, and this is not an area that they have very much depth on. In a particularly fast-moving situation like this, they need the Pakistanis. They don't altogether rely on them, they have their reservations. I don't think their agendas are in perfect sync. But I think over particularly the last decade, they've figured out ways to be relatively joined up on this, a little bit more so than they were.[16]

The Chinese, Small says, 'need the Pakistanis if they want to nudge the Taliban on all of the issues that they're concerned about'. Beijing does have direct links and its own (largely economic) leverage, but the fact is, as Small notes, 'Ultimately, the reason for this relationship [with the Taliban], and the reason that China is able to have a certain quality of relationship with the Taliban, is still, quite heavily, Pakistan.'

Beijing has also appeared to come to the conclusion that India's growing closeness to the US, and the return of the Quad (the US–India–Australia–Japan security grouping), suggested an inevitability of India drifting closer to the American orbit. In the view of some strategists, the border clashes between India and China in the summer of 2020, and the PLA's extraordinary amassing of troops along the Line of Actual Control and disregarding the carefully built border agreements that had maintained a fragile peace for decades, were in part driven by a Chinese view that India was 'strategically unreliable' and needed to be given a message because it was being 'emboldened' by the US.[17]

As much as the PLA is driving hostile relations with India, it is a key force behind the growing closeness with Pakistan. Hu Shisheng, a leading Chinese strategic expert on India and Pakistan at the influential China Institutes of Contemporary International Relations, says the CPEC has changed the China–Pakistan equation dramatically. It is effectively pushing both countries in a direction where they 'will become mutual stakeholders of each other'. 'This means any disturbance in Pakistan,' he cautions, 'will get Chinese interests disturbed.' It is hence unavoidable, in Hu's opinion, that Pakistan will increasingly become 'a bigger factor' in India–China relations.[18]

Privately, many Chinese officials see the military as the most favourable interlocutor in Pakistan, including in pushing the CPEC, rather than a weak civilian government. One of the CPEC's most important projects is the upgradation of infrastructure in PoK, starting with the Karakoram highway. In the event of a conflict between India and Pakistan, this link will allow China to rapidly transport materials and assistance, even if it is unlikely to involve its own troops directly. Officials believe it is only a matter of time before the PLA has boots on the ground in PoK, ostensibly to protect Chinese personnel. In 2016, China and Pakistan for the first time began joint patrols in areas bordering PoK and Xinjiang.

Zhang Chunxiang, a former Chinese ambassador in Pakistan posted there shortly after the 11 September 2001 attacks, reflects much of the thinking in Beijing when he bristles at the suggestion of differences between the two countries he calls 'iron brothers' on the terrorism issue. Zhang says Pakistan is 'the only country we have a solid relationship with'. Zhang became visibly angry when asked about terror links between Uighur groups and Pakistani organizations and whether Pakistani agencies were doing enough to crack down on terror.

'Has the US eradicated terrorism? Has India? It's not possible. So why do you people only ask about Pakistan?' Zhang said. Echoing the Pakistani establishment's repeated (and unfounded) accusations claiming Indian intelligence agencies were behind attacks on Chinese investments in Pakistan, Zhang alleged that an attack during his time as envoy at Gwadar port was carried out not by Pakistani terrorists but by a 'foreign country'. Zhang wouldn't name it, but added, with dramatic effect, it was 'one everybody knows'.[19]

10

The View from India

WHEN THE TALIBAN CAME TO POWER IN 1996, INDIA, like most other countries, shut its embassy in Kabul and pulled back its mission. India, then, also endorsed UN Security Council Resolution 1076, which stated that the continuation of the conflict in Afghanistan provided fertile ground for terrorism and drug trafficking which destabilized the region and beyond.

The resolution also denounced 'the discrimination against girls and women and other violations of human rights and international humanitarian law in Afghanistan (under the Taliban)'.[1] Taking a firm stand, India decided it would not open political contact with the Taliban and, instead, channelled its support for Massoud's anti-Taliban forces in the north.

Four years later, in December 2000, India co-sponsored the UN Security Council Resolution 1333, along with the United States and Russia, that called for a ban on all military assistance to the Taliban, imposed harsh new sanctions and demanded the swift closure of 'all camps where terrorists are trained within the territory under its control'. The resolution also reiterated the UNSC's 'deep concern over the continuing violation of international humanitarian law and of human rights, particularly discrimination against women and girls'.[2] The resolution practically cut off the Taliban regime from the rest of the world.

In a sense, India's unease with the Taliban at the helm was consistent with its past approach to Afghanistan. Decades earlier, India had watched the rise of Islamist insurgency in Afghanistan as a threat to its core interests, a reason why it decided to tone down its opposition towards the Soviet intervention. Delhi decided it would deal with whichever government was in effective power in Afghanistan, which J.N. Dixit called 'a classical and formally correct stand', and stop criticizing the Soviet intervention publicly.[3] In bilateral meetings, India would continue to raise the issue of Soviet presence in the country as well as the atrocities the Soviet troops were committing in the name of fighting counter-revolutionaries, but it had no impact on bilateral cooperation. Afghanistan would see many upheavals in the following decades. But this pragmatic realism India had shown in the early 1980s would largely continue to guide its approach towards the country for many more years.

The King and the Comrades

India had historically enjoyed friendly ties with Afghanistan. Both countries signed a Treaty of Friendship in 1950, 'affirming everlasting peace and friendship', establishing full diplomatic relations with each other and opening embassies.[4] Afghanistan was one of the twenty-nine countries that attended the 1955 Afro-Asian Conference in Bandung, Indonesia, which brought together, according to India, 'the first post-colonial generation of leaders from the two continents with the aim of identifying and assessing world issues at the time and pursuing out joint policies in international relations'.[5] The Bandung conference, which raised a collective voice against colonialism and called for self-determination and peaceful coexistence, laid the foundations for the Non-Aligned Movement in which both India and Afghanistan were members.[6]

While India and Afghanistan were cooperating on issues like non-alignment, Pakistan remained a critical factor that shaped their bilateral ties. Kabul's relations with neighbouring Pakistan were not particularly good. During the colonial period, the British saw Afghanistan as a buffer state between British India and the Russian empire. The British strategic calculation was that they should have some leverage over Afghanistan's foreign policy to stop a potential Russian advance to the landlocked country, which would bring the ever-expanding empire closer to the borders of undivided India. The British tried to manage Afghanistan through invasions; when they found that unsustainable, they withdrew from the country but later imposed a border on the Afghans, carving up the tribal territories that traditionally fell under the jurisdiction of the Afghan monarchs. This border came to be called the Durand Line.

King Zahir Shah, who stabilized Afghanistan in the 1930s and 1940s following a brief period of chaos and anarchy, raised the boundary issue with the British several times. In November 1944, the Afghan government wrote a note to London seeking a settlement of the issue. But the British rejected the plea. In 1949, Afghanistan unilaterally declared that 'it doesn't recognise the Durand Line or any similar line'.[7] No Afghan regime ever since, including the Taliban, has accepted the Durand Line.[8] According to Zahir Shah, Pakistan's large Pashtun belt, including parts of Khyber Pakhtunkhwa and Balochistan, was part of Afghanistan.

The disputed border remained an irritant in bilateral relations between the two countries.

Despite his disputes with Pakistan and warm ties with India, Zahir Shah, who became the monarch in 1933 at the age of nineteen and would go on to rule the country for forty years, was careful not to upset the balance in Afghanistan's ties with its two bigger and more powerful neighbours. Even when India and Pakistan fought several wars in Afghanistan's neighbourhood, Shah's regime remained non-aligned. He never supported India, but he did not take a public position critical of India's interests either. Shah's balancing act would pave the way for deeper relations between the two countries after his cousin, Mohammed Daoud Khan, deposed him in a bloodless coup in 1973 and declared the country a republic. Daoud, backed by Afghanistan's expanding middle classes and the surging left-wing movement, was becoming increasingly critical of Shah's feudal way of governance and traditional policies. India was the second country, after the Soviet Union, that recognized the new regime, within two days of the coup.[9]

Relations between Pakistan and Afghanistan hit a low during Daoud's prime ministership, in 1953–63. A strong supporter of the unification of the Pashtun heartlands of Pakistan with Afghanistan, Daoud supported a Pashtun insurgency in Pakistan's tribal lands in the 1960s. The conflict occasionally resulted in direct fighting between Afghan and Pakistani forces in which hundreds of Afghan soldiers were killed. An angry Pakistan sealed the border with Afghanistan, cutting off all supplies to the landlocked country. Daoud was forced out of power by Zahir Shah in 1963 as hostilities with Pakistan were at their peak and opposition from non-Pashtun ethnic groups as well as the country's rural tribal leaders was rising. But ten years later, Daoud returned to power as President and was now free to pursue his policies without any checks from the palace.[10] In his first speech to the nation after seizing power,

Daoud said, 'The political disputes with Pakistan which had not been solved' would be the centrepiece of his foreign policy.[11]

As President Daoud stepped up his rhetoric for Pashtunistan, his regime also offered support for the Baloch insurgency, which brought the country to the brink of war with Pakistan. On the other hand, Daoud steadily deepened his partnership with a willing India. When Pakistan's Prime Minister Zulfikar Ali Bhutto deployed troops on the Afghan border to press Daoud to stop his support for the Baloch insurgency, the Afghan leader said, 'If Pakistan attacks Afghanistan, India and other countries (Soviet Union) will come to the rescue of Afghanistan.'[12]

It is not clear whether India had made any military commitment to Daoud, but New Delhi was keen to strengthen ties with Afghanistan during this period. In October 1973, a few months after Daoud's coup, a Ministry of External Affairs (MEA) delegation led by Foreign Minister Swaran Singh visited Afghanistan and held talks with the President and his top aides. According to the MEA, 'Bilateral and general questions were discussed at these meetings. Further measures of economic and technical collaboration have been decided upon and the Government of India looks forward to increasing friendly cooperation with Afghanistan.'[13] In 1975, India hosted Daoud in New Delhi. The countries also started military cooperation during this period, which deepened Pakistan's insecurity. The Daoud regime, however, did not last long.

India and the Soviets

Daoud was overthrown and executed by the PDPA in 1978. India was 'surprised' by the coup. India's ambassador in Kabul, S.K. Singh, was of the opinion that despite internal turbulence, President Daoud's regime was 'stable and that prospects were of consolidating his position with general support'.[14] But the surprise factor did not deter India from adapting to the new reality in Kabul. India would offer diplomatic recognition to the new government and remain the only country in South Asia with full diplomatic ties with the Soviet-backed communist regime throughout the 1980s.[15] When Pakistan, Saudi Arabia and the US stepped up their intervention in Afghanistan through their proxies, India's stake in the Soviet presence in Afghanistan increased.

Late in the night of 27 December 1979, Arvind Deo, joint secretary in charge of East Europe at the ministry of external affairs, got a call from the Soviet embassy in New Delhi. Yuli Vorontsov, the Soviet ambassador, was on the line. Vorontsov, a fifty-year-old diplomat, had been in Washington before he was posted to India the year before. The late-night call from the embassy was unusual. The ambassador told Secretary Deo he wanted to meet the Prime Minister urgently to deliver a message from Leonid Brezhnev, the General Secretary of the Communist Party of the Soviet Union. Prime Minister Charan Singh was not available for a meeting at that time. Nor was Foreign Minister Shyam Nandan Mishra. But the ambassador wouldn't relent. He wanted to meet a top Indian official that same night. Finally, Deo managed to fix a meeting with R.D. Sathe, India's foreign secretary, around midnight. At the meeting, Vorontsov told Sathe about the Russian intervention in Afghanistan, which had started on Christmas Eve. He said he would like to deliver the message from Brezhnev to the Prime Minister in person.

The next day, the ambassador met the Prime Minister. Charan Singh was on his way out of power. His government, formed after the collapse of the Janata government, had lost its majority and the country was preparing for the next general elections. There would be a new government within weeks. But India couldn't wait till then to articulate a position on Afghanistan, where the situation was quickly deteriorating. The ambassador explained the Soviet rationale behind the intervention and asked for India's support. India was clearly in a dilemma.

The Soviet Union was a friendly superpower. India had signed a friendship treaty with Moscow in August 1971.[16] The same year, the Soviets had come to India's help during the Bangladesh Liberation War. India was also dependent on the Soviet Union for economic assistance and critical supplies, including fuel, and political support at global fora. So Soviet sensitivities carried weight in the corridors of Delhi. At the same time, India was not a member of any Soviet-backed alliance system. It remained a champion of non-alignment. In the case of Afghanistan, what had happened was a military intervention in a non-aligned third world country by a superpower. India had historically opposed superpower military interventions in the third world. India also feared that the Soviet intervention in Afghanistan would prompt the US to take countermeasures to check Soviet influence, bringing the Cold War closer to India's borders.

Charan Singh's response to Vorontsov was 'cut and dry'. He told the ambassador that military intervention in a non-aligned country that was also a close neighbour of India was 'unacceptable'. He added that New Delhi would take the same position in the United Nations. The ambassador left the meeting disappointed.[17] As the Prime Minister had asserted, India would voice its opposition at the UN to the Russian intervention and re-emphasize the moral aspect of its foreign policy. But India would not be free of the dilemma the Soviet intervention had posed. By January end, 1980, Indira Gandhi was back in power. She reviewed India's position towards Afghanistan.

An Islamist resistance was already taking shape in the country. And it was an open secret that Pakistan was supporting the anti-communist rebels even before the Soviets arrived in Afghanistan. In the late 1970s, there was an upsurge in Islamic radicalism in several parts of the world. In Iran, the hard-line Shia clergy captured power in an Islamic revolution. In Saudi Arabia, Islamists briefly laid siege to the Grand Mosque in Mecca. In Pakistan, Islamists raided the American embassy in Islamabad. Afghan Islamists, influenced and inspired by the ideology of the Jamaat-e-Islami and the Iranian revolution, wanted to overthrow the communist PDPA regime and turn the country into an Islamic republic.

The Soviet withdrawal from Afghanistan in February 1989 posed new challenges to India's Afghan policy. Even so, New Delhi decided to step up assistance to the regime of Mohammad Najibullah.

In March 1989, the Afghan foreign minister Abdul Wakil visited New Delhi, seeking material, diplomatic and security assistance. Afghanistan was going through severe food and fuel shortages and the Mujahideen had captured much of the countryside. Most of the West and East European countries had withdrawn their diplomatic missions from Kabul as many expected an imminent collapse of the Najibullah regime. But India retained its diplomatic presence in Kabul. In New Delhi, Wakil blasted Pakistan and Iran for their support for Mujahideen factions. He said India should put pressure on Pakistan to stop arming the Mujahideen and alleged that Iran wanted to establish a fundamentalist Islamist regime in Kabul. In meetings with Wakil, India agreed to provide 'humanitarian and technical aid' to the Afghan government.[18]

But India's attempts to prop up the internally broken communist regime amidst an Islamist insurgence in Afghanistan would unravel along with the collapse of communism in East Europe and the Soviet Union. After the disintegration of the Soviet Union, Kabul would lose critical supplies and financial assistance from Moscow, sounding the death knell for the Najibullah regime. Najibullah himself knew that the forces of history had turned hostile towards him. He would send his family to India, seek UN-backed assurances of safety from the Mujahideen commanders and offer to leave power. The Mujahideen had surrounded Kabul. It was only a matter of time before Islamist commanders, who were directly backed by Pakistan, captured power. For India, it was a moment of reckoning. The Cold War was over. The superpower India was close to had vanished. The regime it had backed in Afghanistan against a possible expansion of Pakistani influence into the country was falling apart brick by brick. The centre in Kabul was not holding. India saw the sands of geopolitics shift under its feet.

From the Mujahideen to the Mullahs

One Sunday morning in April 1992, Benon Sevan, the UN Secretary General's Special Envoy for Afghanistan, came to the Indian High Commission in Islamabad. The UN was negotiating with President Najibullah, the Mujahideen and Pakistani authorities for an orderly transition of power in Afghanistan. Najibullah had offered the resignation of his entire cabinet. Earlier in the day, Sevan had met Pakistani Prime Minister Nawaz Sharif. He requested India to offer political asylum to Najibullah.

M.K. Bhadrakumar, an Indian diplomat posted at the embassy, immediately spoke to Foreign Secretary J.N. Dixit 'on an open line in Malayalam and sought instructions'. New Delhi's response came within an hour. Prime Minister P.V. Narasimha Rao ordered that 'Najib would be our state guest'.[19] The plan was to take Najibullah out of Afghanistan on 17 April. In the wee hours, a plane was ready on the tarmac of Kabul airport with Sevan waiting for the once-all-powerful communist leader. Najibullah drove past many Mujahideen checkposts. But before reaching the airport, he was stopped by the forces of Abdul Rashid Dostum, who, a few months ago, had defected to the Coalition of the North, the Mujahideen alliance commanded by Ahmad Shah Massoud, the Tajik warlord. The Mujahideen would not let Najibullah leave the country.

Najibullah had no friends left in Kabul. Most of his former allies, including the army chief, had defected. Instead of returning to the presidential palace – because he was not sure he would be safe there any more – he went to the UN building. Later, Sevan would request India to offer Najibullah asylum in the Indian embassy in Kabul. India refused because New Delhi thought Najibullah, who had already become a hated figure in the new Afghanistan, staying at its embassy would complicate matters further for India. India did not want to alienate the Mujahideen further by hosting their enemy number one in its embassy. This incident demonstrated the limited options India faced in a changing Afghanistan and its shrinking influence. Even after offering political asylum to an ally, it could neither exfiltrate him nor offer him protection within Afghanistan.

India faced an even bigger challenge in the Mujahideen's rise to power. For the first time since Independence, New Delhi's policymakers were staring at the prospect of a hostile government in Kabul. On 26 April 1992, less than ten days after Najibullah's aborted escape attempt, the Peshawar Accord was signed between different Mujahideen parties, announcing an interim government called the Islamic Republic of Afghanistan. According to the agreement, Sibghatullah Mujaddedi, a relatively independent religious leader with a small political party, was chosen as the head of the interim government for a period of two months. After that, the Jamiat-e Islami's Burhanuddin Rabbani, an ally of Massoud, would be acting President for four months. After Rabbani's term, a council of elders would choose another interim government for eighteen months, which would be followed by elections.[20] By bringing together almost all Mujahideen groups and brokering a power-sharing agreement, Pakistan demonstrated its growing political clout in the new Afghanistan. India's embassy in Kabul, on the other hand, was vandalized and its vehicles stolen. India evacuated its diplomats and shut down the mission.

This was not the end of India's engagement with the Mujahideen. The internal contradictions within the Mujahideen and the role Pakistan played to keep Kabul under its control would open up opportunities for India to find some strategic space for itself in the complex Afghan theatre. Four months after the Mujahideen government was formed, the MEA received 'a curious query' from Kabul. Rabbani had taken over as President after Mujaddedi ended his two-month term according to the Peshawar Accord. President Rabbani's office wanted to know whether the plane carrying the President and his delegation to Jakarta for the Non-Aligned Movement summit could refuel in India. Bhadrakumar, who was heading the Iran–Pakistan–Afghanistan division in South Block, sensed it was a 'feeler' from the Afghans that they wanted to improve ties with India, and reported it to his bosses. The Indian government allowed the Afghan request. Rabbani and a 'planeload of Mujahideen' landed in New Delhi.[21] K. Srinivasan, a senior official in the MEA, went to the airport to welcome the Afghan President and his delegation.

Rabbani's stopover prompted a serious rethink in New Delhi's approach towards the Mujahideen government. Bhadrakumar was asked to draft a policy paper on Afghanistan and the MEA wanted to send it to Prime Minister Rao. The PMO's response came months later, but Rao, in his response, 'put down thoughtful markers' so that South Block could articulate a durable policy decision. The MEA came up with a manifold approach: deal with all Mujahideen groups without fear or favour and establish contacts with anyone who was willing to talk irrespective of their militancy or Islamism; engage with the government in Kabul, despite its proximity to

Pakistan, and cultivate friendly ties; neither arm nor ostracize any Mujahideen group; and focus on people-to-people relationships and provide help for Afghanistan's economic welfare.[22]

As part of the new approach, the Indian government sent Bhadrakumar to Afghanistan to meet with Massoud and Rabbani. In the winter of 1994, Bhadrakumar met Massoud in Panjshir, north of Kabul, which was home to the northern guerrillas. Massoud was the defence minister, but as the commander of the most powerful guerrillas as well as the security forces of the Rabbani administration, he was 'the king of Kabul'. Bhadrakumar requested Massoud to let Najibullah, who was languishing in Kabul's UN compound, leave the country. 'I would be privileged to escort him to Delhi,' the Indian diplomat told him.

Massoud rejected the request, saying other Mujahideen would misunderstand him if he let Najib go. But in the meeting, Massoud laid out his concerns about Pakistan's interference in Afghanistan, urged India to reopen its diplomatic mission and offered full protection.[23] Massoud made it clear that he wanted a new start with New Delhi. It was the beginning of a long relationship. Two years after India established contacts with the Mujahideen government, the Taliban would reach Kabul. Massoud, Rabbani and their associates would retreat to Panjshir. Najibullah would be killed by the Taliban. For India, it was another moment of crisis. It had developed relations, after initial ambiguity, with one Islamist group that had taken Kabul; and then another Islamist group, this time directly backed by Pakistan, had captured Kabul.

Foes in Kabul, Friends in Panjshir

If, as we have seen, India took a clear stand in 1996 on not dealing with the Taliban, the new rulers at the helm in Kabul, for their part, saw India as a country that consistently adopted 'anti-Afghan' policies, meaning that India supported forces in Afghanistan that the Taliban considered their enemies. In an interview in June 1997, Mullah Abdul Jajil, the Taliban's deputy foreign minister, said,

> It [India] supported the communist regime till Najibullah's downfall. Later, it backed discredited Mujahideen leaders who killed their own people and plundered the country. India never criticised the Soviet invasion, the root cause of all our sufferings. Even now, India is unwilling to accept ground realities in Afghanistan and is backing our opponents. Is it possible to have normal ties in such a situation? [24]

But at the same time, the Taliban had sent feelers to New Delhi, like the Mujahideen did in 1992, that they wanted 'friendly ties with all countries, both Islamic and non-Islamic'. Abdul Jajil said the Taliban 'will be waiting for signs that indicate a change of heart in New Delhi'.[25]

But New Delhi would not change its approach.

It saw differences between the Taliban and the Mujahideen, and understood the context in which the Taliban operated. First of all, there were ideological differences. While both the Mujahideen and the Taliban were Islamist, Massoud seemed relatively modern and tolerant compared to the Taliban's medievalism and violence. But that alone was not necessarily the primary concern of policymakers in Delhi. India had supported the communist regime even when tens of thousands of Afghans were getting killed every year during the civil war. It was that the conditions which allowed India to pursue its interests in the past irrespective of who was in power in Kabul had changed with the Taliban seizing power.

Take the case of the Mujahideen. The Mujahideen were not a unified bloc. There were different factions, from Massoud's Jamiat-e

Islami to Ittihad-e Islami, Harakat Inquilab i-Islami and Hizb-e-Wahdat, which were brought together by Pakistan in Peshawar after the fall of the communist regime. Gulbuddin Hekmatyar's Hezb-e-Islami, the favourite of Pakistan's security establishment, did not accept the Peshawar Accord. According to the agreement, the post of Prime Minister was given to Hekmatyar. But Hekmatyar, the Pashtun warlord who wanted Kabul for himself, did not sign the agreement and threatened to continue the war. So the Mujahideen government was off to a wrong start.

Once they started ruling a divided country, the fault lines started widening. The Peshawar Accord unravelled within months when Rabbani, who was to hand over power to a council of elders after four months, refused to do so. With help from Massoud, Rabbani convened the council of representatives under the Peshawar Accord to 're-elect' the new government. Several Mujahideen factions, including the pro-Iran Wahdat and Hezb-e Islami, boycotted the vote. Rabbani was re-elected President by his supporters and he stated that he would stay in power for eighteen months before the elections.[26] Pakistan was upset with Rabbani's power grab. When Hekmatyar, joined by others, started attacking Kabul, Pakistan would gradually shift its weight behind him. This would push Rabbani and Massoud to seek better ties with India. So the internal contradictions within the Mujahideen opened up opportunities for India, and the Rao government swiftly made use of them, establishing ties with the Mujahideen regime.

In the case of the Taliban, the situation was different. Compared to the fractious Mujahideen, the Taliban were a united force commanded by Mullah Omar, who in turn was supported directly by Pakistan's ISI. The possibility of exploring ties with factions within the Taliban was non-existent. Second, despite the Taliban's feelers to India, Afghanistan under the Taliban's control continued to host training camps for a multitude of terrorist/militant outfits, including Harkat ul-Ansar and Lashkar-e-Taiba. It was also a period when India was battling heightened militancy and violence in Jammu and Kashmir.

Violence in Kashmir had picked up towards the end of the 1980s. After the Soviet withdrawal from Afghanistan, sections of militants had shifted their focus to Kashmir, launching a wave of militancy in the Valley. The training camps inside Afghanistan, which were allegedly run by the ISI, posed a direct threat to India's security. The ISI relocated many of its Kashmir-focused proxies to eastern Afghanistan to evade US pressure on Pakistan to curb militancy. Pakistan's strategy of supporting asymmetric warfare against the Soviets in Afghanistan was a success. The ISI wanted to follow the same strategy in Kashmir, turning the region's scattered militancy into an organized insurgency.[27] Throughout their regime, the Taliban remained heavily dependent on Pakistan, and were either unwilling or incapable of shutting down the training facilities.

Finally, the hijacking in December 1999 of IC 814, an Indian Airlines Airbus A300 flying from Kathmandu to New Delhi with 180 passengers and crew on board, to Kandahar by Islamist terrorists underscored Indian fears that the Taliban continued to work with the ISI. The plane was hijacked by five Harkat ul-Ansar terrorists, who took it first to Amritsar and then to Lahore and Dubai before landing in Kandahar. Twenty-seven of the 176 passengers were released in Dubai and one was killed. The hijackers wanted three terrorists – Maulana Masood Azhar, Ahmed Omar Saeed Sheikh and Mushtaq Ahmed Zargar – who were in Indian prisons to be released. India dispatched a high-level team, including intelligence official Ajit Doval, who is currently National Security Advisor, to Kabul to negotiate with the hijackers.

After eight days of negotiations, India released the three militants and the hostages were subsequently freed. When Masood Azhar and others were taken to Kandahar airport, Mullah Mansour Akhtar, a top Taliban leader who would become the movement's emir after Mullah Omar's death, was waiting on the tarmac to greet him. Masood Azhar was hugged and welcomed by Akhtar.[28] Doval later said the whole hijacking operation was supported by the ISI. The Taliban were guarding the airport with weapons. 'Two ISI men were on the tarmac and others soon joined them. One was a lieutenant colonel and the other a major, who had spent many years serving in Pakistan,' said Doval. 'To make matters worse, the Indian officials realised the hijackers were communicating directly with ISI officers in Kandahar.'[29]

The Taliban repeatedly claimed they had nothing to do with the hijacking. But as soon as the crisis was over, the Taliban let the militants and the hijackers leave the country. Masood Azhar would surface in Pakistan days later and establish Jaish-e-Mohammed, which would carry out the December 2001 Parliament attack in India. Saeed Sheikh would be arrested in Pakistan in 2002 for the abduction and beheading of American journalist Daniel Pearl. The Taliban would later send India a bill of $111,324 for food, fuel and other services it offered during the eight days of the crisis.[30]

Kashmir militants and their patrons continued to use Afghanistan as a safe haven for their operations, which India saw as a major security challenge. Moreover, the Taliban's total dependence on Pakistan was seen as a significant strategic problem. So India, throughout the period the Taliban were in power, deepened its engagement with the Northern Alliance (NA) commanded by Massoud. India, along with Russia and Iran, offered military and financial aid to the NA via Tajikistan and Iran. The Indian

Air Force opened its first base outside the country in Farkhor, Tajikistan, about 2 km from the Afghan border, mainly to supply Massoud's forces and service his Soviet-era helicopters.[31]

When the US launched the Afghan invasion in 2001, after the 9/11 terrorist attacks, the NA emerged as America's key ally on the battlefield. Massoud had been killed, but his comrades and other commanders came together in an anti-Taliban alliance and fought alongside the Americans. In the post-Taliban administration, the Panjshiris, India's friends who made up the core of the NA, took a critical role. India was naturally in an advantageous position to strengthen ties with the new rulers of Afghanistan. New Delhi saw the period 1996–2001, the only time it supported an opposition militancy, as an interregnum in an otherwise stable relationship with Kabul.

The following two decades saw India and Afghanistan, now under a democratically elected government, deepening their partnership, from economic and security cooperation to counterterrorism and defence. India emerged as the biggest regional investor in post-Taliban Afghanistan. Its investments and commitments ran into $3 billion.[32] India built the Afghan–India Friendship Dam (formerly known as the Salma Dam) in Herat and Kabul's national Parliament building (which came under Taliban attack in June 2015), and developed trade corridors bypassing Pakistan. If India–Afghan trade was virtually non-existent when the Taliban were in power in the 1990s, in 2019–20, it ballooned to $1.5 billion.[33] In 2011, the countries signed a Strategic Partnership Agreement that committed New Delhi to 'assist, as mutually determined, in training, equipping and capacity building programs for Afghan National Security Forces'.[34] India also opened four consulates in Afghanistan – Kandahar, Herat, Mazar-e-Sharif and Jalalabad – besides its embassy in Kabul.

When India returned to its original and consistent approach of working with the government in Kabul, Pakistan, fearing that its strategic depth was at risk, returned to what it had always done in Afghanistan: supporting insurgency. Pakistan saw Indian consulates as outposts for intelligence gathering. It blamed Indian intelligence agents based in Afghanistan for creating instabilities inside Pakistan. Pakistan wanted to undercut India's influence in Afghanistan and install a pro-Islamabad government in Kabul.

The Indian position, however, had a weak spot. It supported Afghanistan's democratic order, made huge investments, deepened security and economic partnership, and built a partnership that stood together on global fora. But India's bet on Afghanistan was heavily dependent on the security provided by American troops in the country. It was almost similar to India's dependence on the Russian presence in Afghanistan in the 1980s for good ties with the Democratic Republic of Afghanistan. When the Americans decided to leave, the Indian position weakened. India had repeatedly called for preserving Afghanistan's 'democracy and constitutional order' but it was not willing to step into the vacuum that would be created by the withdrawal of US forces.[35] The result was that its investments in, and partnership with, the Islamic Republic unravelled quickly as Kabul fell to the Taliban.

Twenty years after the Taliban regime was toppled, Pakistan is once more in an advantageous position with its proxy recapturing Kabul. India, on the other side, faces the same dilemma it faced in 1992 and 1996. An Islamist government, backed by Pakistan, has been formed in Kabul. What should India do? When it faced similar circumstances in 1992 and 1996, it adopted divergent sets of policies. Should India today engage with Taliban 2.0 as it did with the Mujahideen in the early 1990s, or should it work to isolate the Taliban regime, as it did in the late 1990s, and prop up the opposition militancy?

The New Reality

In the past when Afghanistan went through several regime changes – be it Daoud Khan's coup, the communist seizure of power, the Soviet intervention or the Mujahideen regime – India had consistently taken the position that it would deal with the government of the day. These regimes represented different sets of ideologies and posed different sets of challenges to New Delhi. India had warm ties with Zahir Shah who presided over a feudal society and wanted to balance ties between New Delhi and Islamabad. Daoud Khan was a left-oriented modernizer who leaned towards India even as he ratcheted up tensions with Pakistan. The communists implemented radical social and economic reforms. The Soviet intervention posed moral questions to India's foreign policy outlook and its commitment to non-alignment. And the Mujahideen were a completely different brand of politicians. They wanted to re-Islamize Afghanistan. The ideological changes in Kabul had mattered little in India's quest to stay engaged in Afghanistan. This position would change after the Taliban captured Kabul in 1996.

In the 1990s, India's policy towards the Taliban had aligned with the overwhelming regional and international approaches. When they captured power, the Taliban enjoyed the direct support of Pakistan and Saudi Arabia, but most of the regional powers had issues with them. Shia theocratic Iran saw the Sunni Deobandi Taliban, in control next door, as a sectarian, security and geopolitical threat. For Russia, which had been forced to withdraw from Afghanistan a few years earlier by Islamist militancy, the Taliban was a source of instability. The Taliban's support for Islamist militant groups such as the Islamic Movement of Uzbekistan posed a major security challenge to Russia and the former Soviet Central Asian republics.

Even China – which had backed the Mujahideen during the Soviet period and opened political contacts with the Taliban towards the end of their reign – looked at the Taliban's hosting of militants from the East Turkestan Islamic Movement (also called the Turkistan Islamic Party) as a major concern. The US was leading the international pressure campaign against the Taliban as it wanted Kabul to hand over Osama bin Laden and other top al-Qaeda operatives, especially after the 2008 embassy bombings in East Africa. So India did not find it challenging from an operational point of view to offer military and financial aid to the rebels in Panjshir.

But the situation today, with the Taliban's second coming, appears to be different. Most countries that opposed the Taliban or supported their opponents in the past are willing to engage with the Taliban now. The US, which toppled the Taliban regime in 2001, started direct negotiations with them in 2018, entered into a formal agreement in 2020 and pulled back all troops from Afghanistan in 2021 as per that agreement. Iran, which had almost gone to war with the Taliban regime in 1998 after its consulate in Mazar-e-Sharif was attacked and diplomats killed, established contact with the Taliban's top leadership at least as early as 2016.

Russia, which was at the forefront of the global campaign to isolate the Taliban regime in the past and one of the co-sponsors of the UNSC Resolution 1333, hosted talks between the Taliban and the Afghan Peace Council, a non-governmental institution that had the backing of Kabul, in November 2018.[36] Russia would continue to maintain official, direct contacts with the Taliban and hold more meetings with them in Moscow in the following months. China had moved faster. In 2015, when Pakistan hosted the first direct talks between the Afghan government and the Taliban in Murree, on the outskirts of Islamabad, China, along with the

US, had sent its diplomats as observers.[37] In 2019, when the US–Taliban talks were on, China held two meetings with the Taliban (one in June and the other in September).[38] On the other hand, there was no attempt from India to open direct official channels of communication with the Taliban until the last moment.

One possible explanation for India's late and reluctant outreach was that the ruling coalition, led by the Hindu nationalist Bharatiya Janata Party (BJP) of Prime Minister Narendra Modi, was hesitant to openly deal with the Islamist extremists in Afghanistan because of domestic political concerns. When the Taliban were making military advances in Afghanistan, BJP leaders signalled that they would use it to drive their political agenda at home. Amid reports of threats to the Hindu and Sikh minorities in Afghanistan, Prime Minister Modi said on 28 August 2021, 'Keeping the [Sikh] gurus' teachings of humanity at the forefront, the country has passed new laws for its own people who were troubled by such circumstances'; this was a veiled reference to the Citizenship Amendment Act (CAA) 2019 that seeks to fast-track citizenship for minorities in the three Muslim-majority countries in India's neighbourhood: Pakistan, Afghanistan and Bangladesh.[39]

Hardeep Singh Puri, India's Minister for Housing and Urban Affairs in Modi's cabinet, was more direct when he linked the CAA with the developments in Afghanistan. 'Recent developments in our volatile neighbourhood & the way Sikhs & Hindus are going through a harrowing time are precisely why it was necessary to enact the Citizenship Amendment Act,' Puri tweeted on 22 August.[40] Mohan Bhagwat, chief of the Rashtriya Swayamsevak Sangh, the ideological parent of the BJP, said on 15 October that India should be militarily alert and be prepared for all possibilities in the wake of the Taliban's takeover of Afghanistan.[41] But while domestic politics remained a factor, this alone was unlikely to have dictated India's policy towards the Taliban.

A closer analysis suggests there were structural factors as well that slowed down India's outreach. For all the other regional countries that opposed the Taliban in the past, be it Russia, Iran or China, the fundamental issue was the Taliban's support for militants. So when the Taliban were returning to power with increased strength, these countries decided to engage the Taliban directly and address their problems that existed between themselves and the Taliban. But in the case of India, there was a Pakistan factor, which it could not wish away even if it directly dealt with the Taliban. The Taliban are as much supported by Pakistan today as they were in the 1990s. And China was in the forefront of welcoming the Taliban regime, albeit with some concerns. With the US withdrawal and the return of the Taliban, giving an upper hand to two of its geopolitical rivals, India's options were limited.

Despite the ideological differences and structural impediments, India articulated a policy of reluctant engagement. In June 2021, when the Taliban offensive in northern Afghanistan was in full swing, Indian officials made a 'quiet visit' to Doha to meet Taliban officials. While the Indian government kept mum on this meeting, a Qatari government official confirmed it at a public event.[42] After the Taliban captured Kabul, India, like other countries, voiced concerns of human rights violations and extremism but sent signals that it was ready to accept the new reality: that the Taliban were in power in Kabul. In October, India sent a high-level MEA delegation to Moscow to attend a conference of ten countries, including Russia, China, Iran and Central Asian republics, with Taliban Deputy Prime Minister Abdul Salam Hanafi and other officials. India signed a communique issued by all the ten countries that called for 'further practical engagement with Afghanistan' and the need to take into account 'the new reality, that is the Taliban coming to power in the country, irrespective of the official recognition of the new Afghan government by the international community'.[43]

Immediately after the Moscow conference, Taliban spokesperson Zabuhulla Mujahid said, 'Both sides considered it necessary to take into account each other's concerns and improve diplomatic and economic relations.' He also revealed that India had 'finally expressed readiness to provide a wide range of humanitarian assistance to the Afghans'.[44] This marked a clear difference from India's policy towards the former Taliban regime, but stopped short of its decision to engage the Mujahideen in the early 1990s, as New Delhi weighed its reluctance to deal with a regime with which it had deep reservations, against an unfolding economic and humanitarian catastrophe in its neighbourhood.

Conclusion: The Tragedy of Afghanistan

HISTORY IS SAID TO REPEAT ITSELF, FIRST AS TRAGEDY, then, as farce. In the case of Afghanistan, it has simply been tragedy, followed by tragedy. In these chapters, we have told the story of power after power entering, and then failing, to remake Afghanistan as per their vision. Each left behind a trail of destruction, devastation and chaos, while trying to install regimes that would struggle for legitimacy, usually being puppets propped up by these foreign hands, and inevitably collapsing for the next civil war to begin.

One common thread running through this book is the perception among these foreign powers of Afghanistan as a mere chessboard, on which they attempted to play their great games. The focus of this book, in a sense, has been their rise and fall; yet, the most important consequence of this seemingly endless cycle of invasion and civil war, played out over centuries, is the enormous cost borne by the people of Afghanistan.

The Afghan people who should be at the centre of any story about their country have been relegated to the sidelines by power after power; the welfare of the people has always been secondary in their calculations in deciding what's best for Afghanistan. The last three decades in Afghanistan have encapsulated this tragic cycle. As we have seen, when the Mujahideen took over in the early 1990s, they found a country devastated by fifteen years of war. Afghanistan had the world's lowest life expectancy, of just fifty-one years.[1] It had the largest refugee problem, with 3.5 million Afghans living in Pakistan and an estimated 3 million in Iran.[2] As with others who found themselves at the helm, the new government promised to unify the country, bring stability, end violence, and address the social and economic problems, but ultimately failed.

Twenty years later, the US invasion quickly put an end to the Taliban regime, but what transpired thereafter did not pan out as Washington had expected. The invasion of Afghanistan would go down in history as America's longest war. And after two decades of fighting that claimed the lives of hundreds of thousands of Afghans, the American presence would come to an end with an agreement with the very same power that it drove underground.

The US exit in August 2021 and the first months of Taliban rule were marked by a humanitarian catastrophe – one that is unfolding as this book goes to print. In October 2021, the World Food Programme (WFP) said Afghanistan was becoming 'the world's largest humanitarian crisis, with needs surpassing those in Ethiopia, South Sudan, Syria and Yemen'. The WFP's Integrated Food Security Phase Classification (IPC) assessment issued that month – an evaluation of a country's food security – found

22.8 million people were 'at acute risk' while 8.7 million faced 'emergency levels of hunger'. In the ten years that the United Nations had been carrying out IPC evaluations in Afghanistan, this was the most dire assessment.[3]

The WFP report warned that Afghanistan was at risk of becoming 'a collective international failure'. Since the Taliban's return, the economy collapsed. Banks ran out of cash, prompting people to stand in long queues every morning to get hold of what little currency they could to purchase daily necessities. Urban food insecurity for the first time rose to 'similar rates' as a countryside already ravaged by two droughts since 2018. Children were at particular risk. The report said, 'a million children are at risk of severe acute malnutrition, and 2 million more are at risk of moderate acute malnutrition'. Jean-Martin Bauer of the WFP, one of the authors of the assessment, described the situation as 'frightening'.[4]

In October 2021, the leaders of China and Pakistan issued what was described as 'a rare joint appeal' asking the international community to send humanitarian assistance as well as 'unfreeze Afghanistan's assets', with the central bank's $9 billion in reserves, held mostly by the New York Federal Reserve, inaccessible to the Taliban regime. This followed a phone call between President Xi Jinping and Prime Minister Imran Khan.[5] In December 2021, India announced it would provide limited humanitarian assistance, sending medical supplies to deal with a rapidly escalating health crisis. The boxes of medicines were marked 'a gift from the people of India to the people of Afghanistan'.[6]

The grim situation underlined the stark but simple truth at the heart of Afghanistan's future: beyond all the debates and discussions about geopolitical great games, the ability of the regime of the day to stabilize the country is what ultimately matters above all else. And the new Taliban regime was certainly beset by enormous challenges on multiple fronts. Amid the humanitarian crisis, economic collapse and a public health emergency, the Islamic State-Khorasan was rising rapidly, posing a serious security challenge to the Taliban across the country. The Panjshir guerrillas had retreated from the valley, but had not been defeated. And there was no shortage of self-inflicted missteps, with the Taliban's move to build a Pashtun men-only regime in Kabul in its early days, despite all of its public utterances and the pleas from the international community, including China, to build an 'inclusive' new government, already creating resentment among the country's powerful ethnic minorities who had been in the battlefront for decades. The Taliban's mindless extremism, keeping young girls out of school and women from government offices, faced resistance from Afghan civil society which had enjoyed relative freedom in the past two decades. If the Taliban hadn't changed, the people of Afghanistan certainly had.

If the Taliban fails to resolve these internal contradictions, it is entirely possible that the country would fall further into chaos. One possibility is that the Taliban would be even more dependent on Pakistan, as in the 1990s. Yet Pakistan, beset by its own domestic challenges, is hardly in a position to prop up another country. And what of China? As we have seen, Chinese strategists are far from enthused by the prospect of committing resources during these times of instability. While China's appetite for risk has certainly grown, there still remain firm limits to its willingness to extend itself. As we have argued, it remains clear that China's priority is to secure its frontiers, and not conquest.

This viewpoint was captured in the assessment of Mei Xinyu, a scholar at the Chinese Ministry of Commerce, who chastised the 'blind revelry' that followed the US exit among some of his peers and the hype about exploiting mineral resources while the Afghan economy teetered on the brink. As Mei cautioned, it was by no means a given that the Taliban would be able to stay in power. He rightly emphasized the burden faced by an economy crippled under the weight of a history of exploitation that had resulted in the 'failure to build a sustainable economic and industrial base'. Food, he reminded his compatriots in Beijing, remained the first and abiding priority for a country still over-reliant on international aid. And with the US and the West unlikely to continue the levels of aid of the past decade and more, the Taliban regime was facing an enormous challenge – a challenge, he argued, that China certainly could not help address on its own, despite the fanciful talk of Beijing being the next great power in Kabul.[7]

Regionalism, not rivalry, is Afghanistan's best hope. It is also the only path towards breaking the familiar cycle of geopolitical great games that left great costs. Writing from our vantage point, we believe India can play a role, working with regional powers, especially Iran, Russia, the Central Asian republics and, to a limited extent, even China despite its nexus with Pakistan, to forge a coordinated response. This would, of course, challenge India's policy of reluctant engagement.

Any policy of future engagement, or lack thereof, should be based on a realistic assessment of India's interests in Afghanistan, the Taliban's responsiveness and, above all, the interests of the Afghan people. As Jayant Prasad, who was India's ambassador in Kabul when the Indian embassy came under attack in 2008, put it succinctly in an interview, 'What India wants in Afghanistan is very simple – our strategic objective will be served fully if the Afghans have a government that stands on its own feet in terms of decision-making – who it can be friends with, cooperate with, and so on.'[8]

Put simply, India's foreign policy objectives in Afghanistan can be categorized into economic, security and strategic. Having made billions of investments over the past twenty years that also generated goodwill among common Afghans, India would like to protect its investments. The second and more pressing objective is that India would not like Afghanistan returning to the 1990s when the country became a safe haven for anti-India terrorist groups. India is already witnessing a surge in violence in Kashmir and the Taliban could make it worse if they continue to offer support for Pakistan-sponsored militants. Third, in the long term, India would not like to see the Taliban – or for that matter, any regime in Kabul – being a Pakistani satellite. The fourth, finally, is the China factor. The question India faces is whether it should sit on the fence, watching China deepen its footprint in an Afghanistan ruled by a Pakistan-controlled Taliban, or continue its investments in the country and explore the possibility of a Taliban free from the complete control of its regional rivals.

It is obvious that India cannot meet any of these objectives if it cuts off ties with the Taliban. This explains the reluctant outreach we have seen so far. The Taliban, for their part, have repeatedly stated that they want to improve ties with India. Sher Mohammad Abbas Stanikzai, a top Taliban leader, said two weeks after the fall of Kabul, that the group wanted to continue Afghanistan's political, economic and cultural ties with India.[9] Regarding Kashmir, however, the Taliban have sent mixed signals. On 1 September 2021, Anas Haqqani, the influential Taliban leader from the Haqqani Network, said, 'Kashmir is not part of our jurisdiction and interference is against our policy.'[10] But two days later Suhail Shaheen, the Taliban's spokesperson, said, 'As Muslims, we also have a right to raise our voice for Muslims in Kashmir, India or any other country.'[11] If on India's first two objectives there is some scope for engagement, on the third, the Taliban haven't shown any sign, as of now, that they would outgrow Pakistan's influence, which will remain a key challenge for India.

In the past forty years, every regime in Kabul, and its regional backers, chased stability. They all failed to find it. Despite the chaos of the US exit that invoked a second fall of Saigon, Afghanistan is, by no means, a closed chapter for American power, just as Vietnam was not. Indeed, the US exit from Afghanistan will, in a sense, free up greater American resources for its competition with China in the Indo-Pacific theatre, as the world looks at the beginning of a new Cold War – even if its two protagonists are reluctant to call it as such – marked by an increasingly intense US–China rivalry and competition.

The past forty years tell us that great power competition has historically had disastrous consequences for Afghanistan. The past forty years also tell us that there has never been a constant winner. Russia, forced to withdraw by the Mujahideen in 1989, ended up supporting them in the second half of the 1990s. Iran, which came to aid anti-Russian rebels in the 1980s, would work with Russia and India in the subsequent decade to prop up Ahmad Shah Massoud's guerrilla army. India initially backed the communists against the Mujahideen, and then backed the Mujahideen against the Taliban. China supported the Mujahideen against the Soviets, and are now, along with the Russians, courting the Taliban. Through all the churn, and the changing positions on the chessboard, there has only been one constant. That is the continued suffering of the Afghan people. That is the tragedy of Afghanistan.

Notes

Introduction

1. Quoted in Alan Axelrod (2009), *Little-Known Wars of Great and Lasting Impact*, Fair Winds Press, Houston, p. 222.

1: America in Afghanistan

1. 'Letter from Pakistani General Zia to President Carter', *Foreign Relations of the United States, 1977–1980, Vol. XII: Afghanistan*, Document 16, Office of the Historian, 9 May 1978.
2. Mukesh Kumar Kayathwal, 'Pak-Afghan Relations: Durand Line Issue', *Indian Journal of Asian Affairs* 7(2) (December 1994): 37–46.
3. 'Letter from Zia', Document 16.

4. 'Letter from President Carter to Pakistani General Zia', *Foreign Relations of the United States, 1977–1980, Vol. XII: Afghanistan*, Document 23, 9 June 1978.
5. For a detailed account of how the anti-communist insurgency started, see P. Goodson, *Afghanistan's Endless War: State Failure, Regional Politics, and the Rise of the Taliban* (Seattle: University of Washington Press, 2001).
6. In a telegram from the American embassy in Kabul to the Department of State dated 16 August 1978, Ambassador Adolph Dubs wrote about a conversation he had with Hafizullah Amin. Amin was certain that Pakistan was supporting insurgents in Afghanistan. He claimed that Kabul had evidence of Pakistan's complicity in a large number of anti-Afghan cross-border operations to support subversion of the Democratic Republic government. As a comment in the telegram, Ambassador Dubs wrote: 'In spite of everything the Pakistani Govt might be trying to do, anti-DRA operations are probably still being supported through the traditionally porous frontier.' 'Telegram from the Embassy in Afghanistan to the Department of State', *Foreign Policy of the United States, 1977–1980, Vol. III: Afghanistan*, Document 28, Office of the Historian, 16 August 1978.
7. 'Memorandum from the Deputy Director of Central Intelligence to the President's Deputy Assistant for National Security', *Foreign Relations of the United States, 1977–1980, Vol. XII: Afghanistan*, Document 34, Office of the Historian, 26 January 1979.
8. 'How Jimmy Carter and I started the Mujahideen', interview with Zbigniew Brzezinski, *Le Nouvel Observateur* (France), 15–21 January 1998; republished in *Outlook*, 15 November 2001, https://www.outlookindia.com/website/story/how-jimmy-carter-and-i-started-the-mujahideen/213722.

9. 'Memorandum from the President's Assistant for National Security Affairs to President Carter', *Foreign Relations of the United States, 1977–1980, Vol. XII: Afghanistan*, Document 97, Office of the Historian, 26 December 1979.
10. Ibid.
11. Arley Munson, *Kipling's India* (New York: Doubleday, Page & Company, 1915), digitized by the Internet Archive in 2008, 90.
12. Stuart Auerbach, 'Zbig holds his fire at Khyber Pass', *The Washington Post*, 4 February 1980, https://www.washingtonpost.com/archive/politics/1980/02/04/zbig-holds-his-fire-at-khyber-pass/c815197b-7878-40cf-b735-aebd24762dbc/.
13. Video footage of Brzezinski's address was telecast on a CNN show in 2001. 'Encore Presentation: Soldiers of God (transcript)', CNN, 29 September 2001, https://transcripts.cnn.com/show/cp/date/2001-09-29/segment/00.
14. Auerbach, 'Zbig holds his fire'.
15. Michael Rubin, 'Who Is Responsible for the Taliban?', The Washington Institute for Near East Policy, 1 May 2002, https://www.washingtoninstitute.org/policy-analysis/who-responsible-taliban.
16. Ahmed Rashid, 'The Taliban: Exporting Extremism', *Foreign Affairs* 78 (6) (November–December 1999): 22–35.
17. 'NSDD 166 United States Policy, Programs, and Strategy in Afghanistan', National Archives Catalog, 27 March 1985, https://catalog.archives.gov/id/6879761.
18. David B. Ottaway and Patrick E. Tyler, 'US sends new arms to rebels', *The Washington Post*, 30 March 1986, https://www.washingtonpost.com/archive/politics/1986/03/30/us-sends-new-arms-to-rebels/4aa67929-f327-43ec-be3a-0649b867ff4c/.

19. For a detailed review of America's Stinger policy towards the Afghan Mujahideen, see Alan J. Kuperman, 'The Stinger Missile and US Intervention in Afghanistan', *Political Science Quarterly* 114 (2) (Summer 1999): 219–63.
20. Christian Parenti, 'America's Jihad: A History of Origins', *Social Justice* 28 (3) (Fall 2001): 31–38.
21. Rod Nordland, 'The empire stopper', *The New York Times*, 29 August 2017, https://www.nytimes.com/2017/08/29/world/asia/afghanistan-graveyard-empires-historical-pictures.html.
22. Robert Fisk, *The Great War for Civilisation* (London: HarperCollins, 2005), 7.
23. Lawrence Wright, *The Looming Tower: Al-Qaeda and the Road to 9/11* (New York: Knopf, 2005), 145.
24. Robert Fisk, 'Anti-Soviet warrior puts his army on the road to peace', *Independent*, 6 December 1993; republished on 4 November 2020, https://www.independent.co.uk/news/long_reads/robert-fisk-osama-bin-laden-interview-sudan-1993-b1562374.html.
25. Ibid.
26. Steve Coll, *Ghost Wars: The Secret History of the CIA, Afghanistan, and Bin Laden, from the Soviet Invasion to September 10, 2001* (New York: Penguin Press, 2005), 72.
27. According to the 9/11 Commission Report, Saudi officials apparently wanted Bin Laden expelled from Sudan. They had already revoked his citizenship, however, and would not tolerate his presence in their country. Also, Bin Laden may have no longer felt safe in Sudan, where he had already escaped at least one assassination attempt that he believed to have been the work of the Egyptian or Saudi regimes, and paid for by the CIA. 'Response to al-Qaeda's Initial Assaults', *The 9/11 Commission*

Report: Final Report of the National Commission on Terrorist Attacks Upon the United States, 22 July 2004. The full report can be downloaded from https://www.govinfo.gov/app/details/GPO-911REPORT/GPO-911REPORT-10/context.

28. For Arabic and English versions of Osama bin Laden's edict, see 'Declaration of Jihad against the Americans Occupying the Land of the Two Holiest Sites', Combating Terrorism Centre, Reference Number: AFGP-2002-003676, https://ctc.usma.edu/harmony-program/declaration-of-jihad-against-the-americans-occupying-the-land-of-the-two-holiest-sites-original-language-2/.
29. 'Jihad Against Jews and Crusaders: World Islamic Front Statement', 23 February 1998, https://irp.fas.org/world/para/docs/980223-fatwa.htm.
30. 'America is under attack: Bush was in Sarasota classroom when grim news came', Fox News, 7 September 2021, https://www.fox13news.com/news/america-is-under-attack-bush-was-in-sarasota-classroom-when-grim-news-came.
31. A former Taliban leader quoted Mullah Omar as saying this in an interview. Steve Coll, 'Looking for Mullah Omar: Will the United States be able to negotiate with a man it has hunted for a decade?', *The New Yorker*, 23 January 2012, https://www.newyorker.com/magazine/2012/01/23/looking-for-mullah-omar.
32. At the end of April 1969 – just over four years after US combat units were deployed in Vietnam – the number of US forces in Southeast Asia reached its peak. That month, approximately 549,500 Americans were stationed in the region. 'Week of April 28', *The USA Vietnam War Commemoration*, https://www.vietnamwar50th.com/education/week_of_april_28/.

33. In his Presidential nomination acceptance speech at the Republican National Convention in Miami, Richard Nixon said, 'I pledge to you tonight that the first priority foreign policy objective of our next Administration will be to bring an honorable end to the war in Vietnam. We shall not stop there – we need a policy to prevent more Vietnams.' Richard M. Nixon, 'Presidential Nomination Acceptance Speech', 8 August 1968, 4President.org, http://www.4president.org/speeches/nixon1968acceptance.htm. After becoming President, he put this policy into practice by launching talks with Vietnamese guerrillas. On 24 January 1973, Nixon gave the 'peace with honor' speech, ending US involvement in the Vietnam war. 'Transcript of the speech by President on Vietnam', 24 January 1973, *The New York Times*, https://www.nytimes.com/1973/01/24/archives/transcript-of-the-speech-by-president-on-vietnam-essential.html.
34. Daniel Ellsberg, 'The Quagmire Myth and the Stalemate Machine', *Public Policy* 19 (2) (Spring 1971): 217–74.
35. Louis Menand, 'What went wrong in Vietnam: The military historian Max Boot takes on the counter-insurgency maven Edward Lansdale', 26 February 2018, *The New Yorker*, https://www.newyorker.com/magazine/2018/02/26/what-went-wrong-in-vietnam.
36. Sam Gollob and Michael E. O'Hanlon, 'Afghanistan Index: Tracking Variables of Reconstruction and Security in Post-9/11 Afghanistan', Foreign Policy at Brookings, August 2020, https://www.brookings.edu/research/afghanistan-index/.
37. 'Agreement for Bringing Peace to Afghanistan between the Islamic Emirate of Afghanistan which is not recognized by the United States as a state and is known as the Taliban and the United States of America', 29 February 2020, US Department of State.

38. Helene Cooper, Thomas Gibbons-Neff and Eric Schmitt, 'Biden to withdraw all combat troops from Afghanistan by Sept. 11', *The New York Times*, 13 April 2021, https://www.nytimes.com/2021/04/13/us/politics/biden-afghanistan-withdrawal.html; Kevin Liptak, Phil Mattingly, Kaitlan Collins and John Harwood, 'Biden keeps August 31 deadline to withdraw from Afghanistan: "The sooner we finish the better"', CNN, 24 August 2021, https://edition.cnn.com/2021/08/24/politics/joe-biden-g7-afghanistan/index.html.
39. 'Remarks by President Biden on the End of the War in Afghanistan', The White House, 31 August 2021, https://www.whitehouse.gov/briefing-room/speeches-remarks/2021/08/31/remarks-by-president-biden-on-the-end-of-the-war-in-afghanistan/.
40. Ibid.
41. 'Remarks by President Biden on the Drawdown of US Forces in Afghanistan', The White House, 8 July 2021, https://www.whitehouse.gov/briefing-room/speeches-remarks/2021/07/08/remarks-by-president-biden-on-the-drawdown-of-u-s-forces-in-afghanistan/.
42. 'Tomorrow the Taliban will start surrendering their weapons. I think we should go home,' the Taliban's spokesman, Mullah Abdul Salam Zaeef, said on 7 December 2001. Quoted in Max Fisher, 'The contradiction that doomed America's mission in Afghanistan', *The New York Times*, 16 April 2021, https://www.nytimes.com/2021/04/16/world/asia/interpreter-afghanistan-war.html; also see Alissa J. Rubin, 'Did the war in Afghanistan have to happen?', *The New York Times*, 23 August 2021, https://www.nytimes.com/2021/08/23/world/middleeast/afghanistan-taliban-deal-united-states.html.
43. During a press briefing, when US State Department spokesperson Ned Price was asked about sharing information regarding the

security of Kabul airport with the Taliban and whether it was extended to the Haqqani Network, Price replied, 'The Taliban and Haqqani Network are two separate entities.' 'Haqqani Network, Taliban separate, says US, as Pakistani terrorist emerges in Afghanistan', NDTV, 28 August 2021, https://www.ndtv.com/world-news/haqqani-network-taliban-separate-says-us-as-pak-terrorist-khalil-haqqani-emerges-in-afghanistan-2521472.

44. 'Address to a Joint Session of Congress and the American People', The White House, 20 September 2001, https://georgewbush-whitehouse.archives.gov/news/releases/2001/09/20010920-8.html.
45. 'Today, the terrorist threat has metastasized beyond Afghanistan. So, we are repositioning our resources and adapting our counterterrorism posture to meet the threats where they are now significantly higher: in South Asia, the Middle East, and Africa,' Biden said on 8 July 2021. 'Remarks by President Biden on the Drawdown of US Forces in Afghanistan'.

2: The Rise of the Mullahs

1. Graeme Wood, 'Security blanket', *The Atlantic*, January/February 2009, https://www.theatlantic.com/magazine/archive/2009/01/security-blanket/307202/.
2. 'The cloak of the Prophet', NPR, 10 January 2002, https://web.archive.org/web/20020118133536/https://www.npr.org/news/specials/response/mobilization/features/2002/jan/cloak/020110.cloak.html.
3. Norimitsu Onishi, 'A tale of the mullah and Muhammad's amazing cloak', *The New York Times*, 19 December 2001, https://www.nytimes.com/2001/12/19/international/asia/a-tale-of-the-mullah-and-muhammads-amazing-cloak.html.

4. Steve Coll, 'Looking for Mullah Omar', *The New Yorker*, 15 January 2012, https://www.newyorker.com/magazine/2012/01/23/looking-for-mullah-omar.
5. Nabi Muhammadi would go on to become the Vice President of the post-communist Mujahideen government. When the Taliban were formed, he dissolved the Harakat Inquilab i-Islami, which was already fading, and urged his supporters to join the Taliban. Diplomatic cable from the US Department of State to Embassies, 3 October 1996. The National Security Archive of George Washington University obtained the cable under the Freedom of Information Act, and published it on its website, https://nsarchive2.gwu.edu/.
6. Steve Coll, 'Looking for Mullah Omar'.
7. Abdul Salam Zaeef, *My Life with the Taliban* (London: Hurst, 2010), Kindle.
8. Ibid.
9. 'Afghanistan Population', World Population Review, 2021, https://worldpopulationreview.com/countries/afghanistan-population.
10. 'Life Expectancy at Birth, Total (Years) – Afghanistan', The World Bank, https://data.worldbank.org/indicator/SP.DYN.LE00.IN?locations=AF.
11. Daniel P. Sullivan, 'Tinder, Spark, Oxygen, and Fuel: The Mysterious Rise of the Taliban', *Journal of Peace Research* 44 (1) (January 2007): 93–108.
12. In *Javid Nama* (Book of Eternity), his Persian book of poetry, Muhammad Iqbal writes: 'Asia is like a human body, made of Water and Clay, and the Afghan nation in that body is like the heart!' Muhammad Iqbal, *Javid Nama* (London: Routledge Library Editions, 2012), Kindle.

13. Olivier Roy and Mariam Abou Zahab, *Islamist Networks: The Afghan-Pakistan Connection*, trans. John King (New York: Columbia University Press, 2004), 14.
14. Ahmad Rashid, *Taliban: The Power of Militant Islam in Afghanistan and Beyond* (London: I.B. Tauris, 2010), Kindle.
15. John F. Burns and Steve Levine, 'How Afghans' stern rulers took hold', *The New York Times*, 31 December 1996, https://www.nytimes.com/1996/12/31/world/how-afghans-stern-rulers-took-hold.html.
16. Ibid.
17. Originally reported by Rahimullah Yusufzai for the Pakistani daily *The News* on 2 February 1995. Cited in Parvez Ahmad, 'Uniqueness of History: Sudden Rise and Rapid Fall of Taliban in Afghanistan', *IOSR Journal of Humanities and Social Science* 19 (2) (February 2014): 40–48.
18. Carlotta Gall, *The Wrong Enemy: America in Afghanistan, 2001–2014* (London: Penguin Books, 2014), 43.
19. 'Afghanistan: Background Information on the Taliban Movement', Research Directorate, Immigration and Refugee Board, Canada, 1 July 1995, https://www.refworld.org/docid/3ae6ad3ac.html.
20. For details on the truck episode, see Sullivan, 'Tinder, Spark, Oxygen, and Fuel'.
21. Burns and Levine, 'How Afghans' stern rulers took hold'.
22. Ahmad, 'Uniqueness of History'.
23. Following the Afghan government's allegations that Pakistan was directly supporting the Taliban, a violent mob of 5,000 protesters stormed the Pakistani embassy in Kabul on 6 September 1995, a day after Herat fell. One employee at the embassy was killed and twenty-six others were injured, including the ambassador. On the same day, Iran closed its border with Afghanistan.

Rizwan Hussain, *Pakistan and the Emergence of Islamic Militancy in Afghanistan* (Farnham: Ashgate, 2005), 203.

24. According to the accord, known as the Mahipar Agreement, both Rabbani and Hekmatyar agreed to cooperate in the organization of fresh elections and establishment of a 'real Islamic government'. In July 1996, Hekmatyar was restored as Prime Minister. But the alliance had little impact on the ground as the Taliban would take Kabul within months. See *A Political Chronology of Central, South and East Asia* (London: Europa Publications, Routledge), 9.
25. The clergy assembled at the Shura pledged their allegiance to Mullah Omar's leadership. 'Afghanistan: Chronology of Events, January 1995–February 1997', Issue Paper by the Immigration and Refugee Board of Canada, 1 October 1997, 12.
26. Ibid., 15.
27. Terence White, 'Flashback: When the Taleban took Kabul', BBC, 15 October 2001, http://news.bbc.co.uk/2/hi/south_asia/1600136.stm.
28. John F. Burns, 'Islamic rule weighs heavily for Afghans', *The New York Times*, 24 September 1997, https://www.nytimes.com/1997/09/24/world/islamic-rule-weighs-heavily-for-afghans.html.
29. On 30 September 1996, Wakil Ahmed, the Taliban's spokesperson, told reporters in Kabul that 'women should not report to work, they should stay home'. Cited in Neamatollah Nojumi, *The Rise of the Taliban in Afghanistan: Mass Mobilisation, Civil War, and the Future of the Region* (New York: Palgrave, 2002), 154.
30. John F. Burns, 'The fiercely faithful – A special report: From Cold War, Afghans inherit brutal new age', *The New York Times*, 14 February 1996, https://www.nytimes.com/1996/02/14/world/fiercely-faithful special-report-cold-war-afghans-inherit-brutal-new-age.html.

31. Nojumi, *The Rise of the Taliban*, 154.
32. Ibid.
33. 'Afghanistan: The World Factbook,' CIA, updated on 29 September 2021, https://www.cia.gov/the-world-factbook/countries/afghanistan/.
34. An investigation by Afghanistan's TOLO News found that the Sikh and Hindu population was 220,000 in the 1980s. That number fell sharply to 15,000 when the Mujahideen were in power during 1992–96 and remained at that level during the Taliban regime. As of 2016, there were only 150 Hindus and Sikhs in the country. 'Nearly 99% of Hindus, Sikhs left Afghanistan in last three decades', TOLO News, 20 June 2016, https://tolonews.com/afghanistan/nearly-99-hindus-sikhs-left-afghanistan-last-three-decades.
35. Nushin Arbabzadah, 'The story of the Afghan Jews is one of remarkable tolerance', *The Guardian*, 28 February 2012, https://www.theguardian.com/commentisfree/belief/2012/feb/28/afghan-jews-tolerance.
36. 'The Taliban's ideology has surprising roots in British-ruled India', NPR, 8 September 2021, https://www.npr.org/2021/09/08/1034754547/taliban-ideology-roots-deobandi-islam-india.
37. Sana Haroon, 'The Rise of Deobandi Islam in the North-West Frontier Province and Its Implications in Colonial India and Pakistan, 1914–1996', *Journal of the Royal Asiatic Society* 18(1) (January 2008): 47–70.
38. Khwaja Khusro Tariq, 'Lessons from Islamic History: Ibn Taymiyyah and the Synthesis of Takfir', HuffPost, 31 May 2016, https://www.huffpost.com/entry/ibn-taymiyyah-and-the-syn_b_10096820.

39. Stanly Johny, *The ISIS Caliphate: From Syria to the Doorsteps of India* (New Delhi: Bloomsbury India, 2018), 58–59.
40. Naseer Ahmed, 'Who and what is a Deobandi?', *New Age Islam*, 24 August 2014, https://www.newageislam.com/islamic-ideology/naseer-ahmed-new-age-islam/-deobandi/d/98711.
41. Ibid.
42. Rashid, *Taliban*, 2010.
43. Hassan Abbas, *The Taliban Revival: Violence and Extremism on the Pakistan–Afghanistan Frontier* (London: Yale University Press, 2014), 67.
44. 'Islamic Parties in Pakistan', International Crisis Group, Report 216, 12 December 2011, https://www.crisisgroup.org/asia/south-asia/pakistan/islamic-parties-pakistan.
45. Shahid Javed Burki, *Historical Dictionary of Pakistan*, 4th edition (New York: Rowman & Littlefield, 2015), 292.
46. Rashid, *Taliban*.
47. Imtiaz Ali, 'The Father of the Taliban: An Interview with Maulana Sami ul-Haq', The Jamestown Foundation, 23 May 2007, https://jamestown.org/interview/the-father-of-the-taliban-an-interview-with-maulana-sami-ul-haq/.
48. 'Maulana Fazlur Rehman', *Dawn*, 5 April 2013, https://www.dawn.com/news/800487.
49. The Deobandi madrassas were estimated to have sent some 30,000 students to join the Taliban over the period of the movement's rise and reign. Abbas, *The Taliban Revival*, 68.
50. Barbara D. Metcalf, 'Traditionalist Islamic Activism: Deoband, Tablighis, and Talibs', Insights from the Social Sciences, Social Science Research Council, 1 November 2001, https://items.ssrc.org/after-september-11/traditionalist-islamic-activism-deoband-tablighis-and-talibs/.

51. Omar issued a decree on 26 February, ordering the elimination of all non-Islamic statues and sanctuaries in Afghanistan. By 14 March, the Taliban announced that it had completed the destruction of the statues. Pierre Centlivres, 'The Death of the Buddhas of Bamiyan', The Middle East Institute, 18 August 2012, https://www.mei.edu/publications/death-buddhas-bamiyan#edn1.
52. Rahimullah Yusufzai, 'Mullah Omar sought to stabilize Afghanistan under Taliban rule', *Al Jazeera*, 6 August 2015, http://america.aljazeera.com/articles/2015/8/6/Mullah-Omar-fighter-on-divine-mission-to-restore-peace-in-Afghanistan.html.
53. Diplomatic cable from the Embassy of the US in Islamabad to the US Secretary of State, 31 December 1998, National Security Archive, George Washington University.
54. According to an April 1998 diplomatic cable from the US embassy in Islamabad, there were deep disagreements between Omar and Rabbani, who was the Taliban's main interlocutor with the international community. But by 1997, Mullah Rabbani and his close associates were 'purged'. Diplomatic cable from the US Embassy in Islamabad to the Department of State, Washington, DC, 7 April 1998, National Security Archive, George Washington University.
55. Diplomatic cable, 31 December 1998.

3: The Generals' Proxies

1. Richard Lei, 'A cloak but no dagger', *The Washington Post*, 18 May 2002, https://www.washingtonpost.com/archive/lifestyle/2002/05/18/a-cloak-but-no-dagger/95bc838e-2beb-4c72-807a-0ab14668c2ca/.

2. US diplomatic cable from the Secretary of State, Washington, DC, to the American Embassy in Islamabad, 13 September 2001, National Security Archive, George Washington University.
3. Hassan Abbas, 'Inside Story of Musharraf–Mahmood Tussle', Harvard Kennedy School: Belfast Center for Science and International Affairs, 26 September 2006, https://www.belfercenter.org/publication/inside-story-musharraf-mahmood-tussle.
4. All quotations in this section are from the US diplomatic cable from the embassy in Islamabad to the Secretary of State, Washington, DC, 13 September 2001, redacted cable obtained by the National Security Archive, George Washington University.
5. George W. Bush, *Decision Points* (London: Virgin Books, 2010), 188.
6. Mary Schons, 'The Durand Line: A historic, disputed border separates Afghanistan and Pakistan', *National Geographic,* 21 January 2011, https://www.nationalgeographic.org/article/durand-line/.
7. Amit Chaturvedi, '"Pakistan our second home, there is peace in Afghanistan": Taliban spokesperson', *Hindustan Times*, 26 August 2021, https://www.hindustantimes.com/world-news/pakistan-our-second-home-there-is-peace-in-afghanistan-taliban-spokesperson-101629960082702.html.
8. Bush, *Decision Points*, 213.
9. Khalid Sheikh Mohammed would provide crucial information to the CIA and FBI regarding al-Qaeda's attack plans during his interrogation. Peter Finn, Joby Warrick and Julie Tate, 'How a detainee became an asset', *The Washington Post*, 29 August 2009, https://www.washingtonpost.com/wp-

dyn/content/article/2009/08/28/AR2009082803874.html?sid=ST2009082804015.

10. Steve Coll, *Directorate S: The CIA and America's Secret Wars in Afghanistan and Pakistan, 2001–2016* (London: Allen Lane, 2018), Kindle.
11. Bette Dam, *A Man and a Motorcycle: How Hamid Karzai Came to Power* (Utrecht: Ipso Facto, 2014), Kindle.
12. Thomas Ruttig, 'With a Little Help From His Friends: A New Biography of Hamed Karzai', Afghanistan Analysts Network, 1 September 2014, https://www.afghanistan-analysts.org/en/reports/context-culture/with-a-little-help-from-his-friends-a-new-biography-of-hamed-karzai/.
13. 'Rumsfeld: Major combat over in Afghanistan', CNN, 1 May 2003, https://edition.cnn.com/2003/WORLD/asiapcf/central/05/01/afghan.combat/.
14. Carlotta Gall, *The Wrong Enemy: America in Afghanistan, 2001–2014* (London: Penguin Books, 2014), 67–68.
15. 'Taliban leaflets urge uprising', CNN, 9 June 2003, http://edition.cnn.com/2003/WORLD/asiapcf/central/06/09/afghan.leaflets/.
16. '"We are hunting Americans like pigs", Interview with Mullah Omar', Rediff, 12 April 2004, https://www.rediff.com/news/2004/apr/12inter.htm.
17. Carlotta Gall, 'U.S. troops still missing after crash in Afghanistan', *The New York Times*, 2 July 2005, https://www.nytimes.com/2005/07/02/world/asia/us-troops-still-missing-after-crash-in-afghanistan.html.
18. Marcus Luttrell, *Lone Survivor: The Incredible True Story of Navy SEALs Under Siege* (London: Sphere, 2014).

19. James Dobbins, Jason H. Campbell, Laurel E. Miller and S. Rebecca Zimmerman, 'DDR in Afghanistan: Disarming, Demobilizing, and Reintegrating Afghan Combatants in Accordance with a Peace Agreement', Rand Corporation, February 2020, https://www.rand.org/pubs/perspectives/PE343.html.
20. Coll, *Directorate S.*
21. Ron Synovitz, 'Afghanistan: Karzai to consult Pakistan about suicide bombings', Radio Free Europe/Radio Liberty, 15 February 2006, https://www.rferl.org/a/1065816.html.
22. Coll, *Directorate S.*
23. Gall, *The Wrong Enemy*, 143.
24. US diplomatic cable from the embassy in Kabul to the Secretary of State, Washington, DC, February 2006, National Security Archive, George Washington University.
25. Bush, *Decision Points*, 215.
26. Matt Waldman, 'The Sun is the Sky: The Relationship between Pakistan's ISI and Afghan Insurgents, Discussion', Paper 18, Destin Development Studies Institute, London School of Economics, June 2010.
27. Eric Schmitt and Mark Mazzetti, 'Taliban widen Afghan attacks from base in Pakistan', *The New York Times*, 23 September 2009, https://www.nytimes.com/2009/09/24/world/asia/24military.html.
28. Mark Mazzetti and Dexter Filkins, 'Secret joint raid captures Taliban's top commander', *The New York Times*, 15 February 2010, https://www.nytimes.com/2010/02/16/world/asia/16intel.html.
29. Dexter Filkins, 'Pakistanis tell of motive in Taliban leader's arrest', *The New York Times*, 22 August 2010, https://www.nytimes.com/2010/08/23/world/asia/23taliban.html.

30. Dexter Filkins, 'Taliban elite, aided by NATO, join talks for Afghan peace', *The New York Times*, 19 October 2020, https://www.nytimes.com/2010/10/20/world/asia/20afghan.html.
31. Jon Boone, 'Fake Taliban leader "dupes Nato negotiators"', *The Guardian*, 23 November 2010, https://www.theguardian.com/world/2010/nov/23/fake-taliban-dupes-nato-negotiators.
32. 'Taliban and Afghan government hold talks in Pakistan', *Al Jazeera*, 8 July 2015, https://www.aljazeera.com/news/2015/7/8/taliban-and-afghan-government-hold-talks-in-pakistan.
33. Lynne O'Donnel, 'Afghanistan says Taliban leader Mullah Omar died 2 years ago', Associated Press, 30 July 2015, https://apnews.com/article/8aea0d55437f4bac9f0356cf0510a69b.
34. Joseph Goldstein and Taimoor Shah, 'Death of Mullah Omar exposes divisions within Taliban', *The New York Times*, 30 July 2015, https://www.nytimes.com/2015/07/31/world/asia/taliban-confirm-death-of-mullah-omar-and-weigh-successor.html.
35. Borhan Osman, 'The Murree Process: Divisive Peace Talks Further Complicated by Mullah Omar's Death', Afghanistan Analysts Network, 5 August 2015, https://www.afghanistan-analysts.org/en/reports/war-and-peace/the-murree-process-divisive-peace-talks-further-complicated-by-mullah-omars-death/.
36. For more on the Haqqani Network, see Jeffrey A. Dressler, 'The Haqqani Network from Pakistan to Afghanistan', Institute for the Study of War, October 2010.
37. 'President Trump outlines new Afghanistan strategy: Full transcript', CBS News, 21 August 2017, https://www.cbsnews.com/news/president-trump-outlines-new-afghanistan-strategy-full-transcript/.

38. Foreign Minister Shah Mehmood Qureshi, after a meeting with US Secretary of State Mike Pompeo in Washington, DC in September 2018, said, 'Today, I told him we fulfilled our promise. The Taliban came to the table. Then you said the delegation should be authoritative and powerful, we did that.' Anwar Iqbal, 'Pakistan wants US to get it off FATF grey list', *Dawn*, 19 January 2020, https://www.dawn.com/news/1529245.
39. Ron Moreau, 'Meet the Taliban's new chief', *Newsweek*, 24 July 2009, https://www.newsweek.com/meet-talibans-new-chief-81727.
40. 'Pakistan: Shoring Up Afghanistan's Peace Process', Briefing 169, International Crisis Group, 30 June 2021, https://www.crisisgroup.org/asia/south-asia/pakistan/b169-pakistan-shoring-afghanistans-peace-process.
41. For the full text of the agreement, see 'Agreement for Bringing Peace to Afghanistan between the Islamic Emirate of Afghanistan which is not recognized by the United States as a state and is known as the Taliban and the United States of America', US Department of State, 29 February 2020.

4: The Fall of Kabul

1. 'Blinken proposes new steps to peace, keeps May 1st pullout option', TOLO News, 7 March 2021, https://tolonews.com/afghanistan-170509, https://tolonews.com/pdf/02.pdf.
2. Dexter Filkins, 'Last exit from Afghanistan', *The New Yorker*, 1 March 2001, https://www.newyorker.com/magazine/2021/03/08/last-exit-from-afghanistan.
3. Gordon Lubold and Yaroslav Trofimov, 'Afghan government could collapse six months after US withdrawal, new intelligence assessment says', *The Wall Street Journal*, 23 June 2021, https://

www.wsj.com/articles/afghan-government-could-collapse-six-months-after-u-s-withdrawal-new-intelligence-assessment-says-11624466743.

4. Dan Lamothe, John Hudson, Shane Harris and Anne Gearan, 'US officials warn collapse of Afghan capital could come sooner than expected', *The Washington Post*, 10 August 2021, https://www.washingtonpost.com/national-security/2021/08/10/afghanistan-intelligence-assessment/.
5. Sayed Salahuddin, 'Do or die: President Ghani rejects idea for interim government in Afghanistan', *Arab News*, 21 February 2021, https://www.arabnews.com/node/1813281/world.
6. Karen DeYoung, 'US proposes interim power-sharing government with Taliban in Afghanistan', *The Washington Post*, 8 March 2021, https://www.washingtonpost.com/national-security/us-afghan-letter-peace-talks/2021/03/07/c30ef2c2-7f75-11eb-9ca6-54e187ee4939_story.html.
7. Rezaul H. Laskar, 'Afghan president Ghani hits out at terror by Pak', *Hindustan Times*, 17 July 2021, https://www.hindustantimes.com/india-news/afghan-president-ghani-hits-out-at-terror-by-pak-101626459194675.html.
8. Suhasini Haidar, 'Taliban has won battles, we will win the war: Afghan President Ghani', *The Hindu*, 17 July 2021, https://www.thehindu.com/news/international/taliban-has-won-battles-we-will-win-war-afghan-president-ghani/article35379659.ece.
9. Ashraf Ghani, *Production and Domination: Afghanistan, 1747–1901* (New York: Columbia University, 1982).
10. Ashraf Ghani, *Fixing Failed States: A Framework for Rebuilding a Fractured World* (London: Oxford University Press, 2009).
11. Stanly Johny, 'The President in his labyrinth', *The Hindu*, 17 July 2021, https://www.thehindu.com/news/international/ashraf-ghani-the-president-in-his-labyrinth/article35385728.ece.

12. George Packer, 'Afghanistan's theorist-in-chief', *The New Yorker*, 4 July 2016, https://www.newyorker.com/magazine/2016/07/04/ashraf-ghani-afghanistans-theorist-in-chief.
13. In 2014, Abdullah Abdullah was made the chief executive of the government, a position created for him as part of a compromise. In 2020, he was appointed the chairman of the High Council for National Reconciliation that was tasked with negotiating with the Taliban. 'Profile: Abdullah Abdullah', *Al Jazeera*, 29 September 2016, https://www.aljazeera.com/features/2014/9/29/profile-abdullah-abdullah.
14. Adam Nossiter, 'Afghan President in "desperate situation" as his power is undermined', *The New York Times*, 10 April 2021, https://www.nytimes.com/2021/04/10/world/asia/afghanistan-ashraf-ghani.html.
15. Mujib Mashal, 'Taliban and US strike deal to withdraw American troops from Afghanistan', *The New York Times*, 29 February 2020, https://www.nytimes.com/2020/02/29/world/asia/us-taliban-deal.html.
16. 'Top US general says Afghan collapse can be traced to Trump–Taliban deal', *The Guardian*, 29 September 2021, https://www.theguardian.com/us-news/2021/sep/29/frank-mckenzie-doha-agreement-trump-taliban.
17. Paul D. Shinkman, 'Number of private contractors in Afghanistan drops precipitously as Biden pushes withdrawal plan', *US News*, 21 July 2021, https://www.usnews.com/news/world-report/articles/2021-07-21/number-of-private-military-contractors-in-afghanistan-drops-precipitously-as-biden-pushes-withdrawal-plan.
18. Phil Stewart and Idrees Ali, Hamid Shalizi, 'Afghan pilots assassinated by Taliban as US withdraws', *Reuters*, 9 July 2021,

https://www.reuters.com/world/asia-pacific/afghan-pilots-assassinated-by-taliban-us-withdraws-2021-07-09/.

19. Yaroslav Trofimov and Ehsanullah Amiri, 'Taliban find new revenues as they seize Afghanistan's US-built border gateway', *The Wall Street Journal*, 5 July 2021, https://www.wsj.com/articles/taliban-find-new-revenues-as-they-seize-afghanistans-u-s-built-border-gateway-11625495521.
20. Yaroslav Trofimov, 'How the Taliban overran the Afghan army, built by the US over 20 years', *The Wall Street Journal*, 14 August 2021, https://www.wsj.com/articles/afghanistan-army-collapse-taliban-11628958253.
21. Yaroslav Trofimov, Alan Cullison and Ehsanullah Amiri, 'Afghan Taliban seize Herat, move into Kandahar after taking Ghazni', *The Wall Street Journal*, 12 August 2021, https://www.wsj.com/articles/afghan-taliban-seize-herat-move-into-kandahar-after-taking-ghazni-11628789620.
22. 'Ghani vows to prevent further instability in Afghanistan', TOLO News, 14 August 2021, https://tolonews.com/afghanistan-174226.
23. Mohamed Madi, Ahmad Khalid and Sayed Abdullah Nizami, 'Chaos and confusion: The frenzied final hours of the Afghan government', BBC, 8 September 2021, https://www.bbc.com/news/world-asia-58477131.
24. After leaving Kabul on 15 August, Ghani re-emerged in the UAE from where he released a video message in which he drew parallels between himself and Najibullah, without naming him. 'The decision was made that whatever happened 25 years ago would be repeated if I had stayed the President of Afghanistan. I would have been hanged in front of the eyes of the people of Afghanistan and this would have been a dreadful disaster in our history,' he said. Mostafa Salem, Tara John, Tim Lister

and Hannah Ritchie, 'Former Afghan President Ashraf Ghani emerges in the UAE', CNN, 18 August 2021, https://edition.cnn.com/2021/08/18/asia/afghanistan-taliban-ashraf-ghani-intl/index.html.

25. Carlotta Gall, Daniel Victor and Ruhullah Khapalwak, 'The Taliban take over the presidential palace', *The New York Times*, 16 August 2021, https://www.nytimes.com/2021/08/16/world/asia/taliban-presidential-palace-afghanistan.html.
26. 'New "inclusive" Afghanistan government to be announced soon: Taliban', Asian News International, 5 September 2021, https://www.aninews.in/news/world/asia/new-inclusive-afghanistan-government-to-be-announced-soon-taliban20210905162757/.
27. Frud Bezhan, 'Taliban imposes new dress code, segregation of women at Afghan universities', Gandhara RFE/RL, 6 September 2021, https://gandhara.rferl.org/a/taliban-dress-code-segregation-women/31446726.html.
28. Yaroslav Trofimov, 'Taliban unveil new Afghan government', *The Wall Street Journal*, 7 September 2021, https://www.wsj.com/articles/taliban-crack-down-on-protest-led-by-women-in-kabul-11631014019.
29. 'Taliban rejects U.N. demand, won't surrender Bin Laden "at any price"', *Los Angeles Times*, 17 October 1999, https://www.latimes.com/archives/la-xpm-1999-oct-17-mn-23280-story.html.
30. 'Consolidated United Nations Security Council Sanctions List', United Nations, generated on 2 October 2015, https://www.un.org/french/sc/committees/consolidated.htm.
31. Diplomatic cable from the US Embassy in Islamabad to the Secretary of State, Washington, DC, December 1997, National Security Archive, George Washington University.

32. US intelligence assessment on Mullah Omar and his Council of Ministers, sent to the Defence Intelligence Agency, 11 November 2001, National Security Archive, George Washington University.
33. Thomas Joscelyn, 'Taliban blames America for 9/11 in video celebrating its own suicide squads', *FDD's Long War Journal*, 3 September 2021, https://www.longwarjournal.org/archives/2021/09/taliban-blames-america-for-9-11-in-video-celebrating-its-own-suicide-squads.php.
34. Steve Coll, *Ghost Wars: The Secret History of the CIA, Afghanistan and Bin Laden, from the Soviet Invasion to September 10, 2001* (London: Penguin Books, 2004), Kindle.
35. Ibid.
36. Jon Boone, 'Osama bin Laden death: Afghanistan "had Abbottabad lead four years ago"', *The Guardian*, 5 May 2011, https://www.theguardian.com/world/2011/may/05/osama-bin-laden-afghan-intelligence-abbottabad-lead.
37. Coll, *Ghost Wars*.
38. Boone, 'Osama bin Laden death'.
39. 'The spy who quit', PBS Frontline, 18 January 2011, https://pbsinternational.org/programs/the-spy-who-quit/.
40. Amrullah Saleh, 'The anti-Taliban constituency', *National Review*, 6 April 2011, https://www.nationalreview.com/2011/04/anti-taliban-constituency-amrullah-saleh/.
41. 'The spy who quit'.
42. Tweet by Amrullah Saleh, 17 August 2021, https://twitter.com/amrullahsaleh2/status/1427631191545589772?lang=en.
43. Ahmad Massoud, 'The mujahideen resistance to the Taliban begins now. But we need help', *The Washington Post*, 18 August 2021, https://www.washingtonpost.com/opinions/2021/08/18/mujahideen-resistance-taliban-ahmad-massoud/.

44. Jon Boone and Sune Engel Rasmussen, 'US drone strike in Pakistan kills Taliban leader Mullah Mansoor', *The Guardian*, 22 May 2016, https://www.theguardian.com/world/2016/may/21/us-airstrike-taliban-leader-mullah-akhtar-mansoor.
45. 'Letter from the Taliban to Abu Bakr al-Baghdadi from the Head of the Shura Council', Lawfare Blog, 27 June 2015, https://www.lawfareblog.com/letter-taliban-abu-bakr-al-baghdadi-head-shura-council.
46. Stanly Johny, *The ISIS Caliphate: From Syria to the Doorsteps of India* (New Delhi: Bloomsbury, 2018), 75.
47. 'Backgrounder: Islamic State Khorasan (IS-K)', Centre for Strategic and International Studies, 9 November 2018, https://www.csis.org/programs/transnational-threats-project/past-projects/terrorism-backgrounders/islamic-state-khorasan.
48. Ibid.
49. Stanly Johny, 'The mystery of the missing twenty-one', *The Hindu*, 23 July 2016, https://www.thehindu.com/news/national/Mystery-of-the-missing-twenty-one/article14504798.ece.
50. Alan Cullison, 'Inside the hidden war between the Taliban and ISIS', *The Wall Street Journal*, 26 August 2021, https://www.wsj.com/articles/isis-taliban-afghanistan-bombing-11630014684.
51. Abdul Sayed, 'Who is the new leader of Islamic State-Khorasan Province?', Lawfare Blog, 2 September 2020, https://www.lawfareblog.com/who-new-leader-islamic-state-khorasan-province.

5: Return of the Silk Road

1. Andrew Small, *The China Pakistan Axis: Asia's New Geopolitics* (Gurgaon: Penguin Random House India, 2015), 122.

2. B.B. Lal, 'India and Afghanistan, Past, Present and Future', in *Xuanzang and the Silk Route*, ed. Lokesh Chandra and Radha Banerjee (New Delhi: Indira Gandhi National Centre for the Arts, 2008), 135.
3. S.K. Pathak, 'Buddhism in Bamiyan', in Chandra and Banerjee, *Xuanzang and the Silk Route*, 47.
4. Marylin M. Rhie, 'Aspects of the Two Colossal Buddhas at Bamiyan', in Chandra and Banerjee, *Xuanzang and the Silk Route*, 2, 27.
5. Ibid., 3, 8.
6. Ibid., 20–21.
7. Pathak, 'Buddhism in Bamiyan', 54.
8. John Keay, *China: A History* (London: HarperPress, 2008), 201.
9. Matthew W. Mosca, *From Frontier Policy to Foreign Policy: The Question of India and the Transformation of Geopolitics in Qing China* (Stanford: Stanford University Press, 2013), 74.
10. Ibid., 75.
11. Keay, *China*, 442.
12. M. Taylor Fravel, *Strong Borders, Secure Nation: Cooperation and Conflict in China's Territorial Disputes* (Princeton: Princeton University Press, 2008), 118–19.
13. From speech delivered by Liu Jinsong, Ambassador of the People's Republic of China to Afghanistan, on 'Forging Peace Together: At the 64th Anniversary of Establishment of Diplomatic Ties', 21 January 2019, http://af.china-embassy.org/eng/zagx/t1630958.htm.
14. Small, *The China Pakistan Axis*, 123.
15. Ibid., 124.
16. Ibid., 128.

17. Ibid., 136.
18. 'Afghanistan's new president starts landmark China visit', BBC, 28 October 2014, https://www.bbc.com/news/world-asia-29803768.
19. Small, *The China Pakistan Axis*, 194.
20. Ibid., 195.
21. Liu Xin and Yang Sheng, 'Initiative "project of the century": President Xi', *Global Times*, 15 May 2017, https://www.globaltimes.cn/content/1046933.shtml.
22. Xi Jinping, 'Achieving Rejuvenation Is the Dream of the Chinese People' (text of speech delivered at the Road to Rejuvenation exhibition), National People's Congress of China, 29 November 2012, http://www.npc.gov.cn/englishnpc/c23934/202006/32191c5bbdb04cbab6df01e5077d1c60.shtml.
23. 'Socialism with Chinese characteristics enters new era: Xi', Xinhua, 18 October 2017, http://www.xinhuanet.com/english/2017-10/18/c_136688475.htm.
24. Bruno Macaes, *Belt and Road: A Chinese World Order* (Gurgaon: Penguin Random House India, 2019), 172.
25. Yan Xuetong, *Ancient Chinese Thought, Modern Chinese Power* (Princeton: Princeton University Press, 2011), 65–66, 219–20.
26. Zheng Bijian, *Economic Globalization and China's Future* (Beijing: Foreign Languages Press, 2018), 13–30.
27. Peter Frankopan, *The New Silk Roads: The Present and Future of the World* (London: Bloomsbury Publishing 2018), 100–04.
28. Niva Yau, 'Expanding China's Central Asia Playbook to Afghanistan', *Jamestown Foundation China Brief* 21 (16) (17 August 2021), https://jamestown.org/program/expanding-chinas-central-asia-playbook-to-afghanistan/.

29. Ibid.
30. Shi Jiangtao, 'Taliban to "actively support" belt and road plan of "trustworthy friend" China', *South China Morning Post*, 3 September 2021, https://www.scmp.com/news/china/diplomacy/article/3147520/taliban-actively-support-belt-and-road-plan-trustworthy-friend.
31. 'Taliban to rely on Chinese funds, spokesperson says', Al Jazeera, 2 September 2021, https://www.aljazeera.com/news/2021/9/2/afghanistan-taliban-to-rely-on-chinese-money-spokesperson-says.
32. Frankopan, *The New Silk Roads*, 100–04.
33. Macaes, *Belt and Road*, 127–28.
34. Small, *The China Pakistan Axis*, 121.

6: Betting on the Taliban

1. Kathy Gannon, 'US left Afghan airfield at night, didn't tell new Afghan Commander', Associated Press, 6 July 2021, https://apnews.com/article/bagram-afghanistan-airfield-us-troops-f3614828364f567593251aaaa167e623.
2. 'Wang Yi Meets with Head of the Afghan Taliban Political Commission Mullah Abdul Ghani Baradar', Ministry of Foreign Affairs, People's Republic of China, 28 July 2021, https://www.mfa.gov.cn/ce/cegh/eng/zgyw/t1895950.htm.
3. Ibid.
4. Geremie R. Barmé, 'The fog of words: Kabul 2021, Beijing 1949', SupChina, 25 August 2021, https://supchina.com/2021/08/25/the-fog-of-words-kabul-2021-beijing-1949/.
5. Yun Sun, 'A reluctant embrace: China's new relationship with the Taliban', War on the Rocks, 10 August 2021, https://

warontherocks.com/2021/08/a-reluctant-embrace-chinas-new-relationship-with-the-taliban/.

6. 'Xi Jinping Speaks with Afghan President Mohammad Ashraf Ghani on the Phone', Ministry of Foreign Affairs, People's Republic of China, 16 July 2021, https://www.fmprc.gov.cn/mfa_eng/topics_665678/kjgzbdfyyq/202107/t20210717_9171139.html.
7. Yun, 'A reluctant embrace'.
8. Ananth Krishnan, 'Suicide bombings cast doubt on China's Pakistan projects', *The Hindu*, 22 August 2021, https://www.thehindu.com/news/international/suicide-bombings-cast-doubt-on-chinas-pakistan-projects/article36037023.ece.
9. Ibid.
10. 'Chinese firms eye resumption of projects in Afghanistan amid power shift', *Global Times*, 17 August 2021, https://www.globaltimes.cn/page/202108/1231749.shtml.
11. Yun, 'A reluctant embrace'.
12. Jun Mai, 'China appoints Afghanistan special envoy as it prepares to play greater role after US troop withdrawal', *South China Morning Post*, 21 July 2021, https://www.scmp.com/news/china/diplomacy/article/3141993/china-appoints-new-afghan-special-envoy-it-prepares-play.
13. All quotes in this section are from Li Shimo's interview with Yue Xiaoyong (Chinese), 'Once the Afghan people seize the opportunity, they will develop very well', Guancha, 29 August 2021, https://www.guancha.cn/internation/2021_08_29_604894_s.shtml.
14. Ibid.

15. Xie Wenting and Bai Yunyi, 'New Afghan govt eyes exchanging visits with China: Taliban spokesperson', *Global Times*, 9 September 2021, https://www.globaltimes.cn/page/202109/1233876.shtml.
16. Ibid.
17. Derek Grossman, 'China and the Taliban begin their romance', *Foreign Policy*, 21 July 2021, https://foreignpolicy.com/2021/07/21/china-taliban-afghanistan-biden-troop-withdrawal-belt-road-geopolitics-strategy/.
18. Ibid.
19. Mei Xinyu, 'No blind revelry about Afghanistan's economy in the post-US era' (Chinese), Aisixiang, 18 August 2021, http://www.aisixiang.com/data/128108.html.
20. Ibid.
21. The quotes in this section attributed to Andrew Small are from his interview with Ananth Krishnan conducted on 17 August 2021. Excerpts of the interview were first published in *The Hindu*. Ananth Krishnan, 'China will not get drawn into serious security role in Afghanistan', 22 August 2021, https://www.thehindu.com/news/international/china-will-not-get-drawn-into-serious-security-role-in-afghanistan/article36046175.ece.

7: Good Terrorists, Bad Terrorists

1. Mahsum is not being identified by his real name. The descriptions of the mosques in Ningxia and Xinjiang in this section come from Ananth Krishnan's multiple visits to the two regions between 2010 and 2014.

2. 'Uygur population in China's Xinjiang doubles in over 40 years', Xinhua, 7 March 2021, http://www.xinhuanet.com/english/2021-03/07/c_139791510.htm.
3. Data from Sixth National Population Census of China, 2010, sourced from University of North Carolina-Chapel Hill Library, https://guides.lib.unc.edu/china_ethnic/statistics.
4. James Leibold, 'Toward a Second Generation of Ethnic Policies?', *Jamestown Foundation China Brief* 12 (13) (6 July 2012), https://jamestown.org/program/toward-a-second-generation-of-ethnic-policies/.
5. M.A. Aldrich and Lukas Nikol, *The Perfumed Palace: Islam's Journey from Mecca to Peking* (Garnet Publishing, 2010), 200–01.
6. Ibid.
7. Nick Cohen, 'Why do Muslim states stay silent over China's abuse of the Uighurs?', *The Guardian*, 4 July 2020 https://www.theguardian.com/commentisfree/2020/jul/04/why-do-muslim-states-stay-silent-over-chinas-uighur-brutality.
8. Gerry Shih, 'Uighurs fighting in Syria take aim at China', Associated Press, 23 December 2017, https://apnews.com/article/syria-ap-top-news-riots-international-news-china-79d6a427b26f4eeab226571956dd256e.
9. Rachel Harris, 'Securitization and mass detentions in Xinjiang: How Uighurs became quarantined from the outside world', *Quartz*, 5 September 2018, https://qz.com/1377394/securitization-and-mass-detentions-in-xinjiang-how-uyghurs-became-quarantined-from-the-outside-world/
10. Sigal Samuel, 'China is treating Islam like a mental illness', *The Atlantic*, 28 August 2018, https://www.theatlantic.com/

international/archive/2018/08/china-pathologizing-uighur-muslims-mental-illness/568525/.

11. Ananth Krishnan, 'China turns to its Muslims to tap the West Asian halal food market', *The Hindu*, 24 September 2011, https://www.thehindu.com/news/international/china-turns-to-its-muslims-to-tap-the-west-asian-halal-food-market/article2482006.ece.
12. Emily Feng, '"Afraid we will become the next Xinjiang": China's Hui Muslims face crackdown', National Public Radio, 26 September 2019, https://www.npr.org/2019/09/26/763356996/afraid-we-will-become-the-next-xinjiang-chinas-hui-muslims-face-crackdown.
13. 'US Muslim groups accuse OIC of abetting China's Uighur "genocide"', Al Jazeera, 18 December 2020, https://www.aljazeera.com/news/2020/12/18/us-muslims-press-organization-of-islamic-cooperation-on-china.
14. Sammy Westfall, 'Pakistan's prime minister embraces China's policy toward Uyghurs', *The Washington Post*, 2 July 2021, https://www.washingtonpost.com/world/2021/07/02/pakistan-prime-minister-backs-china-on-uyghurs/.
15. Ananth Krishnan, 'Shielding terrorists at the UNSC: Why China won't budge', *India Today*, 27 April 2016, https://www.indiatoday.in/magazine/special-report/story/20160509-china-pakistan-india-unsc-masood-azhar-terrorist-828808-2016-04-27.
16. Shubhajit Roy, 'NSC listing: India silence on China's BRI helped seal Azhar deal', *Indian Express*, 3 May 2019, https://indianexpress.com/article/india/unsc-listing-india-silence-on-chinas-bri-helped-seal-masood-azhar-deal-5707862/.
17. 'Pan Guang: The Taliban may be different from 20 years ago, but their essence has not changed', Guancha

(Chinese), 20 August 2021, https://www.guancha.cn/PanGuang/2021_08_20_603675_s.shtml.

18. Bai Yunyi, 'Seven questions on the complex and anxious situation in Afghanistan', *Global Times* (Chinese), 13 July 2021, https://mil.news.sina.com.cn/2021-07-13/doc-ikqciyzk5197156.shtml.

8: The Xinjiang Factor

1. Austin Ramzy and Chris Buckley, '"Absolutely no mercy": Leaked files expose how China organized mass detentions of Muslims", *The New York Times*, 16 November 2019, https://www.nytimes.com/2019/11/24/world/asia/leak-chinas-internment-camps.html.
2. Reid Standish, 'From a secret base in Tajikistan, China's war on terror adjusts to a new reality', Radio Free Europe, 14 October 2021, https://gandhara.rferl.org/a/tajikistan-china-war-on-terror-afghan/31509370.html.
3. Reid Standish, 'Tajikistan approves construction of new Chinese base as Beijing's security presence in Central Asia grows', Radio Free Europe, 27 October 2021, https://www.rferl.org/a/tajikistan-approves-chinese-base/31532078.html.
4. 'China, Pak conduct joint patrol along PoK border', Press Trust of India, 22 July 2016, https://www.thehindu.com/todays-paper/tp-international/China-Pak.-conduct-joint-patrol-along-PoK-border/article14502700.ece.
5. John Keay, *China: A History* (London: HarperPress, 2008), 442.
6. 'US imposes sanctions on Chinese "state-within-a-state" linked to Xinjiang abuses', *The Guardian*, 31 July 2020, https://www.theguardian.com/world/2020/jul/31/us-sanctions-china-xinjiang-uighurs.

7. Darren Byler, 'Why Xinjiang is an internal settler colony', SupChina, 1 September 2021, https://supchina.com/2021/09/01/why-xinjiang-is-an-internal-settler-colony/.
8. Ibid.
9. Ibid.
10. James Millward, *Eurasian Crossroads: A History of Xinjiang* (New York: Columbia University Press, 2007), 331.
11. Ibid., 333.
12. Ibid., 355.
13. The observations on Xinjiang in this chapter are sourced from Ananth Krishnan's visits to the region between 2010 and 2014.
14. 'China imposes customary ban on civil servants, students from fasting during Ramadan', *Indian Express*, 6 June 2016, https://indianexpress.com/article/world/world-news/china-imposes-customary-ban-on-civil-servants-students-from-fasting-during-ramadan-2838128/.
15. 'Hu Jintao leaves G8 as troops pour into Xinjiang capital', Agence France Presse, 9 July 2009, https://www.france24.com/en/20090708-hu-jintao-leaves-g8-troops-pour-xinjiang-capital-.
16. Ananth Krishnan, 'Faith against odds', *The Hindu*, 7 August 2010, https://www.thehindu.com/features/friday-review/religion/Faith-against-odds/article12902046.ece.
17. 'Xinjiang unrest: China raises death toll to 50', BBC, 26 September 2014, https://www.bbc.com/news/world-asia-china-29373158.
18. Liu Zhun, 'Kunming attack shows spread of terror threat', *Global Times*, 2 March 2014, https://www.globaltimes.cn/content/845642.shtml.

19. Zhou Zunyou, 'US hypocrisy on full view over Kunming knife terror attack', *Global Times*, 10 March 2014, https://www.globaltimes.cn/content/847410.shtml.
20. Ramzy and Buckley, '"Absolutely no mercy"'.
21. Gerry Shih, 'China's mass internment camps evoke Cultural Revolution', Associated Press, 18 May 2018, https://apnews.com/article/kazakhstan-ap-top-news-international-news-china-china-clamps-down-6e151296fb194f85ba69a8babd972e4b.
22. Ramzy and Buckley, '"Absolutely no mercy"'.
23. David Brunnstrom and Robin Emmott, 'West sanctions China over Xinjiang abuses, Beijing hits back at EU', Reuters, 23 March 2021, https://www.reuters.com/article/uk-usa-china-eu-sanctions-idUSKBN2BE2LF.
24. Dake Kang, 'Terror and tourism: Xinjiang eases its grip, but fear remains', Associated Press, 10 October 2021, https://apnews.com/article/coronavirus-pandemic-lifestyle-china-health-travel-7a6967f335f97ca868cc618ea84b98b9.
25. Ibid.
26. Ramzy and Buckley, '"Absolutely no mercy"'.
27. Ibid.

9: Iron Brothers

1. 'Wang Yi and Shah Mahmood Qureshi Hold the 3rd Round of China–Pakistan Foreign Ministers' Strategic Dialogue', Ministry of Foreign Affairs, People's Republic of China, 25 July 2021, https://www.fmprc.gov.cn/mfa_eng/topics_665678/kjgzbdfyyq/202107/t20210725_9171162.html.
2. 'Wang Yi Talks about Terrorist Attack in Dasu: Find Out the Truth, Punish Perpetrators and Prevent Similar Incidents from

Happening Again', Ministry of Foreign Affairs, People's Republic of China, 25 July 2021, https://www.mfa.gov.cn/ce/cegv/eng/zgyw/t1894917.htm.

3. 'China and Pakistan Decide to Launch Joint Actions on Afghan Issue', Ministry of Foreign Affairs, People's Republic of China, 25 July 2021, https://www.mfa.gov.cn/ce/cehu/hu/zgyw/t1894919.htm.
4. 'Wang Yi Attends First Foreign Ministers' Meeting on the Afghan Issue Among the Neighbouring Countries of Afghanistan', Ministry of Foreign Affairs, People's Republic of China, 8 September 2021, https://www.fmprc.gov.cn/ce/cohk/eng/Topics/gjfz/t1905753.htm.
5. Khurram Husain, 'CPEC masterplan revealed', *Dawn*, 21 June 2017, https://www.dawn.com/news/1333101.
6. Kazim Alam, 'China helps as FDI in Pakistan surges 38.8%', *Express Tribune*, 20 July 2016, https://tribune.com.pk/story/1146075/2015-16-china-helps-fdi-pakistan-surges-38-8.
7. Snigdhendu Bhattacharya, 'Pakistan prostrating before Chinese imperialist designs, Pak scholar says', *Hindustan Times*, 13 June 2017, https://www.hindustantimes.com/kolkata/cpec-pakistan-prostrating-before-chinese-imperialist-designs-pak-scholar-says-in-kolkata/story-qt9ZdydBVjcoiOYAHFDLtK.html.
8. Ananth Krishnan, 'Pakistan China's new colony? Leaked papers reveal Beijing's stake in economy, key projects', *India Today*, 21 July 2017, https://www.indiatoday.in/magazine/cover-story/story/20170731-china-pakistan-relations-implication-for-india-cpec-obor-1025308-2017-07-21.
9. Ibid.
10. Husain, 'CPEC masterplan revealed'.

11. Ananth Krishnan, 'Brothers in arms', *India Today*, 24 October 2016, https://www.indiatoday.in/magazine/cover-story/story/20161024-india-china-pakistan-xi-jinping-narendra-modi-829717-2016-10-13.
12. Ibid.
13. Ibid.
14. 'Li Shimo interview with Yue Xiaoyong, China's Special Envoy to Afghanistan: Once the Afghan people seize the opportunity, they will develop very well', Guancha (Chinese), 29 August 2021, https://www.guancha.cn/internation/2021_08_29_604894_s.shtml.
15. Ibid.
16. The quotes in this section attributed to Andrew Small are from his interview with Ananth Krishnan conducted on 17 August 2021. Excerpts of the interview were first published in *The Hindu*. See Ananth Krishnan, 'China will not get drawn into serious security role in Afghanistan', *The Hindu*, 22 August 2021, https://www.thehindu.com/news/international/china-will-not-get-drawn-into-serious-security-role-in-afghanistan/article36046175.ece.
17. Yun Sun, 'China's strategic assessment of the Ladakh clash', War on the Rocks, 17 June 2020, https://warontherocks.com/2020/06/chinas-strategic-assessment-of-the-ladakh-clash/.
18. Krishnan, 'Brothers in arms'.
19. Ibid.

10: The View from India

1. 'Resolution 1076, The Situation in Afghanistan', UNSC, 22 October 1996, http://unscr.com/en/resolutions/1076.

2. 'Resolution 1333: The situation in Afghanistan', UNSC, 19 December 2000, http://unscr.com/en/resolutions/1333; also see Barbara Crossette, 'Tough sanctions imposed on Taliban government split U.N.', *The New York Times*, 20 December 2000, https://www.nytimes.com/2000/12/20/world/tough-sanctions-imposed-on-taliban-government-split-un.html.
3. Ibid.
4. 'Treaty of Friendship between the Government of India and the Royal Government of Afghanistan', Ministry of External Affairs, Government of India, 4 January 1950, https://mea.gov.in/bilateral-documents.htm?dtl/6584/Treaty+of+Friendship.
5. 'History and Evolution of Non-Aligned Movement', Ministry of External Affairs, Government of India, 22 August 2012, https://mea.gov.in/in-focus-article.htm?20349/History+and+Evolution+of+NonAligned+Movement.
6. 'Final Communiqué of the Asian-African conference of Bandung', 24 April 1955, available at CVCE, University of Luxembourg, https://www.cvce.eu/en/obj/final_communique_of_the_asian_african_conference_of_bandung_24_april_1955-en-676237bd-72f7-471f-949a-88b6ae513585.html; also see 'Bandung Conference (Asian-African Conference), 1955, Milestones: 1953–1960', Office of the Historian, US Department of State, https://history.state.gov/milestones/1953-1960/bandung-conf.
7. *The Pashtunistan Issue, in Afghanistan: A Country Study*, ed Peter R. Blood, The Library of Congress, US 2001. http://countrystudies.us/afghanistan/
8. Vinay Kaura, 'The Durand Line: A British Legacy Plaguing Afghan-Pakistani Relations', Middle East Institute, 27 June 2017, https://www.mei.edu/publications/durand-line-british-legacy-plaguing-afghan-pakistani-relations.

9. Dilip Mukerjee, 'Afghanistan under Daud: Relations with Neighboring States', *Asian Survey* 15 (4) (April 1975): 301–12.
10. Nushin Arbabzadah, 'Remembering Afghanistan's first president', *The Guardian*, 21 March 2009, https://www.theguardian.com/commentisfree/2009/mar/21/afghanistan.
11. Feisal Khan, 'Why Borrow Trouble for Yourself and Lend It to Neighbors? Understanding the Historical Roots of Pakistan's Afghan Policy', *Asian Affairs: An American Review* 37 (4) (October–December, 2010): 171–89.
12. Quoted in Rizwan Hussain, *Pakistan and the Emergence of Islamic Militancy in Afghanistan* (Aldershot, England: Ashgate, 2005), 78–79.
13. 'Annual Report 1973–74', Ministry of External Affairs, Government of India, https://mealib.nic.in/?2500?000.
14. J.N. Dixit, *An Afghan Diary: Zahir Shah to Taliban* (New Delhi: Konark Publishers, 2000), 19.
15. Lt. Gen. Shokin Chauhan, 'India post-Taliban takeover in Afghanistan assessing the risks', *Financial Express*, 16 August 2021, https://www.financialexpress.com/defence/india-post-taliban-takeover-in-afghanistan assessing-the-risks/2311802/.
16. 'Treaty of Peace, Friendship and Co-operation', Ministry of External Affairs, Government of India, 9 August 1971, https://mea.gov.in/bilateral-documents.htm?dtl/5139/Treaty+of.
17. J.N. Dixit, India's ambassador to Afghanistan in the early years of the Soviet intervention and a former Foreign Secretary, has given this account in his book. J.N. Dixit, *An Afghan Diary: Zahir Shah to Taliban* (New Delhi: Konark Publishers, 2000), 20–21.
18. Crossette, 'India to provide aid'.
19. M.K. Bhadrakumar, 'Manmohan Singh resets Afghan policy', *The Hindu*, 15 May 2011, https://www.thehindu.com/opinion/lead/manmohan-singh-resets-afghan-policy/article2021653.ece.

20. 'Peshawar Accord', 24 April 1992; the document can be downloaded from UN Peacemaker: https://peacemaker.un.org/node/635.
21. Bhadrakumar, 'Manmohan Singh resets'.
22. Ibid.
23. M.K. Bhadrakumar, 'How India reached out to the Afghan Mujahideen', Rediff, 14 September 2016, https://www.rediff.com/news/special/exclusive-how-india-reached-out-to-the-exclusive-how-india-reached-out-to-the-afghan-mujahideen/20160914.htm.
24. Rahimullah Yusufzai, 'India must not treat the Taliban as enemy, interview with Mulla Abdul Jalil', *Outlook*, 11 June 1997, https://www.outlookindia.com/magazine/story/india-must-not-treat-the-taliban-as-enemy/203662.
25. Ibid.
26. 'Blood-Stained Hands: Past Atrocities in Kabul and Afghanistan's Legacy of Impunity', Human Rights Watch, 6 July 2005, https://www.hrw.org/report/2005/07/06/blood-stained-hands/past-atrocities-kabul-and-afghanistans-legacy-impunity#7ea268.
27. Zachary Constantino, 'The India–Pakistan Rivalry in Afghanistan', United States Institute of Peace, Special Report (462), January 2020, 1–24.
28. Nirupama Subramanian, 'IC-814 hijacking: New Taliban chief Mullah Akhtar Mansour escorted Maulana Masood Azhar, says ex-RAW officer', *The Indian Express*, 3 August 2015, https://indianexpress.com/article/india/india-others/new-taliban-chief-mullah-akhtar-mansour-escorted-maulana-masood-azhar-ex-raw-officer/.

29. Quoted in Myra Macdonald, *Defeat Is an Orphan: How Pakistan Lost the Great South Asian War* (New Delhi: Penguin Random House India, 2017), Kindle.
30. Avinash Paliwal, *My Enemy's Enemy: India in Afghanistan: From the Soviet Invasion to the US Withdrawal* (New Delhi: HarperCollins, 2017), Kindle.
31. India operated a small military hospital at Farkhor but also used the base to ship high-altitude warfare supplies to the Northern Alliance, service the group's Soviet Union-built MI-17 and MI-38 helicopters, and execute electronic intelligence-gathering operations. Praveen Swami, 'Making the water boil in Afghanistan', *The Hindu*, 9 July 2008, http://www.hindu.com/2008/07/09/stories/2008070955191000.htm.
32. Rudra Chaudhuri and Shreyas Shende, 'Dealing with the Taliban: India's Strategy in Afghanistan after US Withdrawal', Carnegie India, Working Paper, June 2020.
33. Aishwarya Paliwal, 'Afghanistan crisis: Indian trade worth $1.5 billion stops abruptly as Afghans stare at bleak future', *India Today*, 24 August 2021, https://www.indiatoday.in/india/story/afghanistan-crisis-indian-bilateral-trade-stops-abruptly-afghans-bleak-future-1844493-2021-08-24.
34. 'Text of Agreement on Strategic Partnership between the Republic of India and the Islamic Republic of Afghanistan', Ministry of External Affairs, Government of India, 4 October 2011, https://mea.gov.in/bilateral-documents.htm?dtl/5383/Text+of+Agreement+on+Strategic+Partnership+between+the+Republic+of+India+and+the+Islamic+Republic+of+Afghanistan.
35. In November 2019, New Delhi's ambassador to the United States, Harsh Vardhan Shringla, avowed, 'Democracy and constitutional

order in Afghanistan are the major gains achieved in the last eighteen years, and we believe these are worth preserving.' 'The India–Afghanistan Relationship: Examining Historical, Political, Economic, and Cultural Ties', Remarks made by Ambassador Harsh Vardhan Shringla at the Hudson Institute, Washington, DC, 21 November 2019, https://s3.amazonaws.com/media.hudson.org/Ambassador%20HV%20Shringla%20India.pdf.

36. Andrew Roth, 'Russia hosts talks between Taliban and Afghan peace council', *The Guardian*, 9 November 2018, https://www.theguardian.com/world/2018/nov/09/russia-hosts-talks-between-taliban-and-afghan-peace-council.
37. Bruce Riedel, 'The longshot Taliban talks', Brookings, 10 July 2015, https://www.brookings.edu/opinions/the-longshot-taliban-talks/.
38. Chaudhuri and Shende, 'Dealing with the Taliban'.
39. Varghese K. George, 'BJP's Taliban worry,' *The Hindu*, 8 September 2021, https://www.thehindu.com/news/national/political-line-bjps-taliban-worry/article36353777.ece.
40. Tweet by Hardeep Singh Puri, 22 August 2021, https://twitter.com/hardeepspuri/status/1429356598686715904?lang=en.
41. Smriti Kak Ramachandran, '"Be prepared for all possibilities": RSS chief Bhagwat ahead of Taliban talks', *Hindustan Times*, 15 October 2021, https://www.hindustantimes.com/india-news/ahead-of-talks-with-taliban-rss-chief-says-india-needs-to-be-prepared-for-all-possibilities-101634274658218.html.
42. Suhasini Haidar, 'Indian delegation met Taliban in Doha, says Qatari official', *The Hindu*, 21 June 2021, https://www.thehindu.com/news/national/indian-delegation-met-taliban-in-doha-says-qatari-official/article34895560.ece.

43. Joint Statement of the Participants in the Moscow Format Consultations on Afghanistan, Ministry of Foreign Affairs of the Russian Federation, 20 October 2021, https://www.mid.ru/en/foreign_policy/news/-/asset_publisher/cKNonkJE02Bw/content/id/4913908.
44. PTI, 'Indian delegation meets Taliban team in Moscow', *The Hindu BusinessLine*, 21 October 2021, https://www.thehindubusinessline.com/news/world/indian-delegation-meets-taliban-team-in-moscow/article37103678.ece.

Conclusion: The Tragedy of Afghanistan

1. 'Life Expectancy at Birth, Total (Years) – Afghanistan', The World Bank, https://data.worldbank.org/indicator/SP.DYN.LE00.IN?locations=AF.
2. Daniel P. Sullivan, 'Tinder, Spark, Oxygen, and Fuel: The Mysterious Rise of the Taliban', *Journal of Peace Research* 44 (1) (January 2007): 93–108.
3. 'Afghanistan set to be world's worst humanitarian crisis, report warns', World Food Programme, 25 October 2021, https://www.wfp.org/stories/afghanistan-climate-crisis-drought-wfp-hunger-cop26-ipc-un.
4. Ibid.
5. 'Pakistan, China urge world to send humanitarian aid to Kabul', Associated Press, 26 October 2021, https://apnews.com/article/afghanistan-china-pakistan-xi-jinping-qatar-aabc2b5c668b0893adb781309271d046.
6. Kallol Bhattacherjee, 'India sends medical aid to Afghanistan', *The Hindu*, 11 December 2021, https://www.thehindu.com/news/national/india-sends-medicines-to-afghanistan/article37930879.ece.

7. Mei Xinyu, 'No blind revelry about Afghanistan's economy in the post-US era' (Chinese), Aisixiang, 18 August 2021, http://www.aisixiang.com/data/128108.html.
8. Interview with Ambassador Jayant Prasad, by Stanly Johny.
9. 'Want to continue our political, trade ties with India: Taliban leader Stanekzai', *Hindustan Times*, 29 August 2021, https://www.hindustantimes.com/world-news/want-to-continue-our-political-trade-ties-with-india-taliban-leader-stanekzai-101630233039985.html.
10. 'Haqqani Network scion Anas Haqqani says Taliban won't "interfere" in Kashmir, clarifies Pakistan connection', News18, 1 September 2021, https://www.news18.com/news/world/exclusive-talibans-anas-haqqani-says-wont-interfere-in-kashmir-clarifies-pakistan-connection-4150346.html.
11. Vineet Khare, 'Afghanistan: Taliban says it will "raise voice for Kashmir Muslims"', BBC, 3 September 2021, https://www.bbc.com/news/world-asia-india-58419719.

Index

About the Authors

Ananth Krishnan is the China correspondent for *The Hindu* and is currently based in Hong Kong. In 2019, he was a visiting fellow at Brookings India. He was previously the Beijing-based associate editor at the India Today Group. He has reported from China for close to a decade and his reporting has taken him to all but three of China's thirty-three provinces and regions. He is the author of *India's China Challenge* (2020).

Stanly Johny is the international affairs editor with *The Hindu*. A PhD in international studies from the Centre for West Asian Studies, Jawaharlal Nehru University, he has been writing on international affairs and Indian foreign policy in The Hindu Group publications for nearly a decade. An IVLP fellow of the US State Department and an India–Australia Youth Dialogue alumnus, he has also contributed to think-tanks such as the Middle East Institute in Washington, DC and the Manohar Parrikar Institute for Defence Studies and Analyses in New Delhi. He is the author of *The ISIS Caliphate: From Syria to the Doorsteps of India* (2018).

THE COMRADES AND THE MULLAHS

THE COMRADES AND THE MULLAHS

CHINA, AFGHANISTAN AND THE NEW ASIAN GEOPOLITICS

ANANTH KRISHNAN
STANLY JOHNY

HarperCollins *Publishers* India

First published in India by HarperCollins *Publishers* 2022

HarperCollins Publishers India, Cyber City, Building 10-A, Gurugram,
Haryana-122002, India
www.harpercollins.co.in

2 4 6 8 10 9 7 5 3 1

P-ISBN: 978-93-5489-521-0
E-ISBN: 978-93-5489-544-9

Cover design: Saurav Das
Cover photograph: Reuters

Map on pages vi–vii by L. Balamurugan

Typeset in 11.5/15.2 Bembo Std at
Manipal Technologies Limited, Manipal

Printed and bound at MicroPrints India, New Delhi

MIX
Paper
FSC FSC® C218906

This product is made of FSC®-certified and other controlled material.

HarperCollins Publishers, Macken House, 39/40 Mayor Street Upper, Dublin 1, D01 C9W8, Ireland

Contents

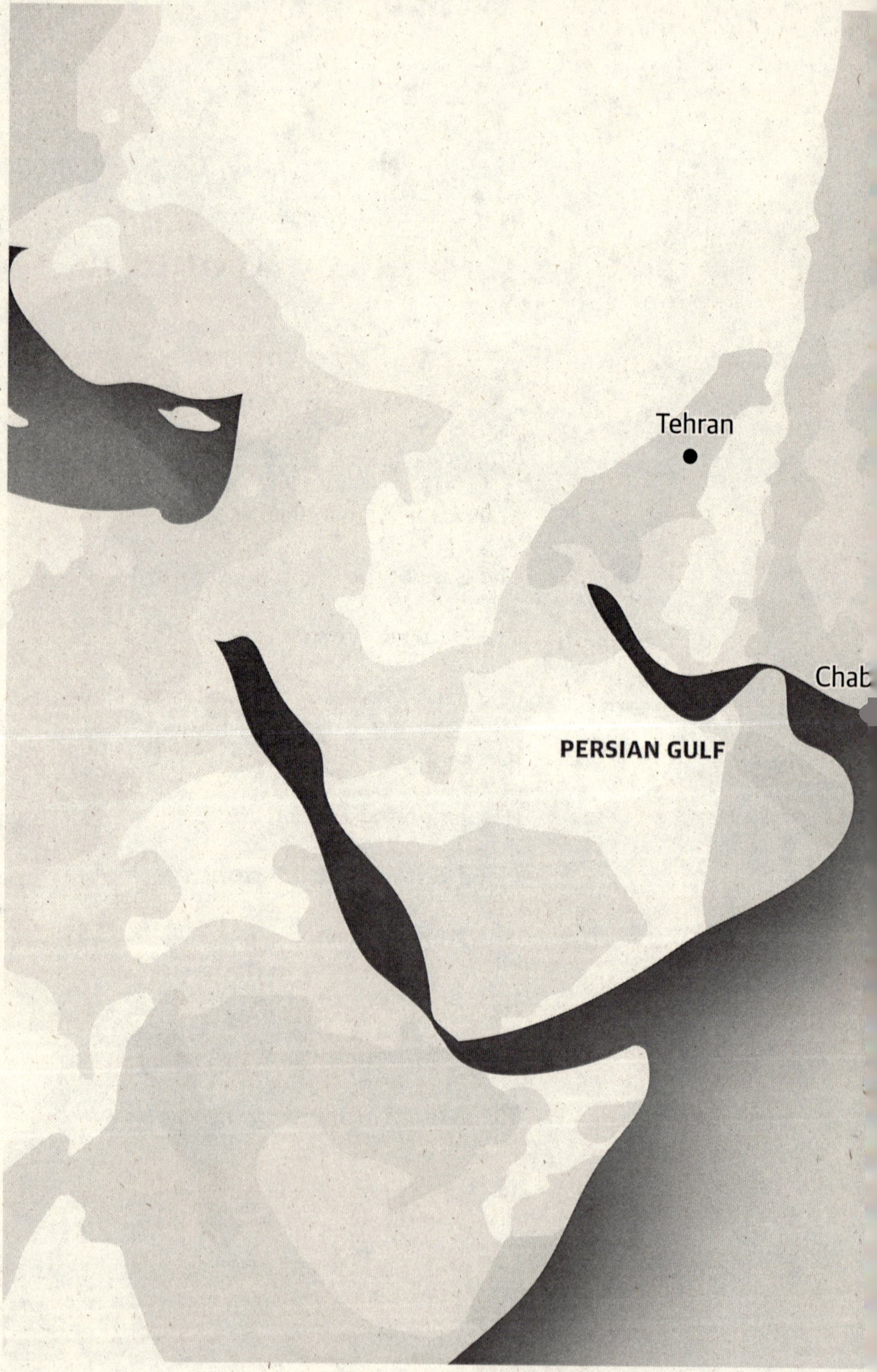
Tehran
Chab
PERSIAN GULF